PROPORTIONALITY
PRINCIPLES
IN AMERICAN LAW

PROPORTIONALITY PRINCIPLES
IN AMERICAN LAW

Controlling Excessive
Government Actions

E. Thomas Sullivan

Richard S. Frase

OXFORD
UNIVERSITY PRESS

2009

OXFORD
UNIVERSITY PRESS

Oxford University Press, Inc., publishes works that further
Oxford University's objective of excellence
in research, scholarship, and education.

Oxford   New York
Auckland   Cape Town   Dar es Salaam   Hong Kong   Karachi
Kuala Lumpur   Madrid   Melbourne   Mexico City   Nairobi
New Delhi   Shanghai   Taipei   Toronto

With offices in
Argentina   Austria   Brazil   Chile   Czech Republic   France   Greece
Guatemala   Hungary   Italy   Japan   Poland   Portugal   Singapore
South Korea   Switzerland   Thailand   Turkey   Ukraine   Vietnam

Copyright © 2009 by Oxford University Press, Inc.

Published by Oxford University Press, Inc.
198 Madison Avenue, New York, New York 10016

www.oup.com

Oxford is a registered trademark of Oxford University Press

Library of Congress Cataloging-in-Publication Data
Sullivan, E. Thomas.
Proportionality principles in American law: controlling excessive government
actions / E. Thomas Sullivan & Richard S. Frase.
    p.   cm.
Includes bibliographical references and index.
ISBN 978-0-19-532493-8
1. Proportionality in law.   I. Frase, Richard S.   II. Title.
K247.S85 2008
340'.11—dc22   2008006939

9 8 7 6 5 4 3 2 1
Printed in the United States of America
on acid-free paper

The only stable form of government is where the rule of law reigns and does not depend on any person.

—IMMANUEL KANT

PREFACE

IN THIS BOOK WE ARGUE for more explicit and consistent application of proportionality principles when courts in the United States are called upon to decide whether a challenged government action is excessive. This normative argument is based in part on a descriptive claim that American courts are already widely applying various proportionality principles. But these courts rarely make explicit reference to proportionality, and when they do, the principles employed lack precise and consistent definition.

Much of the problem is semantic. In the United States, when most people think of proportionality, they think of symmetry or balance (the relationship between a part and the whole, especially in human features, art, and architecture) or a constant ratio between two quantities (so that one varies in direct relation to the other). If people are thinking about government, they might think of proportional voting strength or representation, and if they are lawyers or philosophers, they might think about retributive theories of criminal punishment, which propose that penalties vary in relation to (or at least not greatly exceed) the offender's culpability or "just deserts." Independent of the latter theory, most American philosophers would also recognize that nonretributive (utilitarian) theories of punishment require that penalties be proportionate to the seriousness of the offense (measured by the social harm caused or risked by the crime, with consideration perhaps also being given to the need for greater penalties because the crime is difficult to detect, hard to discourage, etc.).

In the legal systems of other Western countries and in international and European regional law, these legal and philosophical proportionality principles are much more fully developed, and they are explicitly and frequently invoked when courts review legislative and executive actions and lower-court decisions. As in the United States, these foreign reviewing courts do not seek to substitute their own preferences as to the optimum or most proportionate solution to the matter at hand; instead, they recognize the greater institutional competence and/or the greater democratic legitimacy of the government actors whose decisions are under review and therefore confine their oversight role to setting meaningful limits on the severity or intrusiveness of government measures. They seek, in other words, to safeguard citizens and other government actors from excessive government measures—to prevent clear cases of *disproportionality*.

However, all proportionality concepts require an analytic or normative frame-work—proportionality relative to what? Foreign and international laws apply several well-defined disproportionality concepts. Criminal penalties must not be disproportionate to retributive notions of culpability, and *all government measures*, whether criminal or civil, must not be disproportionate in two distinctive utilitarian senses: First, the costs or burdens of the measure must not clearly exceed the likely benefits (a concept we refer to as "ends" or "ends-benefits" proportionality). Second, the measure must not be clearly more costly or more burdensome than equally effective alternative measures (a concept of necessity and narrow tailoring that we refer to as "means" or "alternative-means" proportionality). American courts often invoke one or more of these three proportionality principles under a variety of doctrines that only occasionally use the language of proportionality.

We discuss the many examples of implicit and occasionally explicit constitutional proportionality principles that U.S. courts apply. We also examine the historical origins of these principles in just war doctrines, briefly survey the use of the principles in foreign and international law, and discuss early common law examples of proportionality concepts in the law of damages. We also note several contemporary uses of these concepts in nonconstitutional American law.

We seek to more clearly define the different types of proportionality principles illustrated by these historical, international, and contemporary U.S. doctrines. By doing so, we hope to encourage American lawyers, judges, legislators, and legal philosophers to apply these principles more frequently and more consistently. However, we do not propose to substitute proportionality analysis for all existing standards of constitutional judicial review. In particular, we would retain strict scrutiny analysis in the areas where it currently applies; although strict scrutiny implicitly incorporates ends- and means-proportionality principles, we believe that fundamental rights and historically protected classes deserve the stronger protections provided by the rulelike presumptions of strict scrutiny. We also recognize that, in certain areas, reviewing courts have rightly applied absolute principles, for example, principles of human dignity that prohibit public whipping even if it is arguably proportional in all three of the senses we identify. Our proposed proportionality analysis would apply in areas now governed by rational basis review, by intermediate scrutiny standards, or by review standards that have not been assigned to any of the Supreme Court's three levels of scrutiny.

This project has benefited greatly from the contributions of our student and administrative assistants, colleagues, and friends. For their diligent research assistance and source checking we are indebted to current and former students Rachel Anderson, Courtney Clixby, John Lassetter, Kelly Loudon, Aaron Marcus, Nick Smith, Eric Steinhoff, and Oleh Vretsona. Preparation of the manuscript was expertly supervised by secretary Julie Hunt. Helpful comments and suggestions on this project and related earlier works were provided by current and former colleagues and friends Brian Bix, Guy Charles, Joshua Dressler, Dan Farber, Barry Feld, Oren Gross, Wayne Logan, John Matheson, Marc Miller, Michael Paulsen, Kevin Reitz, Adam Samaha, Michael Tonry, David Weissbrodt, Ron Wright, and Frank Zimring. We also have benefited greatly from the careful reading and useful comments of the publisher's outside reviewers and from the suggestions and corrections of our editors.

MINNEAPOLIS
E.T.S. AND R.S.F.

CONTENTS

PROPORTIONALITY
PRINCIPLES
IN AMERICAN LAW

INTRODUCTION

AS STATES FIND THEMSELVES MORE heavily involved in new areas of public life and as citizens are being further integrated into the polity, the tensions between the need for administrative and penal regulation, the advancement of social welfare, and individual autonomy become increasingly visible. True to their traditional role of upholding the rule of law and recognizing the vulnerability of the individual faced with coercive state power, courts in the United States and other Western nations have developed a variety of mechanisms to curtail government intrusion where it excessively impinges on individual rights and autonomy. Courts have also ruled on whether governmental action unduly invades the powers of another branch or level of government or whether an individual action invades the rights of other citizens. These issues have in common the need for courts to determine when a challenged action is excessive. More precisely, we argue, a reviewing court must decide whether the challenged action is disproportionate in one or more of the following senses—to the benefits likely to be achieved by the action; to alternative methods of achieving those benefits; or to the blameworthiness of a party subject to a penalty or compensation order. As discussed more fully below, we refer to the principles underlying these three review standards, respectively, as "ends-benefits," "alternative-means," and "limiting retributive" proportionality principles.

3

Proportionality principles can take many forms, most of which are more familiar to readers than the three just described, so it is important to understand how the principles we discuss differ from those found in other contexts. In art and architecture, for example, proportionality refers to the balanced relationship between a part and the whole; in math and science it refers to a constant relationship between two quantities that vary in a fixed ratio. The latter usage also occurs in political theory and election law, where writers and courts speak of proportional voting strength or representation; similar fixed-ratio proportionality concepts appear in legal or informal contexts where co-owners or beneficiaries expect to vote or receive proceeds corresponding to their respective fractional shares. In criminal law and philosophy, proportionality is often discussed in relation to theories of punishment. The most common usage refers to the retributive punishment theories that underlie the limiting retributive principle we identify. A lesser-known usage, found in nonretributive (utilitarian) theories of punishment, corresponds to our ends-benefits proportionality principle. A proportionality concept similar to the ends-benefits principle has also been invoked as a limitation on rights to use force in self-defense, to arrest, or to protect property and prevent crime.

One of the earliest applications of proportionality principles in law and philosophy is evident in the ancient concept of just war developed by prominent public and secular figures such as Cicero, Saint Augustine, Saint Aquinas, and Hugo Grotius. More recently, with the rise of the administrative state following World War II, proportionality principles have become important elements of the rule of law.[1] These principles provide essential checks on government power, thus serving to preserve formal legality,[2] maintain a just legal order, and reconcile the interests of the state, the polity, and its citizens so that state regulation produces more benefit to the public interest than harm to individual autonomy.[3]

In each country the scope of application of the principle of proportionality depends largely on the extent of its acceptance and recognition of individual rights. In this matter, the differences among countries are ordinarily observed in the areas of social, economic, and cultural rights because the majority of government intervention takes place there, and countries usually differ in their level of recognition and enforcement of these rights. Civil and political rights generate more uniform government acceptance and protection. The welfare states (e.g., Germany and, to a lesser extent, France), as well as supranational political formations like the European Union, which afford comprehensive humanitarian protection, extensively use the principle of proportionality in testing the fairness of their legislation and administrative law. The principle enjoys limited application in laissez-faire countries such as the United States.[4]

The system of constitutional review in the United States affords the highest degree of protection to fundamental rights that are either enumerated in the

Constitution[5] or, while unenumerated, are "deeply rooted in the Nation's history and tradition," such as when the public has well-settled expectations.[6] The Supreme Court cautiously avoids expressly deriving any of these rights from natural law principles,[7] perhaps out of fear that the natural rights theory has no limiting principle that could curtail the power of the judiciary. The Court, nevertheless, recognizes that certain unenumerated rights are protected because they form part of the implicit, ordered liberty.[8] Similar concerns with the prospect of vesting the Court with unlimited power to strike down federal and state laws whose general thrust does not coincide with the opinions of its majority[9] have caused the Court to avoid widely using the Ninth Amendment[10] for support of unenumerated rights.[11]

Rights that are considered less foundational to ordered liberty are afforded less protection under the rational basis review, and the majority of social, cultural, and economic rights fall under this category.[12] Very limited review, perhaps not substantially exceeding rational basis, is also applied to the liberty interests of convicted offenders when they challenge lengthy prison terms imposed by statutes or courts.[13] There is a strong presumption of constitutionality of government action involving these rights and liberty interests, with the Court affording a great amount of deference to the government.[14] The Court reserves a more rigorous standard of judicial review, "strict scrutiny," for the protection of a narrow category of fundamental rights—the rights and equal protection of certain discrete and insular minorities—and of the political processes designed to safeguard the rights of such minorities.[15] An approach of intermediate scrutiny provides medium-to-high protection in certain contexts, including gender discrimination,[16] state encroachment of federal powers,[17] and violation of the freedom of speech by content-neutral regulation of speech.[18] As discussed in later chapters, intermediate scrutiny (albeit implicit rather than explicit) is also the approach applied to criminal procedure standards, imposition of criminal liability without fair notice, eligibility for the death penalty, and the use of severe fines and forfeitures. The narrow definition of fundamental rights that are afforded strong judicial protection in American jurisprudence, combined with the presumption of constitutionality, deprive many individual, social, and economic rights of meaningful protection against government intrusion.

The Supreme Court has recently identified several areas of economic and social regulation that require heightened scrutiny, and the Court has explicitly invoked proportionality principles. These areas include the use of punitive damages,[19] land-use permit conditions,[20] civil forfeitures,[21] and criminal punishment.[22] Finally, the Court's concern that Congress's broad remedial powers under Section 5 of the Fourteenth Amendment, if unchecked, would be damaging to the states, has led to the judicial curtailment of these powers through the principle of "congruence and proportionality."[23]

The Court's express move in these areas toward proportionality as an instrumental principle of review is commendable. It is also in line with the specific forms of proportionality analysis described later, which, as we show, are implicit in many of the Court's doctrines. Yet, the Court's arbitrary application of express notions of proportionality in a few select areas, while failing to recognize its importance in other areas of judicial review, undermines the doctrinal value of the principle of proportionality: It seems that the Court's intention in using the term "proportionality" was to increase the intensity of judicial review in the select areas from rational basis to a more rigorous standard of review, thus reducing proportionality to a role of a quasi standard of review placed somewhere between rational basis and intermediate scrutiny on a continuum of intensity of judicial review. A better approach for the Court, we argue, would be to recognize the instrumental role of proportionality in any standard of judicial review of government action.

This book first identifies the many forms that proportionality standards have taken and categorizes and more clearly defines them. Our principal theses are the following: (1) that proportionality review is emerging in U.S. law but is not yet a unified theory; (2) that proportionality, even when explicitly invoked, has not been applied in a coherent fashion; (3) that proportionality standards should be more clearly defined along the lines we suggest; and (4) that every intrusive government measure that limits or threatens individual rights and autonomy should undergo some form of proportionality review. We do, however, suggest retaining the more restrictive, context-specific standards that apply under strict scrutiny review, as well as certain absolute prohibitions such as those imposed by principles of human dignity. Our focus is thus on public law and civil liberties. However, to demonstrate the wide variety of proportionality principles and the broad support for them, we also discuss examples broader than government-versus-citizen issues. In addition, we cite instances from foreign, regional, and international law in which proportionality review is explicitly and frequently employed.[24]

Courts and legislatures use a number of retributive and utilitarian proportionality principles as guides when deciding whether a given measure is excessive.[25] Retributive proportionality strives to ensure a proportional relation between the punishment or award of damages and the actor's blameworthiness, as measured by the harm caused and the actor's intent, motives, mental capacity, and contributory role in joint conduct. While a pure retributivist approach recognizes blameworthiness as the sole evaluative criterion, limiting retributivism, or modified just deserts, utilizes retributive proportionality principles to define a range of appropriate sanctions by setting upper and lower limits. Thus, the limiting retributivism approach controls both who may be held liable and how severely that person may be punished. In this book we refer when applicable to these two proportionality limits, respectively, as limiting retributive liability principles and limiting retributive severity principles.

Other proportionality principles focus on excessiveness relative to the achievement of practical purposes, such as crime control or regulatory goals, rather than to an actor's blameworthiness. This utilitarian paradigm was a central feature of just war doctrine and eighteenth-century utilitarian philosophy. Under this approach, a measure is deemed disproportionate if the costs or burdens it imposes exceed the likely benefits or if the measure is unnecessarily severe considering other equally effective, less burdensome means. We refer to these principles, respectively, as "ends" (or "ends-benefits") proportionality and "means" (or "alternative-means") proportionality.

Ends proportionality usually involves a comparison of a single measure to its expected benefits, whereas means proportionality involves comparison of the costs and burdens imposed by equally effective alternative measures designed to achieve the same benefits. But assessments of alternative measures can also involve a form of ends proportionality; if one of the measures imposes higher costs or burdens but is also more effective, the question is whether the greater benefits of that measure justify the added costs or burdens it imposes. A clear example of the latter form of ends-proportionality analysis appears in a well-known decision of the Israeli Supreme Court that involves a challenge to the construction of a lengthy security fence between Jewish and Arab residential areas. The court held, inter alia, that the fence violated the principle of proportionality "in the narrow sense" (involving assessment of whether expected benefits justify the burdens imposed) because, although the government's routing of the fence would slightly increase security, compared to the challengers' proposed alternative route, the former would impose much more severe burdens on local residents.[26]

Courts apply the preceding proportionality principles in a number of ways; they can be adapted to fit any context. The intensity of judicial review can be custom fit to each legal system's normative policy choices and unique history.[27] The principles can be applied categorically either as a rule or on a case-by-case basis as a standard. Courts may also adopt a hybrid approach somewhere between a rule and standard, or they may fashion their proportionality review by combining elements of both approaches.[28] Depending on the context, a finding of disproportionality can be viewed as problematic per se or may play only an evidentiary role (for example, as a way to infer the true intent of government or private actors).

Courts most often utilize proportionality review in the criminal justice and civil liberties arena to ensure that government encroachment on citizens' rights does not become excessive. Sometimes, however, citizens' rights may be *curtailed* under a utilitarian proportionality regime; a finding of disproportionality favors the government, not the citizen. Proportionality principles can also guide a court in settling disputes between two branches of government or two adverse parties. Proportionality principles determine both the legality of government or private action and, if legal, whether the action was excessive in scope, intensity, and duration. Proportionality analysis was utilized in a similar fashion with regard to just war doctrine, where proportionality regulated both the decision to declare war (*jus ad bellum*) and the conduct of war (*jus in bello*).

Proportionality analysis has some points in common with the balancing of competing interests. In particular, the ends-benefits proportionality principle described earlier involves a type of cost-benefit analysis often invoked when courts engage in balancing. However, alternative-means proportionality calls for a very different kind of balance (if "balance" is even the right word to use); it involves comparing a particular measure with less costly or burdensome alternative means of achieving the same goal. Limiting retributive proportionality also involves a comparison—between the severity of a measure and the degree of individual fault of the person subject to the measure. This, too, could be viewed as a kind of balancing, although that term is not used in opinions and writings that invoke retributive theory.

Even if proportionality and balancing analysis have points in common, we argue that the proportionality principles we have identified are better suited to serve as limiting principles in guiding judicial review of excessive government measures. The balancing metaphor suggests a specific, optimum solution. But asking courts to determine that optimum solution implies a degree of judicial power and precision that is usually unattainable and often inappropriate. It is easier and more appropriate for a reviewing court to say "this is clearly too much" than to say "this is (or would be) the optimum." Courts have limited ability to gather and weigh empirical data, limited legitimacy in making complex policy choices, and limited power to enforce their judgments. Legislative and executive officials and private actors are the primary decision makers, and they must be accorded substantial deference and allowed a considerable margin for error or difference of view. However, courts must still impose some meaningful limits on these decisions. Although proportionality analysis requires courts to make difficult factual determinations and value judgments, this is true whenever courts review challenged government measures for excessiveness. Thus, some degree of judicial review is both necessary and inevitable—courts already engage in review under a variety of standards, and as this book shows, many of these standards implicitly or imprecisely incorporate proportionality principles. We argue that more explicit and precise application of such principles will produce more consistent and defensible exercise of essential judicial oversight.

Foundations for the exercise of any of these principles of proportionality may be found in federal and state constitutional law, common law, or legislative principles. Although the Supreme Court has adopted expressly retributive proportionality in some contexts under the federal constitution, its proportionality review based on that document has been limited, perhaps because of concerns about federalism and democratic legitimacy. These concerns, however, are reduced or nonexistent when a state court bases its proportionality review on the state constitution or when courts and legislatures apply proportionality review to nonconstitutional issues. Despite solid legal foundations and the lack of strong concerns to the contrary, U.S. courts and policy makers have failed to implement proportionality review on a broader scale.

As such, U.S. courts have had a difficult time protecting citizens in a systematic and coherent fashion from excessive government encroachment. Widespread acceptance of proportionality principles has been hindered by the courts' failure to properly identify proportionality review when it is utilized. Furthermore, they have been reluctant to adopt explicit proportionality review outside of a very narrowly defined fault-based analysis. Normatively, courts should employ a consistent basis for their decisions so that those rulings are understood, command respect, and provide a predictable guide to the efficient resolution of future claims and disputes.

The diversity of contexts in which proportionality review has been and can be invoked indicates that the principles outlined earlier are flexible and useful analytic tools. By recognizing proportionality principles in their variable forms and implementing them broadly, courts could adopt a more consistent approach to resolving legal dilemmas, thereby improving not only the decisions they must make but also how those decisions are received and acted upon.

Questions may arise as to whether American courts are capable of competently applying the principle. To do so, courts will be forced to move beyond the rigid categorization that the current jurisprudence requires. In light of the recent moves by the Supreme Court toward applying proportionality and the experience of other courts in successfully applying these principles, we argue that the American judicial system possesses the institutional competency to use proportionality to protect individual rights and set meaningful limits on state regulation and punishment. Proportionality may also be utilized by the legislative branch when drafting and passing regulations.[29]

The described beneficial values of proportionality can best be understood through an examination of domestic, foreign, and international experience,[30] as well as its history. Examination of proportionality in broad comparative and historical perspective demonstrates the universality of these principles in space and time—these are fundamental, long-standing, and widespread concepts in European and American jurisprudence. Of course, when making comparisons across doctrines, even within domestic law, the specific doctrinal context of the rules is important. Nevertheless, there is great value in comparing rules or underlying principles in differing doctrinal contexts—a kind of interdoctrinal comparative law. Like more traditional uses of comparative law, examination of the similarities and differences across legal doctrines opens our eyes to new ways of thinking about familiar rules. It also helps us to make the rules more coherent and consistent or at least as consistent as they can be, considering differences in context.

Part I of this work explores the conceptual underpinnings of the principle of proportionality, traces its gradual development under the auspices of the ancient concept of just war, and describes the experience of foreign legal regimes, including the European Union, in their use of proportionality principles to control government regulation. Part I also discusses both common law notions of proportionality in the assessment of reasonableness of compensatory and liquidated damages and implicit proportionality principles applied in fashioning antitrust remedies.

We have chosen to discuss most of the foreign, international, and common law examples first, even though some readers may question the relevance of this material or be impatient to get to the discussions of contemporary U.S. constitutional law in chapters 3 to 7. We begin with foreign and historical examples because we want to emphasize the universality of proportionality principles, as well as their common themes and important variations. Examining these examples at the outset lays the foundation for our principal descriptive and normative claims, summarized earlier. The proportionality principles we discuss in this book are fundamental, long-standing, and widespread concepts in European and American jurisprudence, and American courts should not hesitate to invoke them. Indeed, as the later chapters show, American courts are already using versions of these core principles; they need to do so more explicitly and with more precise definitions, as foreign courts have already done.

Part II examines the general doctrinal standards of judicial review under the Fourteenth Amendment's due process clause and equal protection clause. It also analyzes the discrete areas of American constitutional jurisprudence in which proportionality is explicitly named as a standard of review by the Court to determine the scope of allowable government intrusion into individual autonomy or the autonomy of the several states, as well as the use of proportionality as a remedial tool for establishing the need for government action to protect a guaranteed freedom or right.

Part III analyzes the importance of the principle of proportionality in the American system of criminal justice. Many implicit examples of the proportionality principles we identify appear in constitutional and subconstitutional rules of criminal procedure and in rules limiting criminal liability. Explicit and implicit federal and state constitutional proportionality limits have also been applied, although not consistently, to the severity of punishments and the treatment of prisoners, and proportionality principles are widely recognized in scholarly writings on sentencing theory and in subconstitutional sentencing laws and practices in the United States and foreign countries.

We recommend that every government intrusion into individual autonomy, be it regulation or penalty, undergo some form of proportionality review unless strict scrutiny or another more restrictive standard applies. Although rational application of the principle of proportionality requires the intensity of judicial scrutiny to vary across different areas of legislative or executive action, we submit that even the minimum degree of judicial control over government regulation must be sufficiently scrupulous to meaningfully reconcile societal and individual interests. Applying these principles will enhance the coherence, consistency, and legitimacy of the courts' decisions. To date, the Supreme Court, in its ad hoc approach to decision making, has not considered a general theory of proportionality, although the principle has found expression in isolated cases. In this work, we explicitly advance such an instrumental theory.

ORIGINS I

From the Annals of History
to the Twenty-first Century

The chapters in this part demonstrate the broad and long-standing acceptance of proportionality principles in Western legal systems. Chapter 1 shows how the tradition of proportionality in government affairs finds its roots in the just war theory that was developed by Cicero, Saint Augustine, and Saint Thomas Aquinas to judge the morality of going to and waging war. Building on the teachings of these prominent figures, the renowned Dutch philosopher and legal scholar Hugo Grotius expanded the use of proportionality to ensure not only that the act of going to war was just but also that its actual conduct corresponded with the war's objectives. In his treatise on war,[1] Hugo Grotius also underscored the key role of natural law in shaping the decisions of governments and individuals. Further importance of the principle of proportionality in the law of war has been recognized by the United Nations. In particular, the UN Charter,[2] adopted after World War II, prohibited the use of force except in self-defense, and Protocol I to the Geneva Convention of 1949[3] condemned excessive suffering in the conduct of war.

The modern limitations on the initiation and conduct of war incorporate both alternative-means and ends-benefits proportionality principles. Recourse to war must be in legitimate self-defense, only as a last resort, and only when necessary and proportionate to the needs of self-defense. In the conduct of war, military actions must seek to minimize unnecessary suffering and destruction and must not be excessive relative to the military objectives they attempt to achieve.

At about the same time that these important developments took place in the international regulation of the law of war, Germany, France, and other European democracies began realizing their transformation into welfare states. As discussed in the second part of chapter 1, the emerging need to balance state regulation and individual autonomy has resulted in the adoption of the constitutional requirement of proportionality of government measures to the objectives sought, including both ends- and means-proportionality assessments. This doctrine was also successfully integrated into the legislative and administrative structure of the European Union. Meanwhile, the United States chose to review government action without an express reference to the principle of proportionality.[4] This is despite the fact that its system of judicial review espouses all of the elements of proportionality recognized in European jurisdictions.[5] The American judiciary, led by the Supreme Court, has used the term "proportionality" only to signify a standard of review stricter than rational basis but less rigorous than intermediate scrutiny.[6]

The second chapter in this part examines the development of proportionality principles in the English and U.S. common law limitations on compensatory damages in contract and tort. Although proportionality principles have subsequently been defined and further developed, the common law originally embraced proportionality in the general sense. Chapter 2 concludes with an examination of implicit proportionality principles applied by U.S. federal courts when fashioning remedies for antitrust violations.

1 PROPORTIONALITY IN INTERNATIONAL AND FOREIGN LAW

A. PROPORTIONALITY IN THE INITIATION AND CONDUCT OF WAR

1. The Concept of Just War

The use of war as an instrument of sovereign policy has emerged with the realization that war is undertaken for the advancement of peace. Cicero said in his *De Officiis* that accepting war as a method of state policy for resolving disputes must come only after the state has had recourse to their peaceful resolution. He urged that "wars should be undertaken for the one purpose of living peaceably without suffering injustice."[1] Any other resort to war at the level of state policy is characteristic of beasts rather than civilized human beings.[2] From this idea emerged the concept of just war—a method for distinguishing barbarity from the use of force as a necessary element of sovereign policy.[3]

Cicero's concept of just war was embraced by ancient writers such as Saint Augustine and Saint Thomas Aquinas. Saint Augustine, a prominent philosopher from Hippo, fifth century AD, wrote about the concept of just war in his treatise *City of God*.[4] He believed that waging war was counter to human nature. Only the injustice of the opposing side could justify and even impose a duty to wage a war.[5]

Even when the war to be waged is just, the person thus compelled should "lament the necessity of just wars."[6]

Saint Thomas Aquinas agreed with this formulation some seven hundred years later in his *Summa Theologica*,[7] in which he mentioned the basic requirements for a war to be just. To begin with, there must be "the authority of the sovereign by whose command the war is to be waged."[8] Individuals are not entitled to take the law into their own hands by resorting to the sword, nor are they authorized to gather people to wage wars.[9] The assumption is that a sovereign will have made a legitimate assessment of the justice of going to war. Also, because war is ordinarily followed by peace, the authority of a sovereign is required to enforce the demands and fulfill the promises or concessions reached in the negotiations of peace.[10] Thus, Aquinas quoted Augustine as saying that "[t]he natural order conducive to peace among mortals demands that the power to declare and counsel war should be in the hands of those who hold the supreme authority."[11]

Moreover, "a just cause is required" for a war to be just: "[T]hose who are attacked, should be attacked because they deserve it on account of some fault."[12] Aquinas finds backing for this proposition in the writings of Augustine, who said that the goal of war is to avenge wrongs inflicted by the other state or its subjects.[13] It is required, Aquinas observed, that "the belligerents should have a rightful intention, so that they intend the advancement of good, or the avoidance of evil."[14] Augustine, said Aquinas, specifically emphasized that only wars undertaken with righteous motives were deemed peaceful by any true religion.[15] Both Augustine and Aquinas agreed that wars guided by vengeance, desire for power, and cruelty should be condemned.[16]

Three hundred years later, prominent natural rights theorist Huig de Groot (Hugo Grotius), disgusted at the Christian world's propensity to go to war without regard to any human or divine law, published his treatise *On the Law of War and Peace (De Jure Belli ac Pacis)*.[17] He attempted to set forth the laws of war binding on and applicable to the whole of humanity.[18] He disagreed with some of his fellow writers that Christians were forbidden to use arms.[19] Instead, Grotius reasoned that war could be used as a means of restoring a violated right against those "who could not be held in check by judicial process."[20] Thus, he contended that not all wars are just and argued that, to be justified, wars "must be carried on with not less scrupulousness than judicial processes are wont to be."[21]

Grotius also reasoned that there cannot be a right to an unjust war.[22] Because "right is that, which is not unjust," he said, there can be no right to resort to unjust war.[23] He defines injustice as that "which is repugnant to the nature of society, established among rational creatures."[24] Grotius agrees with Cicero that only when it is impossible to use normal human understanding can there be resort to force in resolving a dispute.[25] He argued that the right of a human being to self-defense is a natural right, one that is not acquired by habit or custom but is "engraven in our hearts and minds with [nature's] own hand."[26] Thus, not all wars are repugnant to nature, but one should discover the just causes for war through natural reason.[27] According to Grotius, the force of natural law is so great that even God cannot appoint things contrary to it if "the law of nature positively forbids or commands."[28]

Grotius refined the theory of just war articulated by Augustine and Aquinas. His requirements of just war were just cause, rightful intention,[29] proper authority and public declaration,[30] war as last resort (necessity),[31] probability of success,[32] and proportionality of response to aggression.[33] "The justifiable causes generally assigned for war are three, defense, indemnity, and punishment...."[34] In pursuance of these causes, just war can be declared in response to a committed or an imminent injury.[35] Just war can also be declared in protection of others.[36]

Quite remarkably, Grotius foreshadowed in his treatise the lawfulness of preemptive wars. He maintained that, although nations may prevent remote or immediate aggression against them, "the suspicion of hostile intentions, on the part of another power, may not justify the commencement of actual war, yet it calls for measures of armed prevention, and will authorise indirect hostility."[37] Accordingly, war cannot be waged as a matter of expediency, as when one nation is feeling uncomfortable about the growing power of a neighboring nation.[38] In this respect, Grotius said that no complete security exists in human life, which is why "[t]he only protection against uncertain fears must be sought, not from violence, but from the divine providence, and defensive precaution."[39] He added that, whenever there is doubt about the justice of the cause of war, one must err on the side of peace.[40] Grotius recommended that, in case of doubt, nations avoid hostilities at all cost and attempt to resolve their disputes peacefully by conference or compromise or by lot or single combat.[41] Even if no doubt exists and a just cause for going to war has been established, said Grotius, nations are to refrain from having recourse to arms.[42]

The application of Grotius's theory of just war was not limited to the *ends* of war. The *means* of war, he said, were "never to be considered by THEMSELVES, but only as they have a tendency to the proposed end."[43] He laid down three basic rules for assessing the proportionality[44] of the means of war to the war's ends. First, the tendency of the desired object to produce good or evil must be determined.[45] Second, if there is uncertainty as to whether the good or the evil will predominate, the use of force may be chosen only if the actor has means to shift the preponderance in favor of the good.[46] Third, the actor may decide in favor of the means—even "if the good and the evil bear no proportion to each other" or the means are inadequate to the end—if the comparative likelihood of the good occurring is greater than the potential excess of the evil over the good, had the evil occurred, or if the potential excess of the good over the evil, had the good occurred, is greater than the comparative likelihood of the evil occurring.[47]

Grotius rephrased these complicated rules by using Cicero's simple analogy to the practice of medicine: Doctors apply weaker remedies to fight weaker diseases and stronger ones to ward off serious illnesses.[48] He observed that "no war should be undertaken, but where the hopes of advantage could be shewn to overbalance the apprehensions of ruin."[49]

Unlike his predecessors, Grotius dedicated several chapters of his treatise to the proportionality of the conduct of war. He established the principle of discriminate application of force and the requirement that the means undertaken in war must be necessary for the attainment of the military objective.[50] The treatise is revolutionary in emphasizing the humanitarian aspects of war and praising the sanctity of human life. For the first time, it offered a global view on the role of the principle of proportionality in reducing unnecessary human suffering in the conduct of war. The values Grotius developed in *On the Law of War and Peace* laid the foundation for gradual restriction of the use of force; the treatise began the introduction of humanitarian law into military affairs.

The purpose of this excursus in history is not to provide a complete account of the development of the principle of proportionality in military affairs but to show its ancient roots. Thus, in the next section we shift our discussion to the modern-day developments of proportionality in military law, skipping several generations of just war philosophers who have built upon the foundation created by Grotius.

2. The Development of the Principle of Proportionality in the Law of War
before the Adoption of the UN Charter and the Geneva Convention of 1949

The world's concern with war was again on a rise in the period between the Geneva Convention of 1864 and the Hague Conventions of 1899 and 1907. The conventions codified a number of important customary international rules and limitations on the conduct of war and the behavior of victors in the occupied territories. This was also the time when the doctrine of proportionality began emerging as a full-fledged principle of the law of armed conflict, restricting the range of available means to inflict damage on the enemy.[51]

Adopted before the St. Petersburg Declaration, the Geneva Convention of 1864 marks the first significant international attempt to limit suffering in the conduct of war. The convention was signed to ameliorate the conditions of wounded soldiers.[52] It contained rules for the treatment of wounded soldiers and established the neutral status of military hospitals and ambulances.[53] To inhabitants of a country who had helped wounded soldiers it guaranteed freedom from harm and even prescribed that, if a household was taking care of a wounded enemy soldier, it would be exempt from the quartering of troops.[54]

Sir Phillimore, a member of the English Privy Council, wrote in 1873 in his *Commentaries upon International Law* that not everything is "'lawful against the enemy,' but only those things which are essential to the vigorous prosecution and speedy termination of the War."[55] He said that ill treatment of "unarmed and unoffending men, much more of women and children" and means of unjustifiable destruction of territory were strictly prohibited.[56] He also declared that the principles of just war forbade the killing of prisoners or wounded or helpless enemies and that such killing would be considered murder.[57]

The Hague Conventions of 1899 and 1907 furthered these principles. They were adopted by the First and the Second International Peace Conferences at The Hague, which convened to codify the generally binding rules of the law of war and warfare.[58] The resulting conventions extensively covered the issue of the accepted law of war embodied in the state of customary law at the time of adoption.[59]

The Hague Convention respecting the Laws and Customs of War on Land focused specifically on limiting the means available to the belligerent parties in the conduct of war.[60] Proportionality figures implicitly in several of the convention's provisions. Most important, the document recognizes that "[t]he right of belligerents to adopt means of injuring the enemy is not unlimited."[61] Several military practices were specifically prohibited as conducive to unnecessary suffering.[62] Finally, several clauses call for a tight fit between the military means and the military objective.[63]

Despite its important pronouncements, the scope of the Hague Convention was limited to prevention of excessive means of conducting a war (*jus in bello*[64]), not unjust war itself (*jus ad bellum*[65]). Proportionality had not found its way into conventional sources of international law regulating the justice of war until the intensification of international security cooperation after World War II, when the UN Charter and the Geneva Conventions were adopted.[66] Sources of customary international law using proportionality for this purpose were likewise scarce. The only significant evidence that proportionality persisted in both *jus in bello* and *jus ad bellum* was the *Caroline* incident,[67] one of those rare occasions in this period when proportionality played an important role in determining the appropriateness of the use of force.

The *Caroline* was a small American steamer that was used to smuggle anti-British insurgents and arms into Canada to support an insurgency against British rule.[68] In 1837 it was destroyed by British forces, who viewed the *Caroline* as an enemy.[69] The Americans considered this an act of aggression, whereas the British contended that the destruction of the ship was in self-defense.[70] After long and heated discussions, the foreign ministers of both countries accepted the principle that the use of force must be proportional to the threat to the sovereign territory of an independent nation: "'Respect for the inviolable character of the territory of independent nations is the most essential foundation of civilization,' and...this can only be legally overridden by 'a necessity of self-defense, instant, overwhelming, leaving no choice of means, and no moment for deliberation,' and 'the act...must be limited by that necessity, and kept clearly within it.'"[71]

3. The UN Charter Regime and the Geneva Conventions

The role of the principle of proportionality in the law of war and the law of warfare was advanced considerably by the adoption of the Charter of the United Nations, the Geneva Conventions, and the Geneva Conventions' Additional Protocols.[72] These international treaties represent the general willingness of world nations, shocked by the cruelties of World Wars I and II, to diminish the use of force in the resolution of international disputes. They also provide greater protection of and respect for human rights in the conduct of war. The treaties embrace the essential force of Cicero's words that resort to force without compromise and negotiation is characteristic of wild beasts, not civilized human beings.[73] The charter and the Geneva Conventions retained the meaningful division of the law of war into *jus ad bellum* and *jus in bello* and preserved in both the role of proportionality.

a. Proportionality of Resort to Force

The Charter of the United Nations prohibits the threat or use of force[74] except in legitimate individual or collective self-defense,[75] thus allowing the customary principle of proportionality to play an important role in the avoidance of the unnecessary use of force. As one of the requirements borrowed from the doctrine of just war, proportionality measures the appropriateness of military response to an armed attack.[76] The recourse to force must be proportionate to the needs of self-defense. In this capacity, proportionality closely correlates with the just war requirements of just cause, last resort (necessity), probability of success, and proper authority. Use of force is not considered proportional if any of these requirements are not met.

Two important cases decided by the International Court of Justice explored the use of proportionality in determining the lawfulness of the use of force in self-defense. Each acknowledged that the requirement of proportionality is not specifically introduced by Article 51 of the charter but rather was incorporated in the charter as part of customary international law.[77]

In the first case, *Military and Paramilitary Activities in and against Nicaragua (Nicaragua v. United States)*, the court held that the "rule whereby self-defense would warrant only measures which are proportional to the armed attack and necessary to respond to it" was a rule "well established in customary international law."[78] The court found that the American activities "relating to the mining of the Nicaraguan ports and the attacks on ports, oil installations, etc.," did not satisfy the requirement of proportionality.[79]

The United States' military attack on Nicaragua, the court held, was so much greater in scope than the perceived dangers to El Salvador, Honduras, and Costa Rica—in protection of whom the United States commenced these attacks, claiming the right to collective self-defense against the military aid provided by Nicaragua to the Salvadorian opposition army—that it failed to satisfy the principle of proportionality.[80] Moreover, the United States continued its assaults well beyond the period in which the dangers from Nicaraguan aid to the Salvadoran opposition army could still be perceived.[81] As a result, the court concluded that the United States' invocation of the right to collective self-defense against an armed attack on El Salvador, Honduras, or Costa Rica to validate its activities against Nicaragua could not be accepted,[82] leaving the United States' attacks on Nicaragua without proper legal support.

In the second case, the court similarly held that United States' strikes on Iranian oil platforms failed to satisfy the principle of proportionality.[83] Two incidents prompted the U.S. military to attack the oil platforms. First, a Kuwaiti oil tanker, sailing under the American flag for protection,[84] was hit by a missile believed to have been launched by Iran.[85] Second, the USS *Samuel B. Roberts*, while traveling in international waters in the Persian Gulf, struck a mine that the United States suspected had been installed by Iran.[86] In addition to considering these strikes unnecessary and finding insufficient evidence for treating the Iranian oil platforms as legitimate military objectives,[87] the court further condemned one of the United States' assaults as disproportional.[88] The attacks in response to the mining of USS *Samuel B. Roberts* were part of a more extensive program named "Operation Praying Mantis."[89] Although this case dealt with the destruction of two oil platforms in the course of this program, the court could not "close its eyes to the scale of the whole operation, which involved, inter alia, the destruction of two Iranian frigates and a number of other naval vessels and aircraft."[90] The court, therefore, held that "neither 'Operation Praying Mantis' as a whole, nor even that part of it that destroyed the Salman and Nasr platforms, [could] be regarded, in the circumstances of this case, as a proportionate use of force in self-defence."[91]

b. Proportionality of the Means of War

The principle of proportionality of the means of war and the rules of combat (*jus in bello*) were codified in Additional Protocol I to the Geneva Convention of 1949

(Protocol I). Protocol I stands for the proposition that, if the resort to force in self-defense is valid, proportionality should be employed to protect combatants and noncombatants from excessive attacks. It is implicitly incorporated in a number of articles that regulate the means and methods of warfare. Customary rules of the law of armed conflict, however, continue in effect with regard to nonparties to the protocol.[92] That the rules of armed conflict and the attendant requirement of proportionality ought not to be suspended with regard to aggressors is indicative of the expanded role of proportionality in the law of war.[93]

Several provisions of Protocol I require special attention in our study of proportionality. Article 35, for instance, embraces the principle of proportionality by declaring that the means and methods of warfare are not unlimited and by prohibiting the use of weapons that may cause excessive and unnecessary suffering. Interestingly, nuclear weapons, whose use without causing excessive and unnecessary suffering is impossible, were not outlawed as disproportionate per se. Having acknowledged that the threat or use of nuclear weapons would generally be contrary to the rules of armed conflict and humanitarian law, the International Court of Justice held that, "in view of the current state of international law" and facts at the court's disposal, "the Court [could not] conclude definitely whether the threat or use of nuclear weapons would be lawful or unlawful in an extreme circumstance of self-defence, in which the very survival of a State would be at stake."[94]

Article 51(4) of Protocol I prohibits attacks that are not directed at a specific military objective, employment of means or methods that cannot be directed at a specific military objective, or the use of means or methods of conduct that are not capable of discrimination. Article 51(5)(b) gives proportionality a central role in avoiding loss of civilian life.[95] This essential provision requires balancing, *ex ante*,[96] the "incidental loss of civilian life, injury to civilians, [and] damage to civilian objects," which is reasonably expected to be caused in the course of a military attack, against "the concrete and direct military advantage anticipated."[97] An attack is unlawful if the undesired collateral effects bear no reasonable relation to the military benefit attained. Article 51(5)(b) requires that both military targets and the means and methods of warfare be reviewed for disproportionality.[98] The rule requires "that proportionality be assessed in relation to each individual attack, rather than on a cumulative basis."[99] Protocol I also specifically provides for the protection from military attack of certain essential objects: cultural and religious items,[100] objects indispensable to the survival of the civilian population,[101] the natural environment,[102] and installations containing dangerous forces.[103] Thus, a proportionality analysis of any method of warfare must take into account a variety of factors, including the importance of the military target, the presence of civilian population and infrastructures in the target area, the potential civilian use of the military target, the ability to provide prior notice to the authorities about the threat to civilian population, the likely short-term and long-term environmental damage,[104] the type of weapon available and its accuracy, and the rights of neutral countries in the target area.

Several important matters of proportionality of means of war were articulated in the documents of the International Criminal Tribunal for the Former Yugoslavia and the Committee Established to Review the NATO Bombing Campaign against the Federal Republic of Yugoslavia. First, with regard to the relative values to be assigned to negative collateral effects and the achieved military advantage balanced under the principle of proportionality, both the tribunal[105] and the committee[106] supported the view that the determination of values be that of a "reasonable military commander." While, as the committee admitted, it would be unlikely for military commanders to agree on the values to be assigned to the collateral damage and military advantages in close cases, in many instances reasonable military leaders would concur on that issue.[107] It is often the case that military objectives are interspersed with or share the use of civilian objects. Moreover, the party responsible for the civilians located in these objects frequently fails to remove them before an attack.[108] Failure of a party in control of the targeted objects to relocate the civilians within or in the vicinity of military objects does not relieve the attacking side from taking these civilians into account in conducting the proportionality analysis before an assault.[109]

The committee also cited with some approval the application in the *Kupreskic Judgment* of a cumulating approach to assessing the scope of collateral harm inflicted in a military campaign:

> [R]egard might be had to considerations such as the cumulative effect of attacks on military objectives causing incidental damage to civilians. In other words, it may happen that single attacks on military objectives causing incidental damage to civilians, although they may raise doubts as to their lawfulness, nevertheless do not appear on their face to fall foul per se of the loose prescriptions of Articles 57 and 58 [of Protocol I to the Geneva Convention of 1949] (or of the corresponding customary rules). However, in case of repeated attacks, all or most of them falling within the grey area between indisputable legality and unlawfulness, it might be warranted to conclude that the cumulative effect of such acts entails that they may not be in keeping with international law.[110]

The committee observed that cumulating collateral damage was useful in conducting the overall assessment of a military campaign, despite the insufficiency of cumulation of instances of collateral damage to constitute a crime.[111] Based on the total casualty figures, the committee decided that there was no sufficient basis for charges of genocide or crimes against humanity.[112] It also found that none of the individual incidents warranted an investigation by the Office of the Prosecutor.[113]

Arguably, proportionality balances between "two opposing goals: the swift achievement of the military goal with the minimum losses of one's own combatants and the protection of the other party's civilian population."[114] This subjective approach is bound to shift the balance in favor of one's own combatants,[115] an effect observed in the first Gulf War. To avoid ground war in Iraq in 1991, the United States launched an extensive air attack that destabilized and weakened Saddam Hussein's army. The swiftness of "Operation Desert Storm" has been praised, but no mention is made of the substantial damage the United States' air strikes caused to the civilian system of Iraq with long-term devastating effects on the civilian population.[116] Despite these drawbacks, the requirement of proportionality of the means and methods of warfare remains an important instrument for the protection of human life in the law of armed conflict.

4. Contemporary Application of Just War Principles

The just war doctrine may also prove an effective tool for assessing contemporary decisions to go to war and for deciding on a method to carry it out. In the wake of the tragedy of September 11, 2001, President George W. Bush promulgated a new national security strategy that focused on "identifying and destroying the [terrorist] threat before it reaches our borders."[117] Affirmative actions would be taken without international support, if necessary, and the president would not hesitate "to exercise our right to self-defense by acting preemptively against such terrorists."[118] President Bush is the first U.S. president to explicitly endorse preemptive strikes as an affirmative national defense strategy.[119]

The president implied that this new strategy was simply an extension of the just war doctrine adapted to the fundamentally different way that terrorist organizations wage war.[120] He argued that when opposing forces manifest an "imminent danger of attack," international law recognizes that one need not wait to be attacked before engaging the threat with force.[121] Historically, an imminent threat was one that the sovereign could observe, such as the mobilization of enemy troops or the strategic placement of weaponry.[122] Preventive war—commenced to defeat an adversary before it is able to gather sufficient forces to launch a successful attack—has largely been condemned as unjust.[123] When the threat is great enough, however, the president expressed a willingness to authorize preemptive strikes "even if uncertainty remains as to the time and place of the enemy's attack."[124]

The president also contended that "emerging threats" and gathering dangers are legitimate targets of preemptive strikes.[125] This propensity for declaring a preemptive strike against uncertain threats stands on an unsure foundation with respect to the principle of proportionality. The president's expansion of the concept of imminent threat necessarily raises the question of whether the standard of evidence used to justify a preemptive strike is satisfied.[126] While resolution of the question is beyond the scope of this book, the missing weapons of mass destruction in Iraq[127] or a 1 percent probability of a threat[128] arguably would not meet this standard.

It is unclear whether Grotius would agree that President Bush's strategy is merely an "adapt[ation of] the concept of imminent threat to the capabilities and objectives of today's adversaries."[129] Although it is possible to view the differences between Grotius and the president as mere semantics, it is important to remember the great cost of waging war.[130] Grotius's repeated appeal to sovereign authority to ensure that every decision to go to war be strictly proportional to the magnitude and imminence of the threat suggests that the use of force based on uncertain circumstances would not be justified. As Grotius urged, prudence dictates that doubts about the justification of a particular war should be resolved in favor of peace.[131]

The United States has also adopted and utilized methods of warfare that raise proportionality concerns. During the buildup to the Gulf War, General Colin Powell articulated a military policy that built on ideas espoused by former secretary of defense Casper Weinberger and centuries of military experience.[132] Now known as the Powell Doctrine, the policy requires decision makers to ask themselves important questions before entering into a war: "Is the political objective important, clearly defined and understood? Have all nonviolent policy means failed? Will military force achieve the objective? At what cost? Have the gains and risks been analyzed? How might the situation to be altered, once it is altered by force, develop further and what might be the consequences?"[133] Later the doctrine was also interpreted to require a viable exit strategy—a "timetable for victory and withdrawal."[134]

Once the decision to go to war is made, the Powell Doctrine calls for massive or overwhelming force to be used[135] in order to minimize the United States' casualties and hasten the end of active hostilities.[136] Thus, when a decision must be made between protecting one's own military forces and objectives and safeguarding the opponent's civilian population, the Powell Doctrine clearly favors the former.[137] The very language used to describe the force required—overwhelming and massive—raises serious proportionality concerns that implicate the just war doctrine and international conventions.[138]

Although the trend in international law has been toward formalizing proportionality analysis and requirements, Powell argued that a rigid national defense policy was imprudent.[139] Ambiguous constraints on the use of force aided deterrence by forcing one's enemy to guess how severely one might respond to a provocation.[140] Powell also argued that adopting a rigid policy would effectively tie the hands of decision makers in adopting the most prudent type of force in any given situation.[141] Instead, Powell favored a pragmatic approach that would allow for the type and magnitude of force necessary to accomplish legitimate military goals.

In sum, the principle of proportionality has an important place in the international system of the laws of war.[142] It reflects the world's growing desire to avoid war and to reduce to a minimum incidental civilian loss. Proportionality offers a meaningful way to balance the evils of war against the benefits of the military objective, with a view of retaining war as a method of last resort in the resolution of international conflicts. The principle of proportionality thus stands not only to limit the number of times nations will choose to go to war but also to limit the number of human lives lost during those wars. Just as the principle as applied in just war doctrine recognizes the importance of human life, proportionality as applied in other contexts recognizes the value of individual rights and autonomy and serves to limit both the quantity and quality of government encroachment of those rights.

B. PROPORTIONALITY IN FOREIGN LEGAL REGIMES

The principle of proportionality has more often been employed in a more peaceful context to measure the fairness of the balance between state regulation and individual autonomy. It has played an important role in the constitutional law of many jurisdictions, where it is used to balance the costs and the benefits of government regulation in the search for the least intrusive and most effective measures. The emergence of the principle of proportionality in European countries was associated with the rise of the social state.[143] The level of government's social involvement in and recognition of basic human rights determines the scope of application of the principle of proportionality. The following examples demonstrate how proportionality measures the balance between the benefits and the costs of the government regulation. Several nations provide illuminating examples of the use of both alternative-means and ends-benefits proportionality principles.

1. Canada

Canadian constitutional jurisprudence derives the principle of proportionality from Section 1 of the Canadian Charter of Rights and Freedoms.[144] It provides that the rights guaranteed in the charter may be "subject only to such reasonable limits prescribed by law as can be demonstrably justified in a free and democratic society."[145]

The Supreme Court of Canada in *R. v. Oakes*[146] developed a two-tier constitutional control test. Once the claimant has proved a violation of a right guaranteed in the charter, the government must satisfy two criteria to establish that the limit on individual rights "can be demonstrably justified in a free and democratic society."[147]

First, measures limiting a constitutionally protected right must serve an important objective that "relate[s] to concerns which are pressing and substantial in a free and democratic society."[148] This requirement can normally be satisfied since courts are generally deferential to legislative choice of action.[149] On several occasions, however, the government has failed to satisfy this requirement.[150] Legislation limiting the rights of English-speaking parents in Quebec to educate their children in English-speaking schools[151] or requiring the Lord's Prayer in secular schools[152] has been found lacking an important public objective. Likewise, the Supreme Court of Canada was unable to find any legitimate public objective that justified denying protection to gays and lesbians under Alberta's human rights law in *Vriend v. Alberta*.[153] In *R. v. Zundel* it also prohibited an intrusive use of a law that was unrelated to the objectives originally contemplated by the Parliament when that law was enacted.[154]

Once an important public objective or end has been established, the selected means to attain it must be "reasonable and demonstrably justified."[155] The court said in *R. v. Big M Drug Mart Ltd.* that this determination involves "a form of proportionality test."[156] Although it varies depending on the facts of the case, the test involves the balancing of public and individual interests based on three principles.[157] First, the means must be rationally related to the objective.[158] The court has infrequently struck down legislation for lack of any rational relation to the objective pursued.[159] It employs a rather deferential and contextual[160] approach to determine the rational relation of a provision to the desired end.[161]

Second, the means should "impair 'as little as possible' the right or freedom in question."[162] This is believed to be the decisive element of proportionality review.[163] It requires that the legislature adopt the least intrusive measure capable of attaining the desired objective.[164] A good example of the application of this element of proportionality appears in a decision of the Supreme Court of Canada in which it invalidated a provision of Quebec legislation prohibiting the use of the English language in signs and posters.[165] The court held that the desired promotion of the French language could be achieved through a less intrusive alternative by "requiring that commercial signs display a marked predominance of French."[166] Most recent cases recognize that the legislatures must be afforded a "zone of discretion within which different legislative choices in derogation of a *Charter* right could be tolerated."[167]

Lastly, the public objective and actual effects[168] of the means adopted for its attainment must be proportionate to an important public end or objective.[169] The court noted that even if the means satisfies the first two criteria, it may be declared unconstitutional in view of its disproportionate harmful effects on an individual.[170] Despite this language, the court has not invalidated a provision solely for failure to balance the costs and benefits of its implementation if it satisfied the first two criteria of proportionality.[171] Rather, courts use balancing to reinforce their conclusions under the "rational relation" and "minimum impairment" components of the proportionality test[172] and to avoid invalidation of legislative provisions for "insubstantial" unconstitutional effects on individual freedoms.[173]

2. Germany

The principle in Germany is an unwritten constitutional rule derived from the principle of the rule of law.[174] The high court of Germany described proportionality "as an expression of general right of the citizen towards the State that his freedom should be limited by the public authorities only to the extent indispensable for the protection of the public interest."[175] The principle of proportionality in German law incorporates three important subprinciples: suitability, necessity, and proportionality in the narrower sense.

According to the high court of Germany, any government interference with basic rights must be suitable and necessary for reaching the ends sought. Its disadvantages to individuals "are generally only permissible if the protection of others or of the public interest requires them, after having due regard to the principle of proportionality."[176] Suitability is the tendency of the course of action to achieve or facilitate the achievement of the desired end. Legislators are given sufficient discretion in determining whether a course of action is suitable.[177] Despite this deferential standard, Germany's high court has not refrained from invalidating the legislative determination of suitability of legislative measures on several occasions.[178] Necessity requires the adoption of the least intrusive, equally efficient alternative. Regarding proportionality in the narrower sense, "the burden resulting from the measure must not be excessive in relation to the public interest concerned."[179] Germany requires meaningful proportionality review of any public interference with a basic right by legislative or administrative action. The importance of the principle of proportionality is largely defined through the measure of guaranteed personal autonomy.

The scope of protection afforded to personal autonomy in Germany is remarkable. The court stated in the *Reiten im Walde Case*:[180] "According to the principles developed in the case law of the Federal Constitutional Court, Art. 2(1) [of the Constitution of Germany[181]] guarantees general freedom of action in a comprehensive [sense]. This does not only protect the limited area of development of the personality. It protects every form of human activity regardless of the weight attaching to it in the context of development of the [personality]."[182] Several basic rights that belong to the "inner core" of one's autonomy are "accorded absolute protection and thus are withdrawn from interference by public authority."[183] Given the social nature of a human being, rights outside the "inner core" are limited by the rights of others, the constitutional order, and the moral code as embodied in the German Constitution.[184]

Responding to the criticism of this broad protection of individual freedom, the court said that limiting the constitutional protection to a narrow set of individual rights "would bring with it difficult demarcation problems which could hardly be satisfactorily resolved in practice."[185] Any interference with the enjoyment of the latter group of rights is subject to judicial proportionality control.[186] Proportionality, according to the court in the *Reiten im Walde Case*, tests, in reference to Article 2(1) of the German Constitution, whether the legal norm that affects the freedom of action "belongs to the constitutional order, that is to say is formally and materially in harmony with the norms of the [Basic Law[187]]."[188] Thus, the court concluded that "the principle of proportionality offers a yardstick by which the general freedom of action may be limited."[189] As such, the principle of proportionality has two purposes. First, it is used to determine whether "the pursuit of the public interest merits precedence generally."[190] Second, it ensures that the measures undertaken are suitable, necessary, and proportionate to the desired end.[191] The court applied the test of proportionality in the following landmark cases.

In the *Cannabis Case*,[192] the Federal Constitutional Court of Germany applied proportionality to determine whether possession, sale, purchase, or use of cannabis should be punishable and whether the criminal sanctions imposed for various cannabis violations were excessive. First, the court used proportionality as a test to determine whether the prohibition of cannabis was proportional to the need of protecting the health, safety, and welfare of the public.[193] It reasoned that the legislature possesses a considerable amount of discretion in determining the sorts of behavior to be punishable by criminal law.[194] Noting that there is no scientifically based information capable of showing which one of the conflicting views about the threat of cannabis to health and public order is correct, the court deferred to the legislature's choice to prohibit cannabis under the threat of criminal punishment.[195] With regard to the criminal penalties, the court focused on assessing the proportionality of criminal sanctions in the narrower sense—whether the restrictions imposed on individual liberty were outweighed by the resulting benefits of protecting the health of society.[196] If the costs of a criminal sanction outweigh its benefits, the right to individual liberty must take precedence.[197]

The court found proportionate all provisions of the Intoxicating Substances Act that imposed criminal sanctions.[198] It explained that the legislature could comply with the principle of proportionality in the narrower sense by taking into account the relative wrongfulness and culpability in certain groups of cases through substantive or procedural provisions.[199] Substantive measures would involve a regime of lower sanctions for petty offenses involving cannabis, while procedural differentiation would be achieved mainly through granting prosecutorial discretion in such cases.[200] The federal legislature opted for procedural differentiation, which, said the court, was entirely consistent with the principle of proportionality.[201]

The *Lebach Case*[202] dealt with the proportionality between media reports about a specific crime and the perpetrator's autonomy. The court observed that when the freedom of reporting news impinges on other protected interests, "the purpose of the individual broadcast, the manner of its presentation, and its actual foreseeable effect may become relevant."[203] When two constitutionally protected interests conflict, said the court, it is important to determine which takes precedence in light of the circumstances of the case and whether its proposed intrusion on the other interest is necessary, suitable, and proportional to the desired end.[204]

The court concluded that the right of personality (personal dignity) of a perpetrator of a crime must give precedence to reporting about the crime in the media because the latter serves the important functions of informing the public about a dangerous crime, publicizing the measures undertaken by the government to solve it, and deterring similar future transgressions.[205] Because the "interest to receive information does not prevail absolutely,"[206] the negative effects of a news report suffered by the perpetrator must still be proportional to the public's need to receive information and to the seriousness of the offense.[207] To protect perpetrators from unwanted intrusion into their personal life and to facilitate their reintegration into society, the balance between the public's right to receive information and a perpetrator's right to "be left alone" begins to shift in favor of the latter following the initial news broadcast.[208]

In *Reiten im Walde Case*,[209] discussed earlier in connection with the scope of the principle of proportionality, the court reviewed the constitutionality of a measure that restricted horseback riding in North Rhine Westphalia to specially designated trails. The claimant argued that he should be able to ride on certain other park trails that were designated for hiking only.[210] The court decided that riding was a form of human activity protected under Article 2(1) of the Constitution of Germany but that it did not belong to the core rights that were exempt from any government intrusion.[211] As such, riding could be subject to statutory limitations aimed at accommodating the rights of others.[212]

The court accepted the local government's explanation that, by restricting the park trails available for horseback riding, the local government intended to protect hikers from the dangers and inconveniences of unwanted encounters with horses and to safeguard hiking trails from damage due to horseback riding.[213] The court considered the regime of designating separate park trails for riding suitable and necessary for the attainment of the desired aims.[214] Finally, the court concluded that the measure was proportionate to the desired end.[215] Acknowledging that riders and hikers have an equal claim to the use of park trails, the court concluded that, because riders represent a smaller proportion of park visitors than hikers, the aims of protecting hikers and maintaining hiking trails would be more appropriately served by designating special tracks for riding rather than vice versa.[216]

3. France

France employs the principle of proportionality to create a means of effective control over growing executive discretion and government intervention into private affairs. The principle of proportionality in France has not been granted general application in administrative law, however.[217] As a general rule, proportionality review has been applied in the following areas: fundamental rights and freedoms, disciplinary action against civil servants, town planning and land development, and environmental protection.[218] In these areas, "[t]he principle of proportionality has been used to ensure that the administration seeks a reasonable balance between the different interests affected by its decisions."[219] Conversely, administrative courts also recognize the need for sufficient administrative discretion for administration "to function with regularity and certainty."[220]

French courts have a sliding scale of judicial review, including minimum control, normal control, and maximum control.[221] The intensity of review depends on the subject matter and the scope of discretion.[222] A recent rise in state social and economic regulations was matched by a corresponding expansion of proportionality review into the areas of minimum control, such as town planning and land development.[223] The threshold for judicial intervention in the areas of minimum control is manifest disproportionality.[224] "Nevertheless, it is still for the judge to evaluate every aspect of the case before him in order to verify whether the principle of proportionality has been respected by the administration."[225] Thus, as a general matter, proportionality review of an administrative action in France generally involves the balancing between advantages and disadvantages of the administrative action.[226] The stricter requirement that an administrative action be the least restrictive of individual liberty is believed to be limited to areas of maximum judicial control, where fundamental individual rights and freedoms are at stake.[227]

4. Eastern Europe

The Constitutional Court of Poland has used the principle of proportionality to determine the constitutionality of a statutory provision requiring that all transactions among legal entities be conducted through banking institutions. This measure was adopted to promote transparency in the national economy and to facilitate the collection of corporate and personal taxes. According to Article 6 of the Constitution of Poland of 1952, as amended in the postcommunist period, "the Republic of Poland shall guarantee freedom of economic activity regardless of the type of ownership; restrictions of this freedom may be imposed only by means of statute."[228] This constitutional provision required not only that any limitation on the freedom of economic activity be implemented by statute but also that any such legislative intrusion not be excessive in relation to the importance of the advancement of the public interest.[229]

To establish excessiveness of a legislative provision, the court considered the nature of the implicated individual rights and freedoms, "because they determine the general boundaries of permissible limitations."[230] This review, said the court, "should provide answers to the following three questions: 1) is the regulation capable of achieving the intended objectives? 2) is this regulation necessary to protect the public interest it refers to? 3) are its results proportional to the burdens imposed on citizens?"[231] Notwithstanding the presumption of constitutionality of legislative actions, the court declared its willingness to intervene should a legislative action exceed the degree of allowable discretion and constitute a drastic violation of the constitution. It noted that, based on the established system of constitutional values, the level of legislative discretion will be highest in regard to economic rights and lowest in regard to political and civil rights.[232]

The court upheld the provision in question because it satisfied all of the elements of the proportionality test, finding that the legislative measure was rationally related to the attainment of the sought objective.[233] It explained that the banking system was well equipped to monitor commercial transactions and to avoid the migration of resources into the shadow economy. The court also held that to require running large commercial transactions through the banking system was necessary for the attainment of the desired market transparency.[234] In this regard, it noted the importance of the ability of the banking system to improve transparency of commercial transactions, monitor cash flow of commercial organizations, and eliminate cheating in taxation.[235] In conclusion, the court determined that the adopted measure was proportional to the desired end because its benefits considerably outweighed the risks of unsecured commercial deposits and bank bankruptcies.[236] In the end, said the court, commercial organizations face a variety of business risks in their everyday operation, which makes the addition of the potential loss of funds due to bank bankruptcy *de minimis*.[237] The three-question test developed in this case "is considered the standard formulation of the proportionality requirement" in Poland.[238]

A similar provision of proportionality was established by the Constitutional Court of Ukraine in its decision reviewing the constitutionality of Article 69 of the Criminal Code of Ukraine.[239] Article 69 authorized the Ukrainian courts to impose a lesser criminal penalty than prescribed by the code on individuals convicted of grievous and intermediate crimes based on mitigating circumstances or *de minimis* social harm,[240] but it did not afford similar treatment to individuals convicted of petty crimes.[241] The Constitutional Court of Ukraine ruled that the principle of proportionality required individualization of criminal punishment to ensure that the burden imposed on an individual charged with a crime is proportional to the social harm the individual caused.[242] It derived the principle of proportionality from the general notion of fairness of the criminal process and from the constitutional principle of the rule of law.[243] The court noted that the requirements of the principle of proportionality were not satisfied in regard to citizens charged with petty crimes, as Article 69 of the Criminal Code of Ukraine did not offer them an option of a lesser sentence in the event that they established the requisite mitigating or character circumstances.[244]

5. The European Union

As with many other general principles of law, the European Union borrowed its general principle of proportionality from its member states. Germany had the most elaborate doctrine of proportionality; after initially employing a much narrower definition of proportionality, the union now has virtually adopted the German system.[245] At the time of its founding, many members of the European Union entertained some notion of proportionality in government regulation, which gave the union grounds for treating proportionality as a general principle of law.[246] The origin of the principle of proportionality was initially not discussed, as had been the case with other general principles.[247]

Scholars have argued that the European Court of Justice made an exception because it might have viewed the principle of proportionality as "such a fundamental and obvious principle that its presence in the Community legal order was deemed self-evident with no need for any further explanation and clarification."[248] Admitting that the national constitutional systems of the member states contributed to the strengthening of the principle of proportionality in its operation to protect fundamental rights, the court rejected national law as one of the plausible origins of the principle of proportionality.[249]

In *Internationale Handelsgesellschaft*,[250] the court determined that the principle of proportionality derived from the general principles of law protected by European Community law.[251] The court did not reject the various articles of the Treaty Establishing the European Community (EC treaty), which contains the words "required"[252] or "necessary"[253] or which "cause[s] the least disturbance to the functioning of the common market,"[254] as the origins of the principle of proportionality. Yet many scholars argue that the principle of proportionality derives its power from the rule of law that underlies the European Community's legal order.[255]

The principle of proportionality is closely linked with the principle of subsidiarity utilized to control EC legislative action.[256] Article 5 of the EC treaty prescribes that the "Community shall act within the limits of the powers conferred upon it by this Treaty and of the objectives assigned to it therein."[257] The principle of subsidiarity derived from this language is interpreted to contain a presumption that "primary responsibility and decision-making competence should rest with the lowest possible level of authority of the political hierarchy."[258] Thus, subsidiarity limits community power in relation to the member states; it determines whether EC action is warranted.[259] The requirement of proportionality contained in Article 5 of the EC treaty—as derived from the words that "[a]ny action by the Community shall not go beyond what is necessary to achieve the objectives of this Treaty"[260]—supplements the principle of proportionality by limiting the breadth of the community action once it is established that one is required.[261] In sum, Article 5 proportionality controls EC legislation, while the judicially established principle of proportionality controls its implementation.

The principle of proportionality applies to community regulation affecting the member states[262] and individuals. The test of proportionality, as developed by the European Court of Justice, contains three elements—suitability, necessity, and proportionality in the narrower sense.[263] The burden of proof is on the contesting party.[264] The court, however, might not apply all three elements in a particular case.[265] Suitability has been assigned a secondary role since most cases involve "complex economic situations" that warrant "wide discretionary powers."[266] As such, the assessment of suitability is limited to determining whether, "at the time when the measure was adopted, it was manifestly unsuitable to achieve the desired end."[267] The test of suitability in European Union jurisprudence is a test of manifest arbitrariness.[268]

Necessity has a leading role in proportionality jurisprudence of the court. It requires that the least intrusive regulatory measure be adopted.[269] Absent manifest error, the court is deferential to the choice of regulatory or legislative action in "the exercise of discretionary powers in the field of economic policy."[270]

The test of proportionality in the narrower sense is ordinarily used to prevent excessive penalty claims and encroachments on fundamental rights recognized as part of the general principles of law or rights granted by the EC treaty.[271] Derogations from EC treaty rights are subject to strict scrutiny and will be allowed in cases of "genuine and serious threats to national interests [of member states]" if the measure is necessary to the attainment of the desired end.[272] Derogations from fundamental rights recognized as part of the general principles of law are subject to suitability, necessity, and proportionality review.[273] Measures are lawful if they are not disproportionate to the end sought in a way that impairs the substance of a fundamental right.[274] This is particularly true in areas of wide discretionary powers, such as in the field of economic policy. Finally, although it recognizes the principle that penalties must not be excessive, the court "is unlikely to intervene unless the disproportionality is reasonably evident."[275] At present, the doctrine of proportionality in the European Union is in a state of constant development to accommodate gradual expansion of community regulation.[276]

European experience with proportionality is indicative of the principle's ability to be flexible to the myriad needs of different countries and governmental systems. Germany's experience—where the principle is most intricately defined and applied because of its constitutional status—demonstrates that proportionality is of sufficient legal character to adequately protect individual autonomy interests in a developed country. The European Community's successful adoption of the principle also demonstrates that proportionality may be used even where different levels of government are involved, effectively curbing unwarranted intrusions into individual autonomy by either level of government and protecting each level of government within its assigned sphere of action.

2 PROPORTIONALITY PRINCIPLES IN THE COMMON LAW OF DAMAGES

THE CONCEPT OF PROPORTIONALITY IS not entirely foreign to the common law. Proportionality, arguably, was embodied in the old common law principle of reasonableness. Indeed, both principles are related, and their application leads to similar results in the majority of cases.[1] The closeness between reasonableness and proportionality on the continuum of limitations on government discretion is instructively suggested by the experience in foreign jurisdictions where the two principles coexist effectively. Reasonableness and proportionality, for instance, have been treated as coordinate principles of German constitutional law deriving from the same source—the requirement of justice for the individual, which is "an integral part of the rule of law."[2]

According to some scholars, however, proportionality and reasonableness represent somewhat different ideas. Proportionality is generally focused on the relationship between two variables, for example, means and ends.[3] By contrast, reasonableness "is used to assess whether the particular circumstances of the person concerned allow the fulfillment of certain duty by him or not"; in other words, it does not necessarily involve the relationship between two variables.[4] Scholars have argued that the principle of proportionality calls for an objective means-ends assessment, whereas reasonableness involves a subjective standard for "the assessment of the totality of the circumstances of the case to which it is to be applied."[5]

The conclusion, nonetheless, is clear—proportionality and reasonableness often work in tandem to determine the justice of a particular situation to an individual.

The common law principle of proportionality (reasonableness) dates back more than a hundred years. Early judicial decisions discuss a need for proportionality in the context of private law, such as contract law, in particular with respect to damage awards. Proportionality analysis extends to the actual damages versus contract price, liquidated damages versus actual or foreseeable damages, and compensatory damages versus contributory fault. What recurs in contract law cases is a concern for fairness, expressed as freedom to contract and honoring a person's reasonable expectations of the deal.

Contract law is the province of the state. Rarely does the Supreme Court of the United States decide contract disputes, with the exception of early admiralty or government contract cases. These rare Supreme Court decisions, combined with those of a few U.S. Courts of Appeal, express some commitment to an idea of proportionality in awarding damages. Though given only cursory treatment by the high court, common law doctrines rooted in proportionality are referenced by early U.S. courts and are also recorded as restatements of contract law. Courts have largely applied ends-means proportionality to ensure that there is a congruent relationship between the evil and the means used to eradicate it.

A. THE RULE OF FORESEEABLE DAMAGES: WHEN LIABILITY IS DISPROPORTIONATE TO THE CONTRACT PRICE

The classic contract law case, *Hadley v. Baxendale*, established the principle that consequential damages should be limited to foreseeable losses, which are those that "may reasonably be supposed to have been in contemplation of both parties at the time they made the contract, as the probable result of the breach of it."[6] The rule of *Hadley v. Baxendale* is based on the idea that "the costs of the untoward consequence of a course of dealings should be borne by that party who was able to avert the consequence at least cost and failed to do so."[7] This rule corresponds to the tort principle that "the amount of care that a person ought to take is a function of the probability and magnitude of the harm that may occur if he does not take care. If he does not know what that probability and magnitude are, he cannot determine how much care to take."[8]

Defendants must have notice of any special circumstances that could give rise to extraordinary or disproportionate liability. Writing for the Seventh Circuit, Judge Richard Posner cited *Hadley v. Baxendale* when explaining and applying the concepts of foreseeable loss in *Evra Corp. v. Swiss Bank Corp.*[9] In *Evra*, Evra Corporation sued Swiss Bank, alleging that the bank's failure to make a timely transfer of funds was negligent and resulted in the cancellation of Evra's contract to charter a ship to carry scrap metal overseas. Evra sued for the additional $2 million it paid to charter the ship under a new contract, the rate of which was double that of the previous contract. The court held that Swiss Bank was not liable to the ship charterer for the two million dollars in consequential damages related to Swiss Bank's improper handling of the wire transfer because it was not on notice of the special circumstances that gave rise to them. The court concluded that "Swiss Bank did not have enough information to infer that if it lost a $27,000 payment order, it would face liability in excess of $2 million."[10]

A court is not required to award damages for all foreseeable losses; it may limit foreseeable damages "if it concludes that in the circumstances justice so requires in order to avoid disproportionate compensation."[11] When there is "an extreme disproportion between the loss and the price charged by the party whose liability for that loss is in question,...[t]he fact that the price is relatively small suggests that it was not intended to cover the risk of such liability."[12] Likewise, if the deal is informal, the parties may not have carefully attempted to allocate all of the risks.[13] The theory behind preventing disproportion is that the liable party did not intend to cover large risks of loss.[14] The great majority of courts that address liability for loss in breach of contract cases are state courts, and many limit foreseeable damages in the circumstance of disproportionate compensation.[15]

Disproportion between contract price and foreseeable damages alone, no matter how excessive, is not enough to convince all courts that the parties did not contemplate that the defendant would bear the risk of liability. In *International Ore & Fertilizer Corp. v. SGS Control Services, Inc.*,[16] a shipper of fertilizer sued the inspection service in contract and in tort for improper inspection and certification of the ship hired by the shipper to transport its fertilizer. When the shipment reached its destination in New Zealand, authorities rejected it because of contamination. The district court denied the plaintiff recovery on its contract claim because the damages were outrageously disproportionate to the contract price. The lower court found that the disparity between the contract price of $150 for inspection service and the $2.4 million in damages indicated that the parties neither anticipated the loss nor intended to allocate the risks that way.[17] There was no meeting of the minds:[18]

> It is not always in the interest of justice to require the party in breach to pay damages for all of the foreseeable loss that he has caused. There are unusual instances in which it appears from the circumstances either that the parties assumed that one of them would not bear the risk of a particular loss or that, although there was no such assumption, it would be unjust to put the risk on that party. One such circumstance is an extreme

disproportion between the loss and the price charged by the party whose liability for that loss is in question. The fact that the price is relatively small suggests that it was not intended to cover the risk of such liability.[19]

The district court awarded damages of $713,666 on the plaintiff's tort claim but reduced them by 50 percent for contributory negligence.[20]

The Second Circuit affirmed the decision. It did not agree, however, with the district court's dismissal of the contract claims on the grounds of disproportion. The Court of Appeals found that the purpose of the inspection "was precisely to guarantee the condition of the hold so as to insure the preservation of the cargo."[21] Since SGS was fully aware that its negligent inspection might cause the loss of an entire cargo, the court reasoned, it must be liable for the consequential damages resulting from its breach.[22]

The purpose of the service rendered may help determine whether a party should be held liable for a loss that is disproportionate to the contract price. The Second Circuit, in *International Ore*, distinguished its holding in *Sundance Cruises v. American Bureau of Shipping*[23] on this basis. In *Sundance Cruises*, the owners of an ocean-going passenger vessel that sank after hitting an underwater rock sued the insurance classification society that had issued it a certificate verifying compliance with international safety conventions.[24] The Second Circuit denied the plaintiff consequential damages and held that the owners were not entitled to rely on the classification certificate as a guarantee that the vessel was soundly constructed, particularly considering the great disparity between the fee charged for the service and the amount of damages sought.[25] "The purpose of the classification certificate [was] not to guarantee safety, but merely to permit [the shipowner] to take advantage of the insurance rates available to a classed vessel."[26] The damages that followed did not flow from the issuance of the certificate since the shipowner was ultimately responsible for the maintenance and operation of the ship.[27]

Not all damages are capable of being anticipated before (or even calculable after) a breach of contract. Contract law, therefore, allows liquidated damages clauses where parties can agree in advance on the amount of damages due after breach. This stipulation of damages facilitates contracting by reducing the risk that would otherwise be associated with unpredictable or inestimable liability.[28]

B. DISPROPORTIONATE LIQUIDATED DAMAGES AS UNENFORCEABLE PENALTIES

Liquidated damages clauses are meant to estimate damages fairly in order to reimburse a party for hardship that occurs from a broken contractual promise.

Damages clauses are not intended to be a punishment for nonperformance, nor are they a threat or an oppressive tool with which to secure performance.

1. Older Common Law Tradition to Void Clauses

The common law of the United States has refused to enforce penalties in contracts because they violate the principle of just compensation. As a comment to the restatement explains, "[p]unishment of a promisor for having broken his promise has no justification on either economic or other grounds and a term providing such a penalty is unenforceable on grounds of public policy."[29] The Supreme Court recognizes that "an exaction of punishment for a breach which could produce no possible damage has long been deemed oppressive and unjust."[30]

Just as it is unfair to impose punishment where there is no damage, it is also unfair to impose liability that is grossly disproportionate to the amount of damage incurred. Regardless of whether the clause provides for damages too large when compared to the harm caused[31] or "fixes an unreasonably small amount as damages,"[32] if the damages are completely disproportionate to the degree of the breach, then "the parties have not adhered to the rule of just compensation."[33]

Courts vary in how they assess the proportionality of liquidated damages clauses. Some have judged the proportionality of a clause using a prospective approach, looking at whether the provision was a reasonable estimate of damages at the time of the contract drafting.[34] Other courts employ a retrospective approach, comparing the stipulated amount to the realized damages.[35] Still other courts consider both the reasonableness of the forecasted damages at the time of drafting and the comparison between the stipulated provision and the actual amount of loss.[36]

The *Restatement (Second) of Contracts* provides: "Damages for breach by either party may be liquidated in the agreement but only at an amount that is reasonable in the light of the anticipated or actual loss caused by the breach and the difficulties of proof of loss. A term fixing unreasonably large liquidated damages is unenforceable on grounds of public policy as a penalty."[37] The more difficult it is to prove actual damages or adequately ascertain their precise amount, the more likely a court will find that the stipulated damages are reasonable.[38] This is so because, when it is objectively difficult to identify actual harm or the precise amount of damages, there is no reason to believe a judge's or jury's estimate will "accord with the principle of just compensation any more than would the advance estimate of the parties."[39] If "it is clear that no loss at all has occurred," the restatement provides that "a provision fixing a substantial sum as damages is unenforceable."[40]

2. Modern Trend to Enforce

The Supreme Court has moved away from the common law practice of voiding liquidated damages provisions. The modern trend, beginning in the early part of the twentieth century, is to respect freedom to contract and enforce liquidated damages provisions if intended by the parties.[41] In *United States v. Bethlehem Steel Co.*, the Court enforced a liquidated damages provision even though the trial court found that there were no actual damages.[42] Although at one time courts "would scarcely admit that there ever was a valid contract providing for liquidated damages," the Supreme Court established that the modern trend is to respect the parties' freedom to contract.[43]

In *Bethlehem Steel*, the Court concluded that the parties intended the contract to provide for liquidated damages because the harm was hard to ascertain in advance and impossible to prove and the parties did not intend the clause to be a penalty. Comparing the stipulated amount to a prospective estimate at the time of contracting, the Court did consider proportion in determining the parties' intentions. The Court concluded, "[t]he amount is not so extraordinarily disproportionate to the damage which might result from the failure to deliver the carriages as to show that the parties must have intended a penalty, and could not have meant liquidated damages."[44]

A court does not have the authority to disregard the parties' provision for liquidated damages merely because the amount is disproportionate to the loss.[45] It is unfair to interfere with a contract in which an owner of property already has "affix[ed] his own estimate of its value" simply because others disagree with it.[46] The parties to a contract are in a more competent position to justly determine a fair amount of damages than a jury concluding after the fact and affected by the partisan testimony of others.[47]

According to the Supreme Court, the proportionality of the stipulated amount to actual harm is relevant only to the extent that it is indicative of intent.[48] The Court established in *Sun Printing & Publishing Ass'n v. Moore*[49] and then followed in *Bethlehem Steel* that modern courts look to the intent of the parties to determine whether the liquidated damages provision is a penalty.[50] If damages are uncertain and have been liquidated by an agreement, it is the duty of the court to enforce the parties' intention as long as it is not to penalize.[51] The Court recognized that disproportion has been relevant in an action at law when the stipulated amount is grossly disproportionate on the face of the contract, thus indicating intent to penalize.[52]

a. Determining Intent of Parties

The Supreme Court has relied on three factors to determine whether the parties intended a penalty: (1) disproportion on the face of the contract; (2) a lump sum rather than one that varies with length of delay; and (3) express language describing the provision as either a "penalty" or "liquidated damages."

1) Disproportion on the Face of the Contract

It seems clear that a clause that provides for the payment of a fixed sum due upon nonperformance is a penalty rather than a liquidated damages provision if a court finds disproportion on the face of the contract.[53] In *Sun Printing*, the Court first explained that when a party alleges disproportion, "it has usually been an excessive disproportion between the stipulated sum and the possible damages resulting from a trivial breach apparent on the face of the contract...."[54] Five years later, in *Bethlehem Steel*, the Court reiterated that if the amount provided in the contract is extraordinarily disproportionate to the damage that might result from the failure to perform, "the parties must have intended a penalty, and could not have meant liquidated damages."[55] In *Kothe v. R.C. Taylor Trust*, the Court refused to honor a residential lease provision that, upon the tenant's filing of bankruptcy, terminated the lease and awarded the landlord rent for the remainder of the two-year term, which ended up being more than a full year's worth.[56] Although recognizing that courts are inclined to enforce the intentions of the parties and allow liquidated damages, the Supreme Court asserted, "agreements to pay fixed sums plainly without reasonable relation to any probable damage which may follow a breach will not be enforced. This circumstance tends to negative any notion that the parties really meant to provide a measure of compensation...."[57] The Court concluded that the provision in *Taylor Trust* was a penalty.[58]

2) A Lump Sum

A provision that provides for a fixed rather than a variable sum for stipulated damages indicates an intent to penalize because it tends to be more disproportional, bearing a lesser relation to an actual amount of damage.[59] In *Tayloe v. Sandiford*,[60] an 1822 construction contract dispute, the Court observed that an agreement to pay a specified sum weekly while the party failed to complete the work would look much more like liquidated damages than reserving the whole sum as one lump payment.[61] The Court summarized, "[i]n general, a sum of money in gross, to be paid for the nonperformance of an agreement, is considered as a penalty...."[62] Likewise, in *Maryland Dredging & Contracting Co. v. United States*,[63] the Court found that an excavating contract provision providing $20 for each division for every day the completion was delayed, had no element of deception or exorbitance, and it could "see no ground upon which the claimant can escape from the terms to which he had agreed."[64] Particularly in construction contracts, courts find liquidated damages provisions that compensate based on each day's delay to be "an appropriate means of inducing due performance" or compensating for failure to perform, and courts will enforce them.[65]

3) Express Language

Courts are more likely to determine that a liquidated damages provision is a penalty if the contract language defines the stipulated amount as a "penalty." As the Supreme Court observed in *Tayloe*, "[m]uch stronger is the inference in favour of it's being a penalty, when it is expressly reserved as one."[66] The covenant at issue in *Tayloe* read: "The said houses to be completely finished on or before the 24th of December next, under a penalty of one thousand dollars, in case of failure."[67] The Court found that the plain language of the contract indicated it was a penalty.[68] Conversely, in *Wise v. United States*,[69] the government construction contract language read: "[I]n view of the difficulty of estimating with exactness the damages which will result, deduct as liquidated damages, and not as a penalty, the sum of two hundred dollars ($200.00) for each and every day during the continuance of such delay and until such work shall be completed...."[70] The Court upheld the validity of the provision.[71]

Although courts have increasingly shown a willingness to enforce liquidated damages provisions, a finding of disproportionality continues to serve as an effective check on the types of provisions that they will uphold. This area of law demonstrates that proportionality may be used to protect not only individual rights from intrusion but also important common law doctrines, such as just compensation. That proportionality has been used effectively in the United States, albeit in a narrow context, indicates that the principle is consistent with the underpinnings of American common law.

C. PROPORTIONALITY OF COMPENSATORY DAMAGES IN TORT

The common law definition of negligence implicitly incorporates an ends-benefits proportionality analysis. The formula developed by Judge Learned Hand[72] balances the probability and severity of the potential harm with the "burden of adequate precaution."[73] Recovery is appropriate when the likelihood or gravity of injury outweighs the cost of providing necessary protection.[74] Compensatory damages issues arise primarily in tort cases, which are generally decided under state law. The rare cases heard by the U.S. Supreme Court have been in the area of admiralty law in the context of joint tortfeasors and apportioning liability among multiple defendants. Drawing from the notion of comparative negligence adopted by most state jurisdictions in the United States[75]—which generally mandated apportionment of damages either in proportion to the fault attributed to the defendant and the plaintiff or among multiple defendants and the plaintiff—the Supreme Court has expressed loyalty to the idea of liability in proportion to fault unless clearly indicated otherwise by statute. This policy corresponds to its position on liquidated damages: Fairness requires proportionality where that is possible to ascertain unless the relevant parties have expressly intended otherwise, in which case the court should not interfere.

1. Liability in Proportion to Fault: Replacing the Divided Damages Rule

In admiralty, like typical state tort cases, where more than one party is at fault, all of the parties should be liable for the harm in proportion to their fault. This is a relatively recent departure from the traditional rule of divided damages. Divided damages operated such that the property damage in a maritime collision or stranding was equally divided whenever two or more parties involved were found to be guilty of contributory fault, regardless of the relative degree of their fault. In *United States v. Reliable Transfer Co.*,[76] the Supreme Court replaced the admiralty rule of divided damages with a new rule requiring, when possible, the allocation of liability for damages in proportion to each party's relative fault.

The Supreme Court reasoned that a vessel should assume a share of the damages in proportion to its share of the blame and that "[a]n equal division of damages is a reasonably satisfactory result only where each vessel's fault is approximately equal...or where proportionate degrees of fault cannot be measured and determined on a rational basis. The rule produces palpably unfair results in every other case."[77] The Court accepted an equal division of damages as equitable "[w]hen it is impossible fairly to allocate degrees of fault."[78] Otherwise, the justices regarded divided damages as an "archaic and unfair rule" and endorsed the apportionment f liability on the basis of fault.[79]

2. Proportionate Liability When One of Multiple Defendants Settles

Even in settlement, the Supreme Court has adhered to the principle that defendants' liability should be apportioned relative to their fault. In *McDermott, Inc. v. AmClyde and River Don Castings, Ltd.*,[80] the Court held that the liability of non-settling defendants in admiralty cases should be calculated with reference to the jury's allocation of proportionate responsibility.[81] This apportionment of liability, referred to as the proportionate share rule, is based on fairness. Since "other defendants are not entitled to a reduction in liability when the plaintiff negotiates a generous settlement,...they are not required to shoulder disproportionate liability when the plaintiff negotiates a meager one."[82]

The Court rejected two *pro tanto* rule alternatives, each of which would subtract the dollar amount of settlement from the total liability for which the nonsettling defendants would be responsible.[83] The first alternative left the nonsettling defendants with a right of contribution against the settling defendants.[84] The second did not.[85] The Court predicted that under a *pro tanto* rule, "a litigating defendant's liability will frequently differ from its equitable share, because a settlement with one defendant for less than its equitable share requires the nonsettling defendant to pay more than its share."[86]

The proportionate share approach, whereby the settlement diminishes the injured party's claim against the nonsettling tortfeasors by the amount of the equitable share of the settling tortfeasor's obligation rather than by the actual dollar amount of settlement, is more consistent with the proportionate fault approach of *Reliable Transfer*; litigating defendants ordinarily pay only their proportionate share of the judgment. Under this approach, "no suits for contribution from the settling defendants are permitted, nor are they necessary, because the nonsettling defendants pay no more than their share of the judgment."[87]

Courts have applied the proportionate share approach in contexts other than admiralty. Lower courts, for instance, have held that the proportionate share judgment reduction formula, endorsed by the Supreme Court in *McDermott*, is appropriate in class action settlement agreements.[88]

D. PRESERVING INTENT

Despite its allegiance to the idea of liability in proportion to fault, the Supreme Court has generally deferred to the relevant parties' intent. In the realm of liquidated damages provisions, the Court honors the parties' freedom to contract and executes their intentions to the extent allowable by law. In the area of compensatory damages, the Court interprets statutes to execute the intentions of Congress.

In *Edmonds v. Compagnie Générale Transatlantique*,[89] the Supreme Court resolved a circuit split over whether, by means of a maritime workers' compensation scheme,[90] Congress intended to impose a proportionate fault rule in admiralty law so as to change the judicially created admiralty rule that the shipowner can be made to pay all the damages not due to the longshoreman's own negligence.[91] The Court held that Congress did not intend to impose a proportionate fault rule, thus preserving joint and several liability. The dissent in *Edmonds* argued that this was "an unfair and unjust result" and that the Court should fashion a rule of comparative negligence in longshoremen workers' compensation cases. Despite the dissenting justices' protests that "[o]ur duty, in such a case, is to adopt the interpretation most consonant with reason, equity, and the underlying purposes Congress sought to achieve,"[92] the Court honored what it felt was the legislature's intent—to preserve joint and several liability.

E. IMPLICIT PROPORTIONALITY PRINCIPLES
IN AMERICAN ANTITRUST LAW

Some notions of proportionality also exist in other areas of American law governing remedies. Despite the fact that most remedies raise issues similar to those informing the Court's analysis in punitive damages cases, the Court has been slow to expressly adopt proportionality as a mode of their review. Antitrust remedies provide a good example of this cautious approach. The Court appears to have implicitly adopted several of the proportionality principles we identify, but has never explicitly used the language of proportionality. These judicially crafted applications of proportionality had their origin in the common law.[93]

There are three aspects in which the Supreme Court's analysis has implicitly leaned toward using proportionality/reasonableness to determine the adequacy of antitrust remedies. The first relates to monetary and injunctive/structural relief in private antitrust actions. The second pertains to damages awards in private antitrust actions. The third is relevant both to monetary relief in private antitrust actions and injunctive/structural relief in private and government antitrust actions.

The first aspect is the requirement of "antitrust injury" established in *Brunswick Corp. v. Pueblo Bowl-O-Mat, Inc.*:

> [T]o recover treble damages on account of § 7 violations, [plaintiffs] must prove more than injury causally linked to an illegal presence in the market. Plaintiffs must prove antitrust injury, which is to say injury of the type the antitrust laws were intended to prevent and that flows from that which makes defendants' acts unlawful. The injury should reflect the anticompetitive effect either of the violation or of anticompetitive acts made possible by the violation. It should, in short, be "the type of loss that the claimed violations... would be likely to cause."[94]

An antitrust remedy, whether damages or injunctive/structural relief, must redress the harm caused by a violation of the antitrust laws. Like suitability, which is an element of the European Union and German test of proportionality, the requirement of "antitrust injury" tests the reasonable relation of a remedy to the harm it is sought to redress.[95] In addition, the requirement that the injury be "the type of loss the claimed violations... would be likely to cause" may reflect an implicit limiting retributive principle—defendants should not held liable for treble damages if they could not have reasonably foreseen that their violation would cause such injury.

The second aspect is the "direct purchaser rule" established in *Illinois Brick Co. v. Illinois*.[96] According to the rule, indirect purchasers are precluded from seeking treble damages in federal antitrust actions.[97] The Third Circuit explained the Supreme Court's adoption of the direct purchaser rule by the need to contain the extraordinary treble damages remedy under Section 4 of the Clayton Act. In particular, it said that, in view of the remedy's extraordinary nature, it must be "confined within reasonable limits."[98] Moreover, the Third Circuit implicitly emphasized that the Supreme Court limited the recovery of treble damages to direct purchasers because it was optimal for deterrence of future antitrust violations, it advanced the judicial efficiency of the private federal antitrust enforcement system, and it prevented the adverse economic effects that could stem from granting access to the treble damages remedy to indirect purchasers.[99] Thus, the adoption of the direct purchaser rule, according to the court, was a result of the balancing of the costs, including excessive treble damages litigation, and benefits of the treble damages remedy in direct and indirect purchaser scenarios. As indicated, the rule reflects a proposition that the costs of the treble damages remedy in the indirect purchaser scenario outweighs its deterrence benefits.[100] This is an implicit form of ends-benefits proportionality.

The third aspect of American remedial antitrust jurisprudence that may have some resemblance to the rule of proportionality is the federal courts' concern over the scope of injunctive/structural relief. Such relief must be proportional to the harm caused by the defendant's antitrust violation to the market[101]—an implicit form of ends-benefits proportionality analysis. What makes the task of assessing the fit between an antitrust remedy in the form of injunctive/structural relief and the harm caused to the market particularly challenging is the fact that, in fashioning a remedy, the courts may address conduct beyond the scope of the conduct that is illegal under the antitrust laws.[102]

The breadth of allowable injunctive/structural antitrust remedies is not without limits. One limit is that the remedy must be fit to redress the loss to the market caused by the defendant's antitrust violation.[103] Another limit on the scope of allowable nonmonetary antitrust remedies was mentioned in *United States v. Microsoft Corp.*[104] The court established a relationship of proportionality between the severity of the remedy and the strength of the causal connection "between the conduct and the creation or maintenance of the market power": "Mere existence of an exclusionary act does not itself justify full feasible relief against the monopolist to create maximum competition. Rather, structural relief, which is designed to eliminate the monopoly altogether...require[s] a clearer indication of a *significant causal connection* between the conduct and creation or maintenance of the market power."[105]

Finally, the scope of a nonmonetary antitrust remedy, similarly to punitive damages,[106] depends on the reprehensibility of the illegal conduct, thus suggesting an implicit version of limiting retributive proportionality.[107] In *United States v. U.S. Gypsum Co.*,[108] the Court specifically emphasized that more reprehensible conduct warrants "call[s] for repression by sterner measures than where the steps could reasonably have been thought permissible."[109]

The principle of proportionality/reasonableness is an ancient one preceding the formation of the U.S. legal system we know today. In antitrust jurisprudence, the Court has relied on implicit notions of proportionality when crafting remedies. The "antitrust injury" requirement reflects the German suitability concept and perhaps also the limiting retributive liability principle that governs who may be held liable, while the requirement of proportionality in the scope of the remedy adheres to both the limiting retributive severity principle and ends-benefits proportionality. The latter principle also informs the "direct purchaser rule," thereby limiting those who may seek treble damages because the ends of such allowance are not justified in light of their overwhelming cost. Common law contract cases reference the concept of proportionality in determining what is fair and just. To the extent that the Supreme Court has decided issues of determining damages, the Court has expressed a commitment to the idea of proportionality. Whether in the context of foreseeable damages, liquidated damages, or compensatory damages, the Court's position seems to be that fairness requires proportionality except (1) when the relevant parties have expressly intended otherwise and (2) when it is impossible to ascertain the proper proportions.

PROPORTIONALITY IN
AMERICAN CIVIL JURISPRUDENCE II

In contrast to the practice of the foreign jurisdictions described in part I, American jurisprudence has made only limited use of the term "proportionality" in the evaluation of government conduct.[1] Proportionality is rarely mentioned as an underlying basis of constitutional decisions.

Despite the reluctance of American courts expressly to employ proportionality as a limit to government discretion, the values promoted by proportionality have not been rejected by American constitutional jurisprudence. Traces of notions akin to proportionality, including balancing of constitutional values,[2] appear in the U.S. system of substantive doctrinal standards of constitutional judicial review.[3] More important, the Supreme Court has explicitly used the term "proportionality" in several matters that came under its review[4]—in particular, punitive damages,[5] property permit conditions,[6] congressional enforcement actions under Section 5 of the Fourteenth Amendment,[7] criminal penalties,[8] and forfeitures.[9] The first three topics are discussed in chapter 4 of this part; criminal penalties and forfeitures are discussed in part III.

However, this presence of proportionality in American law can be quite misleading. The prevailing two-tier system of judicial review[10] is a set of categorical rules that allow courts to decide cases based on a characterization at the outset of the aspects of individual autonomy implicated by government regulation. This system excludes a meaningful reconciliation, usually present in foreign decisions applying proportionality, of individual autonomy values and the goals justifying the government action.[11] If the only protection for which an individual's interest or right qualifies is rational basis, the individual's case against government regulation is frequently lost. Likewise, if the government happens to venture into an area governed by strict scrutiny, the individual is likely to prevail.[12]

Even in its express resort to proportionality, the Supreme Court is either inconsistent or frequently unaware of the doctrine's broader application. The inconsistency is well illustrated by the fact that defendants enjoy the strong protection of the principle of proportionality from excessive punitive damages and forfeitures,[13] but they are virtually unprotected from excessive imprisonment.[14] With respect to punitive damages and land-use permit conditions—both socioeconomic matters that traditionally fall under rational basis review—the Court employs proportionality not to embrace the principle that government regulation must be proportional to the ends sought and attendant harm to an individual but rather to create a standard of review stricter than rational basis but more deferential to government than intermediate scrutiny. This practice unjustifiably transforms the versatile and flexible principle of proportionality into a narrow standard applicable to only a few narrow matters of constitutional law. Finally, the Court, by requiring "rough" proportionality, marginalizes the principle of proportionality in land-use permit conditions and federal enforcement actions under Section 5 of the Fourteenth Amendment.[15] By definition, proportionality as a measure of constitutional compliance is never exact; thus, the use of the word "rough" in conjunction with the principle of proportionality suggests the Court's intention to dilute further the principle's force.

In this part we provide a brief, critical analysis of the Supreme Court's general substantive standards of judicial constitutional review and the related doctrine of fundamental rights (chapter 3). We then touch on modern proportionality trends in the Supreme Court's constitutional jurisprudence and discuss the internal inconsistencies in the Court's analysis (chapter 4).

3 IMPLICIT PROPORTIONALITY PRINCIPLES IN AMERICAN STANDARDS OF CONSTITUTIONAL REVIEW

DESPITE CALLS FOR A SLIDING scale of judicial constitutional review,[1] the high court has for the most part retained its two rigid standards of strict and rational basis scrutiny.[2] These standards generally apply to challenges of state or federal legislation under the due process and equal protection clauses of the U.S. Constitution. Although these tests are often called standards of judicial review, they are more similar to legal rules than standards.[3] Indeed, they help the Court to categorize cases that involve a variety of competing interests into either strict or rational basis scrutiny.[4]

The Court, however, has deviated from this rigid categorization of constitutional issues in limited circumstances, developing what is known as a rational basis standard with bite, an intermediate scrutiny standard, and recently a softer version of strict scrutiny.[5] It is not surprising that these exceptions involve some balancing of competing constitutional interests implicated by a government action. After all, the move to a more flexible mode of constitutional review in several limited areas is consistent with the ideal of a sliding-scale judicial review that usually involves a degree of constitutional balancing. Such balancing of competing interests resembles ends-benefits proportionality analysis, although the Court rarely uses the language of proportionality. In contrast, the Court's traditional rational basis and strict scrutiny tests apply implicit ends-proportionality principles more crudely. The importance of the government's asserted goals, the likely benefits, and the resulting burdens on individual autonomy are evaluated in a categoric fashion, which, depending on the categorization, determines the outcome. On the other hand, the traditional "narrow-tailoring" requirement of strict scrutiny has always permitted case-specific analysis in a manner quite consistent with alternative-means proportionality principles.

A. STRICT SCRUTINY

If a government action is subject to strict scrutiny, the action is almost always invalidated.[6] To survive strict scrutiny, a government action must be necessary to achieve a compelling government interest.[7] This method of constitutional analysis employs several inquiries that are also present in traditional proportionality review. First, the Court must determine whether the government action infringes on a fundamental right or discriminates against a suspect class.[8] If it does, the Court must invalidate the government action unless it is necessary for the attainment of a compelling government interest.[9] The government interest involved must be sufficiently important to justify a suspect classification or government invasion of individual autonomy.[10] The result is that the government action is invalidated if the Court is able to find a less restrictive, yet equally effective, alternative to the proposed method.

Strict scrutiny in substantive due process and equal protection cases derives its force from the famous footnote 4 in the Supreme Court case *United States v. Carolene Products Co.*, which indicates that the presumption of constitutionality of government action will have a significantly lesser force in situations involving "prejudice against discrete and insular minorities" or an infringement of a fundamental right.[11] In some respects, strict scrutiny is similar to the absolute protection of "inner core" autonomy in Germany, as only a rare statute can survive strict scrutiny.[12] However, a recent case shows the Court's move toward a softer strict scrutiny standard at least in the area of affirmative action.

In *Grutter v. Bollinger*, the Supreme Court declared that "strict scrutiny is not strict in theory, but fatal in fact."[13] Using racial classification as an example, the Court explained that, although people suffer injury under the Equal Protection Clause whenever a government action treats them unequally based on their race, the suspect action must not be automatically invalidated.[14] The Court went on to point out that the goal of strict scrutiny is to assist the Court in determining whether the government interest underlying the proposed classification is sincere and sufficiently compelling to outweigh the right of an individual to equal protection.[15] In other words, the Court said that not all use of race in government regulation is prohibited; the Court's decision will consider the context in which race is used.

Using this line of reasoning, the Court approved the affirmative action program at the University of Michigan Law School.[16] The Court considered student diversity a sufficiently compelling government interest to allow the law school to take race into account when making admissions decisions.[17] The Court's decision is unusual when viewed from the standpoint of conventional strict scrutiny. Rather than review the compelling nature of student diversity—the goal that the school claimed justified using race in the admissions process—and the means used for its attainment with the usual thoroughness and skepticism characteristic of strict scrutiny review, the Court deferred to the law school's educational judgment.[18] The dissenting justices criticized the majority's decision, arguing that deference has no place in strict scrutiny.[19]

The Court performed its analysis of the law school's race-conscious admissions program in a similar deferential fashion under the "narrowly tailored" prong.[20] It was satisfied that the program was narrowly tailored to the compelling state objective of student diversity.[21] According to the Court, if a race-conscious admissions program uses race as a plus factor and allows individualized consideration of a variety of other factors bearing on diversity, the members of other racial or ethnic groups will not be foreclosed from competing for enrollment.[22] The Court found that the law school's admissions program allowed this result since it required that students be selected who demonstrate the greatest potential to enhance diversity, irrespective of the nature of diversity-enhancing factors.[23]

Grutter marks a substantial relaxing of the strict scrutiny analysis, at least in the context of higher education. According to the principles pronounced by the Court in *Grutter*, the invalidation of a government action is no longer predetermined merely because it falls within the ambits of strict scrutiny. Instead, the fate of a government action is decided by balancing the competing constitutional interests in specific contextual circumstances. This type of balancing is characteristic of the ends-benefits proportionality principle employed in foreign jurisdictions[24] and of intermediate scrutiny used by the Supreme Court in gender discrimination cases, dormant commerce clause cases, and some First Amendment scenarios.

Similar softening of strict scrutiny review has also occurred in the field of substantive due process, where strict scrutiny is employed to protect fundamental rights from government intrusion. *Planned Parenthood of Southeastern Pennsylvania v. Casey*[25] is an example in which the Court applied a less rigid strict scrutiny approach. In *Casey*, the Court adopted an "undue burden" method of balancing a woman's right to terminate her pregnancy with the state's "profound interest in potential life."[26] The government is permitted to promote its pro-life interests as long as it does not impose an undue burden on a woman's freedom to have an abortion.[27] In other words, instead of allowing one of the competing interests to override the other, the Court established a standard that accommodated both of them.

By contrast, conventional strict scrutiny allows one of the competing interests to completely override, not accommodate, the other. The overridden interest regains its power only when the right or freedom protected by strict scrutiny is abused and causes harm to others. This type of overriding analysis is found in *Roe v. Wade*,[28] which established a woman's limited right to terminate her pregnancy. *Roe* prohibited any interference with a woman's decision to terminate her pregnancy during the first trimester.[29] The state's interest in the potentiality of human life was suspended until after viability, when, in the Court's opinion, a woman's decision to have an abortion could harm a viable human organism.[30]

A similar conventional approach was employed in relation to several other freedoms such as the right to marry;[31] the right to have children;[32] the right of parents to control the upbringing of their children;[33] the right to marital privacy, including the right to procreate or not to procreate;[34] the right to use contraception;[35] the right to bodily integrity;[36] the right to refuse medical treatment;[37] and other fundamental rights.[38] None of these rights is absolute; strict scrutiny is employed to ensure that their exercise is suspended only when necessary to accommodate an overriding state interest such as public safety and health. In a sense, the Court engages in balancing when contemplating the enforcement of these rights, but the extent of this balancing is narrower than under the standard proposed in *Casey* and *Grutter*.

Further, the Court did much more in *Casey* than just soften the strict scrutiny standard of review and allow for balancing. It gave the constitutional doctrine of fundamental rights a semblance of proportionality to review the constitutional validity of government interference. The Court arguably used the language "undue burden"[39] to signal its intention to inquire into the proportionality of the benefits of a state action to the harm inflicted on the bearer of a fundamental right to have an abortion. The concept of undue burden contemplates the existence of some due, or fair, burden. There is little doubt that to constitute a due burden, the beneficial effects of a state action must be proportional to the inconvenience suffered by the bearer of the right to abortion. Otherwise, the burden would be undue; the utility of the state action would then be outweighed by its disutility.

Strict scrutiny has traditionally been observed to result in a virtually automatic invalidation of a challenged federal or state action.[40] The situation may change, however, in light of the constitutional developments described earlier, which indicate that the Court is willing to consider strict scrutiny's less rigid alternatives. There is also much potential for the application of the principle of proportionality in the field of constitutional protection of fundamental rights, primarily because these rights are not absolute and their exercise may be subject to government interference. Indeed, the principle of proportionality is very well suited for limiting regulatory or legislative discretion to means that are necessary and proportionate to the desired results. In short, proportionality is an essential tool that the Supreme Court could use to detect unnecessary government usurpation of individual autonomy because, in addition to the suitability and necessity of a government action, proportionality weighs the corresponding burden on individual autonomy against the proposed action's anticipated beneficial outcome.

B. INTERMEDIATE SCRUTINY

Intermediate scrutiny is a less exacting test applied when there is no objective basis for a strong presumption in favor of or against the validity of a government action.[41] This occurs when competing constitutional interests have relatively equal constitutional standing. For instance, nondiscriminatory state legislation is reviewed with intermediate scrutiny under the dormant commerce clause[42] because it carries sufficient constitutional weight to compete with the federal interest on an equal footing. By contrast, facially or otherwise discriminatory laws are subject to a more rigorous scrutiny mainly because their discriminatory nature provides a sufficient assurance of their invalidity and diminishes the weight of the underlying state interest.[43]

The Supreme Court formulated the test for nondiscriminatory state legislation in *Pike v. Bruce Church, Inc.*:[44] "[W]here the statute regulates even-handedly to effectuate a legitimate local public interest, and its effects on interstate commerce are only incidental, it will be upheld unless the burden imposed on such commerce is clearly excessive in relation to the putative local benefits."[45] This is an American rendition of the principle of proportionality found in German and European Union law; all of the elements of proportionality are present.

First, the extent of the burden tolerated depends on the importance of the state interest. In the same way, the comparative weight of competing constitutional interests is instrumental in German constitutional law[46] for determining the extent of deference to a government regulation. Second, the requirement of suitability is either implicit or represented by the words "the statute regulates... to effectuate a legitimate local public interest." Because a statute cannot regulate to effectuate a legitimate state interest unless it is suitable for such effectuation, under this test, the Court will have to consider whether the statute is suitable to achieve the desired public objective.[47] Third, the Court pronounced the requirement of necessity of the state action in *Pike* when it said that "the extent of the burden that will be tolerated will... depend... on whether it could be promoted as well with a lesser impact on interstate activities."[48] Finally, the *Pike* Court laid out the third requirement of the principle of proportionality—proportionality in the narrower sense—by specifically commanding that the burden the state statute imposed on interstate commerce could not be "clearly excessive in relation to the putative local benefits."[49] The weighing of the evils and benefits of a state action is a quintessential characteristic of the requirement of proportionality in the narrower sense.[50]

1. First Amendment Protections of Speech

A similar approach may be observed in some First Amendment cases. In fact, Justice Breyer, who is a strong proponent of the principle of proportionality,[51] expressly suggested that it be used in such situations to find a constitutional equilibrium. In *Nixon v. Shrink Missouri Government PAC*, he stated:

> In such circumstances—where a law significantly implicates competing constitutionally protected interests in complex ways—the Court has closely scrutinized the statute's impact on those interests, but refrained from employing a simple test that effectively presumes unconstitutionality. Rather, it has balanced interests. And in practice that has meant asking whether the statute burdens any one such interest in a manner out of proportion to the statute's salutary effects upon the others (perhaps, but not necessarily, because of the existence of a clearly superior, less restrictive alternative). Where a legislature has significantly greater institutional expertise, as, for example, in the field of election regulation, the Court in practice defers to empirical legislative judgments—at least where that deference does not risk such constitutional evils as, say, permitting incumbents to insulate themselves from effective electoral challenge.[52]

Justice Breyer's language proposed to apply a standard that balances competing constitutional interests—a characteristic of intermediate scrutiny—to all cases in which the protection of First Amendment free speech rights faces competition from a similarly important constitutional right. The Court did not expressly adopt this proposition. It did, however, create an intermediate scrutiny standard for all "content-neutral" regulation of speech,[53] arguing that the government's burden to justify "time, place, and manner" regulations addressing the "secondary effects" of speech should be lower than strict scrutiny because they did not pose such a serious threat to the right to free speech as "content-based" regulations would pose.[54] "Content-based" regulations of speech are still subject to the strict scrutiny standard of judicial review.[55]

In *United States v. O'Brien*,[56] the Court established the requirements for the application of the intermediate scrutiny standard to regulations affecting speech. Such a regulation must be within the government's constitutional power and must be adopted in furtherance of an important or substantial government interest.[57] The former requirement resonates with that of suitability, one of the elements of the test of proportionality in Germany and the European Union, but the *O'Brien* test goes further: The insistence on an important or substantial government interest represents an implicit form of categoric ends-proportionality analysis (whereas the third German and EU test, proportionality in the narrow sense, is an ends-proportionality standard that evaluates government interests on a sliding scale).[58] The requirement mentioned in *O'Brien* that government regulation be unrelated to the suppression of free expression also pertains to suitability.[59] The notion of necessity, the test of proportionality in Germany and the European Union,[60] was reflected[61] in *O'Brien*'s requirement that a government regulation restrict no more protected interests than were needed for addressing the government's legitimate interests.[62] Unlike the European and German tests,[63] however, intermediate scrutiny does not require strict necessity (least restrictive means).[64]

a. The Overbreadth Doctrine

In addition to the listed requirements, the test of intermediate scrutiny regarding "content-neutral" regulation affecting speech is modified by the so-called overbreadth doctrine. This doctrine has elements of both the second and the third tests of proportionality in German and EU law;[65] the Court examines not only the availability of more narrowly tailored means (necessity) but also the degree of interference with protected activity (proportionality in the narrow sense).

The overbreadth doctrine allows facial challenges of a law if it punishes a "substantial" amount of protected speech, "judged in relation to the statute's plainly legitimate sweep."[66] A finding of overbreadth allows the plaintiff to request a complete invalidation of the law "until and unless a limiting construction or partial invalidation so narrows it as to remove the seeming threat or deterrence to constitutionally protected expression."[67] The Court explained the availability of this remedy based on the concern that the threat of enforcement of an overbroad content-neutral law may "'chill' constitutionally protected speech."[68]

The relation of the overbreadth doctrine to proportionality is based on more than a mere implication from the language adopted by the Supreme Court to describe the doctrine. In fact, Justice Scalia, delivering the Court's opinion in *Virginia v. Hicks*[69]—and, incidentally, rejecting the plaintiff's request to apply the overbreadth doctrine in that case[70]—explicitly criticized the decision of the Supreme Court of Virginia under consideration as erroneous for ignoring "the proportionality aspect of [the Court's] overbreadth doctrine."[71] He said that a facial challenge of a law based on its overbroad application to protected speech required substantial effects on the protected speech "not only in an absolute sense, but also relative to the scope of the law's plainly legitimate application."[72] He added that it was the effect of the law on protected speech "taken as a whole" that was considered for the purposes of determining its overbreadth.[73]

In the conclusion of his opinion in *Hicks*, Justice Scalia added one other caveat to the application of the overbreadth doctrine: "[T]he overbreadth doctrine's concern with 'chilling' protected speech 'attenuates as the otherwise unprotected behavior that it forbids the State to sanction moves from "pure speech" toward conduct.' "[74] A law will rarely be invalidated with the use of the overbreadth doctrine, then, if it is not directed at speech or conduct substantially related to speech.[75]

b. Commercial Speech

Proportionality is also present in cases that deal with the "commercial speech doctrine," a matter related to trade and antitrust regulation, as well as to the protection of the freedom of speech rights under the First Amendment. Under the commercial speech doctrine, the government cannot regulate speech that does not threaten the asserted state interest, "nor can it completely suppress information when narrower restrictions on expression would serve its interest as well."[76] This formulation implicitly invokes alternative-means proportionality principles.

In determining whether a government regulation of commercial speech is overbroad or excessive, the court must first determine whether an expression is protected by the First Amendment.[77] To qualify, commercial speech must concern lawful activity and not be misleading.[78] The next inquiry is whether the government's interest is substantial,[79] a test that invokes implicit ends-benefits proportionality principles in a categoric rule: The potential benefits associated with less than "substantial" government interests can never justify burdens on commercial speech. If that test is met, the court "must determine whether the regulation directly advances the governmental interest asserted and whether it is not *more extensive than necessary* to serve that interest."[80] The Court has expressly invoked proportionality principles in some of these cases, but the justices continue to debate the level of proportionality necessitated by this fourth and final requirement.[81]

In *Central Hudson*,[82] the Court found that the contested advertising of electric energy could advance valid business goals that were not related to the asserted government interest of conserving energy.[83] The Court said: "To the extent that the Commission's order suppresses speech that in no way impairs the State's interest in energy conservation, the Commission's order violates the First and Fourteenth Amendments…"[84] The Court also held that the regulation was overbroad because the commission could not prove that a narrower means would be completely ineffective.[85] Note that the commercial speech doctrine is not a subspecies of the overbreadth doctrine we discussed earlier in this book because, under the commercial speech doctrine, the plaintiff is asserting its own First Amendment rights, not the rights of *chilled* third parties.[86]

To summarize, the constitutional standards that govern the regulation of commercial speech implicitly incorporate both ends- and means-proportionality principles. Ends proportionality is implicit in the requirement of a substantial government interest; means-proportionality analysis is implicit when courts consider the availability and effectiveness of narrower restrictions on the speech.

2. Gender

The intermediate scrutiny used in gender discrimination appears to be more rigorous than that employed in constitutional review of state actions under the dormant commerce clause and the First Amendment. The state bears the burden of justification for a classification based on gender.[87] The justification must be "exceedingly persuasive."[88] The Court admitted the existence of inherent differences between men and women but cautioned that these differences justify only actions "to compensate women 'for particular economic disabilities [they have] suffered,'"[89] "to 'promot[e] equal employment opportunity,'"[90] and "to advance full development of the talent and capacities of our Nation's people."[91] However, they cannot be used to promote "legal, social, and economic inferiority of women."[92]

Intermediate scrutiny has been instrumental in embedding the roots of the principle of proportionality in American constitutional jurisprudence. It is arguably an effective tool for harmonizing competing constitutional interests. In spite of this, intermediate scrutiny should not be used to assess the validity of government interference with strong overriding interests. Otherwise, the constitutional weight of the interest will be diminished by the concomitant deference to the state.

C. RATIONAL BASIS

Rational basis review is employed in situations where strict or intermediate scrutiny is inapplicable. All laws must meet this minimum level of constitutional scrutiny.[93] Like strict scrutiny, the traditional rational basis standard is outcome determinative—government action subject to rational basis review is afforded a strong presumption of constitutional validity. As such, it is rarely invalidated.[94]

Such minimal scrutiny corresponds to the suitability test of proportionality in Germany and the European Union. However, where it applies, rational basis is the only test, whereas Germany and the EU also apply two additional tests (necessity and proportionality in the narrow sense) corresponding to means and ends proportionality. Recent Supreme Court decisions that adopt somewhat stricter standards reflect dissatisfaction with the toothlessness of rational basis review.

1. Traditional Standards

The traditional rational basis test is highly deferential to the government.[95] It merely requires that the law be rationally related to a legitimate government purpose.[96] The purpose does not have to be actual; for rational basis review, the Court can accept any conceivable government objective.[97] For example, in *Federal Communications Commission v. Beach Communications, Inc.*, the Court said that "those attacking the rationality of the legislative classification have the burden 'to negative every conceivable basis which might support it.'"[98]

The rational basis standard tolerates both under-[99] and overinclusiveness[100] of a legislative act. Thus, for rational basis purposes, a law does not have to affect everyone similarly situated the same. Courts "are compelled under rational-basis review to accept a legislature's generalizations even when there is an imperfect fit between means and ends."[101]

As indicated, the rational basis standard is applied to the majority of state and federal economic and social legislation that does not involve a fundamental right or suspect classification.[102] The extreme deference to the government that courts exercise when reviewing state action under the rational basis test emerged as a response to excessive judicial interference with the states' police powers during the so-called *Lochner* era.[103]

Under *Lochner v. New York*,[104] the Court showed little or no deference to the states' political and economic judgment. Economic and social laws were overturned on the finding that they were not reasonably related to the declared end. The principle of rational relation of regulatory means to the desired objectives proclaimed in *Lochner* bears some notion of proportionality in that it was intended to protect the freedom of individuals from government interference with their economic activity. In *Lochner*, for example, the Court overturned as unduly intrusive a law restricting bakers' working hours, holding: "The [state] act must have a more direct relation, as a means to an end, and the end itself must be appropriate and legitimate, before an act can be held to be valid which interferes with the general right of an individual to be free in his person and in his power to contract in relation to his own labor."[105]

Although the legislature based the law on perceived threats to "the safety, the morals, [or] the welfare...of the public," the Court was unable to find any such danger caused by allowing bakers the freedom to set their working hours.[106] It held that, bearing no rational relation to its declared objectives, the challenged state action unduly interfered with the freedom of individuals "to make contracts regarding labor upon such terms as they may think best."[107]

The fallacy in the *Lochner* Court's application of balancing under the adopted rational basis test was that it did not balance the competing interests. Rather, the Court used heightened scrutiny to invalidate the state law at issue in that case without giving any weight to its social purpose and utility.[108] The Court limited the state interests that could compete with the individual economic freedom to public health, safety, and morals.[109] Along similar lines, it invalidated minimum wage laws,[110] laws protecting unionizing,[111] and consumer protection laws.[112]

A significant jurisprudential change occurred nearly thirty years later in 1934, when the Court in *Nebbia v. New York* sustained price regulations for milk.[113] Regarding the groundwork for an inquiry into the proportionality of government measures, the Court said:

> Under our form of government the use of property and the making of contracts are normally matters of private and not of public concern. The general rule is that both shall be free of governmental interference. But neither property rights nor contract rights are absolute; for government cannot exist if the citizen may at will use his property to the detriment of his fellows, or exercise his freedom of contract to work them harm. Equally fundamental with the private right is that of the public to regulate it in the common interest.[114]

Implicit in this language is the notion that the Court is willing to engage in constitutional balancing as a means to harmonize the competing individual and public constitutional interests in the socioeconomic field. Regrettably, the Court failed to advance this idea into an overarching requirement of proportionality of government action. Eventually the Court moved from the position of no deference to that of broad deference to state socioeconomic legislation.[115]

2. Rational Basis with a Bite

A positive shift in the direction of a more searching rational basis review outside the areas traditionally reserved for strict or intermediate scrutiny can be gleaned from several recent Supreme Court decisions. The first group of cases reveals congressional or state desire to harm a politically unpopular or disadvantaged group;

the Court focuses on the hurtful legislative intent, declares it to be illegitimate, and declines to consider or posit possible valid government purposes (as is done under traditional rational basis review, discussed earlier). The second group deals with the protection of individuals, entities, and states from excessive civil penalties and unconstitutional enforcement actions. In this part we focus primarily on the first group. The second group of cases is discussed in chapter 4.

The first important decision of the Supreme Court to invalidate a piece of federal legislation because it failed the rational basis test was *United States Department of Agriculture v. Moreno.*[116] The Court invalidated § 3(e) of the Food Stamp Act of 1964, which, "with certain exceptions, exclude[d] from participation in the food stamp program any household containing an individual who [was] unrelated to any other member of the household."[117] Sensing that the challenged legislation would primarily harm "those persons who are so desperately in need of aid that they cannot even afford to alter their living arrangements so as to retain their eligibility" under the food stamp program, the Court concluded that the challenged classification was not related rationally to the stated purpose of the act, which was to stimulate the agricultural economy by purchasing farm surpluses.[118]

The Court, moreover, rejected an additional government objective of preventing "so-called 'hippies' and 'hippie communities' from participation in the food stamp program" found in the legislative history.[119] In particular, the Court pointed out that "a bare congressional desire to harm a politically unpopular group cannot constitute a legitimate government interest."[120] Finally, the Court rejected the government's contention that preventing "hippie communities" from participating in the food stamp program served the purpose of minimizing fraud in the administration of the program. It reasoned that the antifraud mechanisms incorporated into the Food Stamp Act were sufficient to fight fraud in this field.[121] According to the Court, the challenged exclusion of households containing unrelated persons from the food stamp program would not so much minimize fraud as harm those who cannot afford separate residences to retain their eligibility under the program.[122]

The Court employed similar reasoning in *City of Cleburne v. Cleburne Living Center, Inc.,* in which the city of Cleburne, Texas, had denied a special use permit for the operation of a group house for persons with a mental disability.[123] As in *Moreno,* the Court perceived a strong hint of prejudice and invalidated the government action.[124]

The Court, however, rejected the proposal to afford a quasi-suspect status to persons with a mental disability because of the state's need to deal with different variations of mental disability, from slight deviations in the functioning of mental facilities to severe impairments of mental activity.[125] The Court found additional support for its decision in an argument similar to that used in gender classification. In particular, it stated that a requirement that a state must justify its efforts in protecting and helping persons with a mental disability would chill much beneficial government action in this field.[126] It added that "given the wide variation in the abilities and needs of the [persons with a mental disability] themselves, governmental bodies must have a certain amount of flexibility and freedom from judicial oversight in shaping and limiting their remedial efforts."[127]

The denial of quasi-suspect status to persons with a mental disability did not prevent the Court from invalidating the permit requirement under the rational basis test. Having analyzed the proffered reasons in this case for denying the permit to the group home for persons with a mental disability, the Court concluded that the city's decision was driven by an "irrational prejudice against the mentally [disabled]."[128] These considerations provided no rational basis for denying the permit.

Other examples of rigorous use of the rational basis test along the same lines include two Supreme Court decisions that deal with state regulation targeting the freedom of sexual orientation and sexual activity. In the first case, *Romer v. Evans*,[129] the Court invalidated a constitutional amendment that deprived gays, lesbians, and bisexuals of state antidiscrimination protection. The Court considered the breadth of the amendment's effect on a single named group to speak of nothing but "animus toward the class it affects."[130] The Court was particularly disturbed by the fact that this animosity may have caused the state to single out the named class from the rest of its citizens to deprive it of any opportunity to seek government protection except by constitutional amendment.[131] As a measure that intends to make gays, lesbians, and bisexuals unequal to everyone else, the amendment was invalidated.

In the second case, *Lawrence v. Texas*,[132] the Court strengthened the protection of the freedom of sexual orientation and sexual activity under the due process clause. The Court reviewed a challenge to a Texas statute that criminalized consensual sodomy between two persons of the same sex in the privacy of their home. Unlike in *Romer*, the Court decided to invalidate the Texas statute under the due process clause[133] to provide protection from government interference with the freedom of sexual orientation and sexual activity irrespective of an individual's membership in a discrete class or group. It held that criminalizing sodomy between members of the same sex in this situation not only gave effect to an unlawful public prejudice against a specific choice of sexual orientation but also constituted an unwarranted government intrusion into a sphere of protected individual liberty.[134]

Generalizing from all of these cases, it seems the Court may be willing to apply a more rigorous scrutiny than the conventional rational basis test in circumstances in which it perceives a strong countervailing interest of individual liberty or senses that a government action implicitly promotes public prejudice against a single named group. This so-called rational basis test with a bite appears to be more flexible than ordinary rational basis review in accommodating a variety of societal and individual interests without denigrating any of them or blindly allowing one interest to override another. Such qualities make it a model for transitioning the two-tier system of constitutional review into a meaningful sliding-scale proportionality analysis.

Furthermore, developments in the field of fundamental rights, such as *Lawrence*'s remarkable expansion of the scope of individual autonomy entitled to more than nominal protection under the due process clause, will require proportionality to play a more prominent role in U.S. constitutional jurisprudence. Foreign experience shows that proportionality is better suited for reconciling the expansion of protected individual autonomy with the rule of law principle that individual autonomy should be preserved insofar as it does not harm others or inhibit the normal functioning of human society.[135] Proportionality can balance competing constitutional interests without allowing the majority to impose its views of morality on the minority unless those views are independently supported by evidence of some important public interest.[136] By contrast, the existing conclusory-oriented tests of strict scrutiny and rational basis simply lack the ability to check the regulatory discretion of the state in accord with the growing realization of individual autonomy, leaving a substantial part of individual autonomy unprotected.

4 EXPLICIT PROPORTIONALITY PRINCIPLES IN DISCRETE AREAS OF AMERICAN JURISPRUDENCE

DESPITE THE TRADITIONAL APPLICATION OF the deferential rational basis standard of judicial review to government action in the sphere of socioeconomic regulation,[1] the U.S. Supreme Court has moved in select areas of its jurisprudence toward a more searching scrutiny than is typically present in rational basis decisions. We have already discussed the effect of the Court's enhanced rational basis review on matters of equal protection and substantive protection of individual autonomy. We now turn to its explicit use of proportionality as a means of increased constitutional oversight of remedial or regulatory actions, including (1) punitive damages, (2) land-use exactions, (3) attorney's fees awards, and (4) federal enforcement measures under Section 5 of the Fourteenth Amendment. As we will see, the Court applies different degrees of proportionality to different remedial measures. It demonstrates an initial, although inconsistent, doctrinal readiness for the gradual importation of the overarching principle of proportionality into U.S. constitutional law.

On the other hand, selective employment of proportionality in various socioeconomic matters may have a negative impact on the prospects of introducing proportionality as a general instrumental tool of constitutional review. It is patently obvious from the cases that follow that the Court uses proportionality as another standard of review, placed in light of its level of intensity between rational basis and intermediate scrutiny. In this manner, the role of proportionality may become marginalized in those areas where the Court chooses not to apply it as an express limitation on government discretion.

A. THE PROPORTIONALITY OF PUNITIVE DAMAGES

Punitive[2] and compensatory damages serve different purposes. Compensatory damages compensate a plaintiff for the loss suffered as a result of the defendant's wrongful conduct.[3] Punitive damages, on the other hand, have no compensatory basis;[4] they serve the broader public functions of deterrence and retribution.[5]

States possess a substantial amount of autonomy in promoting private enforcement of public interests through the mechanism of punitive or exemplary damages.[6] As a general matter, the Supreme Court found this autonomy to be consistent with the guarantees of fundamental fairness enshrined in the due process clause of the Fourteenth Amendment[7] and refused, in large measure because of its consistent common law history, to declare the common law method of assessing punitive damages unconstitutional per se.[8] The Court, nonetheless, acknowledged very early in the history of punitive damages that they may become suspect under the due process clause when they are "wholly disproportioned to the offense and obviously unreasonable."[9] This position remained largely symbolic throughout the twentieth century until *BMW v. Gore*, when the Court invalidated a punitive damages award as excessive under the due process clause.[10]

As discussed later, the factors used by the Court in identifying unconstitutionally disproportionate punitive damages awards seem to incorporate all three principles we have identified: limiting retributive, ends-benefits, and alternative-means proportionality. When the Court's punitive damages standards and holdings are compared to those in prison-duration cases (discussed in chapter 7), it appears that the Court grants more protection to the security of civil defendants' property than to criminal defendants' liberty.

1. Pre-*BMW* Jurisprudence

Several important principles that govern matters of constitutional validity of punitive damages were elaborated prior to *BMW*.

In *Browning-Ferris Industries of Vermont, Inc. v. Kelco Disposal, Inc.,*[11] the Court held that the excessive fines clause of the Eighth Amendment did not apply to punitive damages. The Court explained that the excessive fines clause was "concerned with criminal punishment and with direct actions initiated by government to inflict punishment."[12] Accordingly, the intent of the Eighth Amendment was to address potential government abuse of its prosecutorial power, not to constrain the state's ability to facilitate private enforcement of public interests through punitive damages.[13] The Court refused to decide whether excessive punitive damages could violate the due process clause because the issue had not been properly raised on appeal.[14] It also rejected the plaintiffs' invitation to impose a common law requirement of reasonableness on state punitive damages awards because common law excessiveness principles, as matters of state law, were outside the Court's jurisdiction.[15]

The next two decisions tested the validity of punitive damages under the due process clause. In *Pacific Mutual Life Insurance Co. v. Haslip,*[16] the Court upheld an award of punitive damages because the award was based on identifiable objective criteria of reasonableness, notwithstanding the facts that it was four times the amount of compensatory damages, two hundred times the amount of the plaintiff's out-of-pocket expenses, and larger than any available applicable criminal fine.[17] The Court refused to find a common law method of assessing punitive damages unconstitutional per se.[18]

Two years later, in *TXO Production Corp. v. Alliance Resources Corp.,*[19] the Court declined to assign a specific level of scrutiny to punitive damages and rejected proposals to apply either heightened scrutiny or rational basis, holding that it would not adopt a bright-line mathematical formula to determine whether an award of punitive damages was constitutionally acceptable or unacceptable.[20] The Court said a punitive damages award resulting from fair procedures was "entitled to a strong presumption of validity."[21] It also indicated that concerns about the reasonableness of punitive damages were valid[22] and that potential harm to the plaintiff could be considered in determining whether punitive damages were excessive.[23]

2. Guideposts of Proportionality under *BMW* and *State Farm*

BMW v. Gore[24] and *State Farm v. Campbell*[25] established the constitutional principles currently governing awards of punitive damages. Both cases express the Supreme Court's approval of using punitive damages to further the state interests of retribution and deterrence.[26] The Court recognized that states and their juries have a substantial degree of flexibility with regard to the amount of punitive damages awards.[27] That said, it cautioned that a punitive damages award may run contrary to the implicit notion of fairness embodied in the due process clause of the Fourteenth Amendment if it can "fairly be categorized as 'grossly excessive' in relation" to the state interests of deterrence and retribution.[28]

Two important principles control the constitutional validity of punitive damages. First, "a State may not impose economic sanctions on violators of its laws with the intent" to punish the defendant for its conduct outside the state's jurisdiction, whether lawful[29] or unlawful.[30] Imposing economic sanctions for lawful out-of-state conduct, according to the Court, would violate other states' constitutional autonomy to promote values and shape conduct falling within their jurisdiction.[31] The state's authority to impose punitive damages for a defendant's unlawful out-of-state conduct without joining the out-of-state victims of such conduct was also considered questionable.[32] Both lawful and unlawful out-of-state conduct, however, could be considered as evidence that bears on the reprehensibility of the defendant's conduct insofar as it is related to the harm suffered by the plaintiff.[33]

Second, to meet the requirements of the due process clause, a punitive damages award must provide the defendant sufficient notice of the severity of the penalty that may be imposed for the defendant's conduct.[34] To facilitate this inquiry, the Court established a test that consists of three guideposts of the reasonableness of a punitive damages award. Implicit in these guideposts is the notion that a punitive damages award must be proportional to the harm inflicted.

a. Guidepost #1: Reprehensibility of Defendant's Conduct

The first and most important guidepost deals with the degree of reprehensibility of the defendant's conduct.[35] The language of "reprehensibility" and repeated references to the defendant's "culpability" and "blameworthy" acts[36] suggest that the Court is imposing implicit limiting retributive caps on punitive damages awards. This interpretation is also supported by the Court's list of factors to consider in determining the reprehensibility of the defendant's conduct. Those include whether "the harm caused was physical as opposed to economic; the tortious conduct evinced an indifference to or a reckless disregard of the health or safety of others; the target of the conduct had financial vulnerability; the conduct involved repeated actions or was an isolated incident; and the harm was the result of intentional malice, trickery, or deceit, or mere accident."[37] The Court treats punitive damages awards as suspect if none of these factors supports the plaintiff's case of punitive damages, but it has cautioned that the existence of any of them still might not be dispositive to the issue of whether a punitive damages award must be affirmed.[38]

With regard to judicial determination of reprehensibility, the Court was particularly troubled by the problem of multiplicity of punitive damages awards. In *State Farm*, it criticized Utah's reliance on the evidence of the defendant's unrelated questionable conduct in determining the degree of reprehensibility of the defendant's conduct that harmed the plaintiff.[39] "A defendant's dissimilar acts, independent from the acts upon which liability was premised, may not serve as the basis for punitive damages."[40] A contrary practice, said the Court, would lead to the adjudication, for the purposes of imposing punitive damages, of unrelated, hypothetical third-party claims and eventually burden the defendant with multiple punitive awards for the same conduct.[41] The same concerns are present in the use of recidivism as an aggravating factor, so the definition of recidivism is limited solely to replication of prior transgressions.[42] The present and past transgressions must be sufficiently related or similar to give rise to the charge of recidivism.[43] Wholly unrelated past conduct may not be used to supply the repetition element of recidivism.[44]

The Court's argument regarding multiple punitive awards is somewhat arbitrary, however, because it condemns only the use of the defendant's unrelated conduct in the calculation of punitive damages.[45] The Court fails to acknowledge that evidence of the defendant's similar or related conduct harming others, if admitted, might create no less a possibility of multiple punitive damages than the evidence of its unrelated conduct. The threat of multiple punitive awards is inversely related to the ability of juries and courts to accurately attribute punitive damages to the plaintiff's harm.[46] The task of correlating punitive damages to the plaintiff's harm is substantially difficult regardless of the relation that conduct has to the plaintiff's harm.

Legal scholars have proposed a variety of solutions to the problem of multiplicity of punitive damages awards, including the societal damages approach to punitive damages[47] and bifurcated class-action punitive damages trials.[48] Both have significant drawbacks. The difficulties with correlating punitive damages to a specific harm are not alleviated in a class action, where juries and courts face the challenge of attributing punitive damages to the harm suffered by a class.[49] The theory of societal harm suggests that a portion of punitive damages represents and should cover two types of compensatory societal damages—*specific harms*, which include absent plaintiffs with cognizable tort claims and "quasi plaintiffs," whose harm caused by the defendant's conduct is not yet recognized as cognizable under any existing damage theory;[50] and *diffuse harms*, which consist of any structural harm inflicted on society by the defendant's conduct.[51]

One point of criticism of allowing absent plaintiffs to participate in the distribution of punitive damages as compensation for their actual harm may be that the defendant's due process protection against arbitrary takings of property may be implicated without adequate adjudication of absent plaintiffs' claims in a direct individual or class action trial. With regard to quasi plaintiffs, it would be more prudent to provide this category of potential claimants with compensation through a less arbitrary process of direct judicial recognition of certain new physical or psychological harms. Admittedly, judicial acceptance of new types of compensatory damages is not always aligned with the emerging empirical notions of harm, though this fact alone cannot provide sufficient basis for avoiding the rigors of judicial debate that usually attends the expansion of the theory of compensatory damages.[52]

Compensation of diffuse harms through punitive damages is fraught with even bigger problems. It would permit a state to avoid the constraints of the excessive fines clause by allowing an individual plaintiff to proceed on behalf of the state rather than having to prosecute the defendant's wrongful conduct directly. More important, contrary to the controversial nature of punitive damages that usually militates in favor of restricting their use, the proposition to compensate diffuse harms through punitive damages would unduly expand their use by adding to the existing traditional purposes of punitive damages in American jurisprudence the goal of compensation of societal harm.

A better solution to the problem of multiplicity of punitive damages awards, at least concerning the difficulties that juries and courts experience in accurately attributing punitive damages to the plaintiff's harm, exists in the form of split-recovery statutes. Under a split-recovery statute, a state allows the court to reallocate a portion of punitive damages back to the state.[53] Properly drafted,[54] a split-recovery statute would reallocate a portion of a punitive damages award, erroneously attributed to the plaintiff's harm, to societal use in the areas that suffered from the defendant's conduct.[55]

b. Guidepost #2: Proportionality to Actual or Potential Harm

Because punitive damages are paid to the plaintiff, the Court in *State Farm* and *BMW* fashioned the second guidepost of reasonableness, or proportionality, to demand a certain proportional correlation between a punitive damages award and the harm inflicted on the plaintiff.[56] The Court seemingly accepted the principle stated in *TXO* that there must be a reasonable relationship between a punitive damages award and the *potential*, as well as *actual*, harm inflicted on the plaintiff.[57] Despite the acceptance of potential harm as an allowable benchmark for the constitutional evaluation of punitive awards, both *BMW* and *State Farm* proceeded on the basis of actual harm, thereby limiting the importance of the inquiry based on potential harm to *TXO*-like situations. The focus on actual or potential harm suggests that the second guidepost reflects implicit ends-benefits proportionality principles.

In *TXO*, the potential harm from the defendant's conduct was sufficiently cognizable to enter the punitive ratio calculus mainly because the defendant's conduct set in motion a chain of events that, unless stopped, would continue causing the plaintiff harm without any additional affirmative action by the defendant.[58]

Embarking on its fraudulent scheme, the defendant in *TXO* did not plan to get caught, and, as a result, the total amount of harm to the plaintiff and gain to the defendant was part of the defendant's wrongful intent, for which the defendant had to be punished.[59] The situation was different in *State Farm* and *BMW*, where the extent of damage to the plaintiff from the defendant's conduct was effectively exhausted before the commencement of the suit.[60]

On the matter of an actual, constitutionally allowable ratio, the Court has given scant guidance. It has consistently refused to impose rigid ratio benchmarks,[61] concluding simply that, "in practice, few awards exceeding a single-digit ratio between punitive and compensatory damages, to a significant degree, will satisfy due process."[62] The Court has given no justifiable reason for treating single-digit ratios as more constitutionally defensible than larger ratios,[63] but in *State Farm* it did express one caveat: Ratios higher than a single-digit may be upheld where especially reprehensible conduct results in small actual damages.[64]

The Court rejected a multiplier formula, under which the total amount of punitive damages would be calculated based on the difficulty of detecting and quantifying the plaintiff's harm caused by the defendant's conduct.[65] It also held that the defendant's wealth alone could not justify a large punitive damages award.[66] Finally, if it is likely that the harm suffered by the plaintiff could be covered by compensatory damages and punished by punitive damages at the same time, a lesser ratio would be appropriate.[67]

c. Guidepost #3: Necessity to Achieve Adequate Deterrence

The third guidepost tests the necessity of a punitive damages award by comparing it to the existing legislative sanctions for comparable conduct.[68] The Court observed that the severity of these legislative sanctions represents what the state expected would be the size of a civil penalty needed to deter the conduct at issue.[69] To comply with due process, a remedy must be necessary and superior to less drastic alternatives. As the Court stated in *BMW*, "[t]he sanction imposed in this case cannot be justified on the ground that it was necessary to deter future misconduct without considering whether less drastic remedies could be expected to achieve that goal."[70] In *BMW* there was no history of statutory noncompliance to test the effectiveness of the existing statutory remedies for comparable conduct, which, in the Court's opinion, made it unreasonable to assume that the public goals of retribution and deterrence could not be achieved with a less intrusive remedy than the punitive damages under consideration.[71]

The State Farm Court added that lower courts should avoid using criminal penalties for the calculation of punitive damages.[72] Admitting that the existence of a criminal penalty reflects the state's assessment of the social disutility of the defendant's action, the Court cautioned that punitive damages should not take the place of criminal penalties without the heightened protection of the criminal process.[73] In sum, said the Court, "the remote possibility of a criminal sanction does not automatically sustain a punitive damages award."[74]

State Farm and *BMW* are among the first few Supreme Court decisions that apply proportionality principles to state socioeconomic regulation. Interestingly, despite the fact that proportionality was the underlying principle of the standard of review newly established in *BMW*, that case omitted the word "proportionality" from the standard's description. It took the Court seven years to finally recognize in *State Farm* that the test in *BMW* embraces the principle of proportionality. "[C]ourts must ensure that the measure of punishment is both reasonable and *proportionate* to the amount of harm to the plaintiff and to the general damages recovered."[75]

B. THE ROUGH PROPORTIONALITY OF LAND-USE PERMIT CONDITIONS

In following its concern over discretionary, ad hoc[76] government interference into the autonomy of entities and individuals, the Supreme Court adopted the doctrine of proportionality in a narrow class of cases to provide protection for private property from unconstitutional takings. In particular, the Court in *Dolan v. City of Tigard*[77] instituted a requirement of "rough proportionality" to measure the reasonableness of the relationship between the severity of individualized conditions imposed by the government on land-use permits and the impact of a proposed land development. The inquiry was designed to supplement the "essential nexus" test developed by the Court in *Nollan v. California Coastal Commission*[78] to ensure that a permit condition is substantially related to the public burden that a proposed land-use development imposes.

Nollan inquired into the existence of a fit between a permit condition and a projected development's impact, while *Dolan* examined the required tightness of that fit. The two inquiries became the prongs of a test employed to assess the constitutional validity of governmental land-use permit conditions.[79] The test recognizes the important role of government exactions in land-use regulation and employs the traditional constituent elements of the German doctrine of proportionality—suitability, necessity (alternative-means proportionality), and proportionality in the narrower sense (ends-benefits proportionality)[80]—to screen constitutionally excessive land-use permit conditions. The application of the *Nollan-Dolan* test has not been limited explicitly to possessory[81] exactions.[82] Yet, the Supreme Court has rejected the test's use in cases involving legislative land-use restrictions[83] or where owners are merely denied land-use permits.[84]

As an initial step in the constitutional protection of private property from excessive land-use permit conditions, *Nollan* established the requirement of essential nexus between land-use permit conditions and projected development impacts.[85] In *Nollan*, the Court dealt with a condition the California Coastal Commission had imposed on its approval of a rebuilding permit requested by the Nollans.[86] The commission held that the new house the Nollans planned to build "would increase blockage of the view of the ocean, thus contributing to the development of 'a wall of residential structures' that would prevent the public 'psychologically... from realizing a stretch of coastline exists nearby that they have every right to visit.'"[87] Thus, the commission required that the Nollans dedicate an easement across their property to provide access to public beaches.[88]

The Supreme Court agreed that states may impose permit conditions that serve the same purpose that a denial of a permit would serve.[89] The Court opined that a permit condition in *Nollan* would be constitutional if it were directed, as a height or width limitation on a structure would be, at the protection of the public's ability to view the beach.[90] Along the same lines, the state would be permitted to condition the land-use permit on the Nollans' providing a viewing spot for the public on their property.[91] Despite the fact that absent attachment to a land-use permit, the latter alternative would have constituted a taking, according to the Court, the commission would be justified in using its police power in this manner as an alternative to denial of a development permit, provided, of course, that such concession of property rights by the owner served the same purpose as the denial of the development permit would serve.[92]

The commission in *Nollan*, however, did not utilize any of these permissible methods of conditioning a land-use permit because dedication of an easement for public passage through the Nollans' property served the purpose of maintaining public access to public beaches, not the objective of preserving the public's view of the beach from the street, which would be served by denial of development.[93] The Court held that, "unless the permit condition serves the same governmental purpose as the development ban, the building restriction is not a valid regulation of land use but an 'out-and-out plan of extortion.'"[94] Because the condition imposed by the commission served a different purpose, the Court held that the condition constituted an unconstitutional taking without compensation.[95]

In *Dolan v. City of Tigard*,[96] the Court added to the requirement of essential nexus the demand for proportionality between a governmental exaction imposed as a condition to a permit and the projected development impact. The City of Tigard Planning Commission required that Mrs. Dolan "dedicate the portion of her properly lying within the 100-year floodplain for improvement of a storm drainage system along [the adjacent creek] and that she dedicate an additional 15-foot strip of land adjacent to the floodplain as a pedestrian/bicycle pathway."[97]

The commission justified the imposed conditions by the need to prevent flooding along the creek and to reduce additional traffic congestion created in the central business district by the proposed development.[98]

Quoting *Agins v. City of Tiburon*,[99] the Court reinforced the notion that "[a] land use regulation does not effect a taking if it 'substantially advance[s] legitimate state interests' and does not 'den[y] an owner economically viable use of his land.'"[100] It then observed two important distinctions of the case at issue from the sort of land-use regulations examined in *Agins*.[101] First, said the Court, the regulations described in *Agins* represented legislative zoning determinations, while the land-use decision here was an "adjudicative decision" imposing an individualized condition on an individual parcel of land.[102] Second, the limitation here did not merely restrict the use of land by the owner as in *Agins* but also required that the owner completely give up portions of her property in favor of the city.[103] Under these circumstances, the Court noted, a person cannot be compelled to give up her constitutional right to receive compensation for condemned property in return for a discretionary governmental benefit unrelated to the property.[104]

The *Dolan* Court had no problem finding an essential nexus between the permit conditions at issue and the projected impact of the proposed development of the property. It said that sufficient nexus existed between preventing flooding and not developing in the floodplain since the proposed expansion of the premises on the property would increase the amount of storm water runoff.[105] Similarly, the Court found it reasonable to reduce traffic congestion created as a result of the proposed development by building new pedestrian/bicycle paths as additional means of access to the city's business district.[106]

Under *Nollan*, the inquiry into the constitutional validity of these permit conditions would end here. The Court, however, went on to add an additional prong to its analysis—whether the degree of government exactions reasonably related to the severity of the projected impact of the proposed development.[107] In other words, the court was to determine whether the public benefit and the property owner's detriment from the imposed condition were roughly proportional to the harm from the proposed land use. To establish a meaningful standard, the Court surveyed a number of applicable state court practices in this area.[108] It rejected the rational basis standard[109] and the test of direct proportionality,[110] reasoning that both of these standards failed to reflect adequately the balance of competing constitutional interests in this type of case. The Court concluded that the test of rough proportionality best corresponded to the needs of constitutional review relative to land-use permit conditions.[111] It said that the test required no mathematical calculation "but that the city must make some sort of individualized determination that the required dedication is related both in nature and extent to the impact of the proposed development."[112]

A detailed review of the Court's examination of the permit condition in question in *Dolan* is necessary for a better understanding of the thrust of the Court's "rough proportionality" test. The Court could find no reasonable relation between dedication of an easement lying within the floodplain and prevention of flooding.[113] In the Court's view, the same goal could have been achieved by the extant zoning requirement that the owner refrain from building within the established floodplain.[114] In other words, the complete abridgment of Mrs. Dolan's right to exclude others from her property was excessive and unnecessary for the attainment of the municipal goal of flood prevention.[115]

Regarding the pedestrian/bicycle path, the Court opined that the city failed to show that the increased number of vehicle and bicycle trips caused by the proposed development reasonably related to the requirement that Mrs. Dolan dedicate a portion of her property as a public easement for a pedestrian/bicycle pathway.[116] The Court emphasized that the city merely provided evidence that the contemplated pedestrian/bicycle pathway *could* reduce some of the additional traffic created by the proposed development instead of offering proof that the path *would* or was *likely to* do so.[117]

Dolan's rough proportionality test bears certain resemblance to the proportionality review of governmental interference with social and economic individual rights in foreign jurisdictions discussed earlier. The intensity of constitutional inquiry introduced by the Court in relation to land-use permit conditions in the United States reflects the position of the protected constitutional interests in the established constitutional hierarchy.[118] The Court shied away from adopting the requirement of strict proportionality, viewing the need for government regulation of land use sufficiently important to allow for a certain flexibility of action.[119] On the other hand, the Court realized that the intensity of government intrusion involving land-use permit conditions warrants the placement of the burden of showing rough proportionality on the government.[120] According to *Nollan*, this is because often the conditions that require the permanent dedication of property to public use "would have to be considered a taking if [they] were not attached to a development permit."[121]

In sum, owners' concessions of property in exchange for land development permits do not constitute a taking per se precisely because they are demanded in exchange for a development permit the government would be authorized to deny.[122] Thus, the owner is vested with the choice whether to forego the contemplated development or make a possessory property concession. This aspect saves uncompensated land-use permit exactions from per se unconstitutionality, but it does not entirely remove the concern that the government will use its leverage, which it possesses by virtue of its being the issuer of land-use permits, to demand excessive exactions. Thus, an inquiry more searching than the rational basis standard is required to protect individual property rights from excessive land-use permit conditions.[123]

Like its counterparts abroad, the inquiry of proportionality contemplated under the aegis of *Dolan*'s rough proportionality test includes the assessment of the imposed condition's suitability, necessity, and proportionality in the narrower sense. Suitability of a land-use permit condition is assessed under *Nollan*'s essential nexus test. Like the inquiry of suitability, the essential nexus test requires that a permit condition be designed to redress the projected harm of the proposed property development.[124] Absent such meaningful connection, a permit condition will be invalidated.[125]

The requirements of necessity and proportionality were conflated in *Dolan*'s analysis of the permit condition. The Court criticized the city for not choosing a less restrictive and more proportional exaction to offer the owner in exchange for a land-use permit.[126] For instance, granting an easement over a strip of land to create a public greenway was neither necessary nor proportional to the reduction of the projected increase of the amount of storm water runoff to the adjacent creek created by the contemplated expansion of retail premises and parking lots.[127] The Court concluded that the same objectives were achievable through the existing restrictions on construction within the floodplain area and that, as a result, dedication of a strip of land within the floodplain area was excessive in relation to the perceived threat of increased flooding caused by the proposed development.[128] This position was further reinforced by the city's concession of the ancillary nature of the recreational easement to "the city's chief purpose in controlling flood hazards."[129]

The Court's necessity and proportionality analysis was less cogent relative to the city's second objective that the permit condition at issue was intended to serve. The necessity and proportionality of the demanded dedication of an easement to the city's objective of reducing traffic congestion created by the proposed expansion of business premises, according to the Court, hinged on individualized evidence showing that dedication of an easement would—not merely could or was likely to—reduce the increased traffic congestion.[130] The Court seems to have mistaken the requirement of "rough proportionality" for that of "essential nexus." In effect, it used the central inquiry of the essential nexus test—whether the permit condition at issue was suitable to attain reduction of traffic congestion created by the proposed development—to invalidate the said condition under the requirement of rough proportionality.[131] In doing so, the Court diminished the value of rough proportionality and its constituent elements of necessity and proportionality in the narrower sense.

Dolan failed to define the scope of the "rough proportionality" test, thereby leaving open the questions of whether it applied to legislative regulation of zoning[132] and/or nonpossessory permit conditions,[133] like impact fees or fees in lieu of dedication. These issues were subsequently raised in *City of Monterey v. Del Monte Dunes at Monterey, Ltd.*[134] The plaintiff contested the city government's zoning regulations, which foreclosed the plaintiff from developing its land. The Court attempted to dispel any ambiguity that existed regarding whether the requirement of rough proportionality applied to general land-use regulation, holding that a meaningful proportionality analysis of takings is necessary only in "the special context of exactions—land-use decisions conditioning approval of development on the dedication of property to public use."[135] Having acknowledged that "in a general sense concerns for proportionality animate the Takings Clause,"[136] the Court nonetheless maintained that in applying the test of rough proportionality the Court had not ventured beyond permit-incentivized land dedications.[137] It concluded that mere denials of development did not call for the heightened protection of rough proportionality because they derived their authority from legislative land-use regulation and did not involve the permit-for-land-dedication scenario present in *Dolan* and *Nollan*.[138]

Several important conclusions flow from *City of Monterey*. The Court recognized that proportionality plays a role in the relationship between the government and property owners. The Court's searching proportionality review has been limited to a specific group of cases in which the Court detected a threat to individual property rights from uncompensated takings disguised as permit conditions.[139]

Despite the possible interpretation of the Court's focus in *City of Monterey* on possessory exactions[140] as an exclusion of nonpossessory exactions from the reach of the test of rough proportionality, there is sufficient jurisprudential evidence to the contrary. The primary weakness of this interpretation is that the Court's language in *City of Monterey* limiting the use of rough proportionality to possessory exactions was dictum with regard to nonpossessory exactions because the case did not deal with a nonpossessory exaction. Moreover, a subsequent reversal and remand by the Supreme Court to consider "in light of *Dolan*" a California decision that a fee imposed on a developer to mitigate the loss of community recreational facilities on the developer's property was valid[141] further supports the view that the Court did not intend to exclude nonpossessory exactions from the reach of the *Dolan* test. On remand, the Supreme Court of California held that the rough proportionality test established in *Dolan* applied to nonpossessory (i.e., monetary, exactions).[142] The Supreme Court denied a petition for a writ of certiorari,[143] perhaps indicating that the *Nollan-Dolan* rough proportionality inquiry is applicable to nonpossessory exactions.

The question whether the *Nollan-Dolan* rough proportionality test was applicable to legislative land-use enactments was resolved finally by the 2005 Supreme Court decision in *Lingle v. Chevron U.S.A., Inc.*[144] The Court determined that neither the "substantially advances" test developed in *Agins v. City of Tiburon*[145] nor similar tests related to due process standards of review were applicable in the context of regulatory takings.[146] The Court explained that the takings clause "does not prohibit the taking of private property, but instead places a condition on the exercise of that power."[147] The proper inquiry, therefore, must focus not on the validity of the government action but on the economic burden imposed on the property to determine whether a taking of property has occurred by reason of that property's having been deprived of all of its economic value as a result of government regulation.[148] The validity of the government action ordering a taking is a separate inquiry that applies the deferential rational basis test used in all economic and social regulation.[149]

Despite its general attack on any heightened judicial scrutiny of takings, the *Chevron* decision did not disturb the application of the rough proportionality test in land-use permit exactions.[150] A land-use permit exaction—a government demand of land or money in return for a permit that the government could deny—constitutes a denial of a constitutionally mandated compensation for taken property. As such, the Court reasoned, the rough proportionality standard was appropriate to test the validity of government intrusion into the enjoyment of that constitutional right;[151] however, it was wholly irrelevant in the context of regulatory takings, as the issue there was whether there was a taking, not whether a constitutional right to receive compensation for condemned property was denied.[152]

It is unfortunate that the use of proportionality in land-use regulation was limited to nonlegislative discretionary adjudicative exactions. This leaves landowners virtually unprotected from government land-use regulation because the deferential rational basis test[153] provides no adequate, thorough balancing of the public interest being advanced by a land-use regulation with the competing individual property rights. Arguably, landowners should be protected from excessive government intrusion into their economic autonomy irrespective of whether the intruder is a legislature or an executive body taking the land in an adjudicative nonlegislative manner.[154]

C. PROPORTIONALITY OF ATTORNEY'S FEES AWARDS IN CIVIL RIGHTS CASES

Punitive damages and attorney's fees play a similar public policy role. The proportionality of attorney's fees has been considered in the context of reasonable attorney's fees awards in civil rights litigation under 42 U.S.C. § 1988.[155] Despite the fact than an award of reasonable attorney's fees to a successful plaintiff in § 1988 actions serves the same goal of deterrence as punitive damages[156]—to which the Court has applied the requirement of proportionality to screen out unconstitutionally excessive punitive damages awards[157]—the Court has refrained from imposing a requirement of proportionality on attorney's fees awards under § 1988 on the ground that it would significantly reduce the incentives plaintiffs have to litigate this type of case.[158] As determined by the Court, proportionality can be used only to test the validity of attorney's fees awards in civil rights cases under § 1988 if it is established that the primary purpose for the civil rights litigation was recovery of damages.[159]

As a general matter of reasonableness, the Court held in *Hensley v. Eckerhart*[160] that a plaintiff's success is an important factor in determining the proper amount of an award of attorney's fees under § 1988.[161] Courts should attempt to detect and exclude excessive and redundant fees.[162]

In some cases, for example, counsel may bring distinct actions against the same or different individuals. If counsel prevails under one cause of action and fails under another, the attorney's fees for the litigation of a distinct cause of action on which the attorney failed to prevail should not be taken into consideration when determining the award of attorney's fees to the plaintiff.[163] By contrast, where counsel obtained "substantial relief" for the client, the award of attorney's fees should not be reduced merely because counsel did not succeed on all theories or claims advanced.[164] However, in a case of limited success, the court should award reasonable attorney's fees relative to the degree of success in the matter.[165]

Hensley's general analysis of reasonableness of attorney's fees in § 1988 actions failed to answer whether there should be any overriding proportional relationship between compensatory damages and attorney's fees, mainly because the matter of the allowable amount of attorney's fees was not raised on the theory of proportionality.[166] The Court nonetheless effectively promoted the notion of proportionality by elevating the plaintiff's success to the level of becoming a crucial determinant of the reasonableness of attorney's fees.[167] It seems that successful claims provided the Court with an assuring assessment of harm suffered by the plaintiff that it could use as an objective benchmark of reasonable attorney's fees. As a logical extension of this reasoning—and not unlike punitive damages cases that use compensatory damages as a proxy for the reprehensibility of the defendant's conduct[168]—the Court could effectively use compensatory damages as a rough equivalent of plaintiff's success to provide a benchmark for assessing the reasonableness of attorney's fees.

The Court rejected this easily administrable test of reasonableness of attorney's fees for an important reason. In *City of Riverside v. Rivera*,[169] the plurality acknowledged that the amount of compensatory damages was pertinent to the issue of attorney's fees awards but denied giving it a decisive role in determining the reasonableness of those awards. The plurality held that the size of a compensatory award in a case brought under § 1988 was merely one of the factors[170] to be considered under the prevailing totality of circumstances analysis.[171] According to the Court, attorney's fees awards should not be pegged to the amount of compensatory damages "[b]ecause damages awards do not reflect fully the public benefit advanced by civil rights cases."[172] Moreover, the *Rivera* plurality expressly rejected the proposition that attorney's fee awards under § 1988 must "necessarily be proportionate to the amount of damages a civil rights plaintiff actually recovers"[173] because, according to the plurality, such a requirement would eliminate virtually all of the incentives that full recovery of attorney's fees creates for private plaintiffs to litigate civil rights violations.[174]

The plurality underscored the narrow application of this decision to § 1988 attorney's fees cases. In particular, it stated that the adopted rationale for rejecting proportionality as a measure of reasonableness of attorney's fees in civil rights cases did not apply to most private law cases, where damages awards, unlike the same in civil rights cases, reflect the harm to the plaintiff and the public benefit arising out of private law litigation.[175] Thus, *Rivera* does not preclude the use of proportionality in private law cases—where, by law or contract, courts may award attorney's fees to the plaintiff—to test the reasonableness of attorney's fees in relation to the plaintiff's success, measured, *inter alia*, by the amount of the plaintiff's compensatory damages award.[176]

Rivera is most interesting for Justice Powell's concurrence, which shifted the result in favor of the plurality and full attorney's fees. He agreed with the plurality that § 1988 attorney's fees do not have to be proportional to damages recovered in a civil rights action.[177] Yet, he urged that the use of proportionality of attorney's fees as a measure of reasonableness hinges on the plaintiff's purpose for engaging in civil rights litigation.[178] If the primary purpose of the civil rights litigation is recovery of damages[179] and no significant public interest is served by vindicating the violated constitutional rights, "a district court, in fixing fees, is obligated to give primary consideration to the amount of damages awarded as compared to the amount sought."[180] This formulation fits within the traditional understanding of the ends-benefits analysis of proportionality. To the contrary, if vindicating a constitutional right, irrespective of the novelty of the constitutional ruling, may substantially serve a public interest, it should be considered in addition to the recovered damages in the calculation of attorney's fees.[181]

Justice Powell's position was subsequently adopted in the majority opinion in *Farrar v. Hobby*.[182] "Having considered the amount and nature of damages awarded, [a district] court may lawfully award low fees or no fees without reciting the 12 factors [from *Hensley*] bearing on reasonableness."[183] In the case *sub judice*, where the plaintiffs requested a large damage amount but recovered only nominal compensatory damages, the Court decided that the measure of reasonableness of attorney's fees had to focus on the extent to which the plaintiffs were able to prove actual injury necessary for the recovery of compensatory damages.[184] This was so because the primary purpose of the litigation, in light of the large amount of requested compensatory damages, was recovery of damages.[185] *Rivera* was never intended to allow windfalls to plaintiffs' attorneys, the Court reasoned.[186] Lower courts have subsequently interpreted *Farrar* as establishing what amounts to an ends-benefits proportionality principle in awarding attorney's fees in civil rights cases, and some of these courts have explicitly mentioned proportionality.[187]

D. USE OF PROPORTIONALITY IN ASSESSING THE VALIDITY OF CONGRESSIONAL ABROGATION OF STATE SOVEREIGNTY UNDER THE FOURTEENTH AMENDMENT ENFORCEMENT CLAUSE

Proportionality, as argued here, is key to preventing excessive government intrusion into individual autonomy and also to striking a meaningful balance between the federal government's limited powers and the states' police power. One point of tension between the federal and state powers, in which proportionality principles are implicitly employed under the guise of intermediate scrutiny, is determining whether nondiscriminatory state laws violate the dormant commerce clause (discussed earlier in this book).[188]

    This section explores the application of proportionality in determining the constitutionality of a congressional enforcement action imposed on state governments under the authority of Section 5 of the Fourteenth Amendment.[189] The Court has indicated in several of its decisions that the Constitution requires such enforcement actions to be "congruent and proportional" to the harm they are intended to redress.[190]

    The primary test was established in *City of Boerne v. Flores.*[191] It resulted from the Court's concern that unchecked congressional enforcement power could lead to unjustifiable abrogation of the states' sovereign immunity as recognized in the Eleventh Amendment.[192] The Supreme Court ruled that the Constitution permits Congress to abrogate state sovereign immunity under Section 5 of the Fourteenth Amendment only when there is an identified pattern and history of constitutional violations by the states and if Congress uses means that are congruent and proportional to those violations to remedy the unconstitutional conduct.[193] Otherwise, the Court could fairly interpret the congressional action as an "attempt [to effect] a substantive change in constitutional protections, proscribing state conduct that the Fourteenth Amendment itself does not prohibit."[194] Such a congressional exercise of constitutional interpretive power is not allowed under Section 5 of the Fourteenth Amendment.[195]

In deciding these matters, the Court begins its inquiry by making certain that Congress has expressed its intent to abrogate Eleventh Amendment immunity. If Congress has done so, the Court then considers the validity of such abrogation by assessing the implicated constitutional right, documented state constitutional violations, and the remedy provided by the abrogation.[196]

The nature of the constitutional right Congress intends to protect is crucial for determining whether the state has violated the right. The Court is more deferential to the state when congressional action intends to protect a right that is normally subject to the rational basis standard of judicial review.[197] By contrast, it will more readily find violations of constitutional rights by state conduct deserving of congressional reaction if the rights are protected by higher scrutiny.[198] Thus, using the level of scrutiny applicable to the constitutional right Congress intended to protect, the Court reviews the congressional findings to ascertain whether the alleged state conduct rises to the level of a constitutional violation. If the proof provided by Congress is sufficient, the Court will find that Congress is entitled to enact remedial legislation.[199]

The final step in the analysis is to determine whether the means used by Congress to remedy a constitutional violation are congruent and proportional to that violation. The Court permits prophylactic legislation with a degree of overbreadth, prohibiting some constitutional conduct, but the scope of the remedy must not greatly exceed the identified violations.[200] This is an example of means-proportionality analysis.[201] However, the Court may have been as concerned with protecting its monopoly on constitutional interpretation from congressional encroachment as it was with protecting the states from excessively broad remedies.

Subsequent Supreme Court decisions confirmed the Court's adherence to the *Boerne* principles. *Florida Prepaid Postsecondary Education Expense Board v. College Savings Bank*[202] held that the *Boerne* test was the primary standard for scrutinizing Section 5 legislation. Following *Florida Prepaid* by a year, *Kimel v. Florida Board of Regents*[203] confirmed that it was the judicial branch's role to determine what constitutes a substantive constitutional violation and that Congress's power under Section 5 of the Fourteenth Amendment must necessarily be of a remedial character. It also held that the level of scrutiny applicable to the constitutional right Congress intended to protect controls the weight of the burden that Congress can impose on the states pursuant to its remedial powers under Section 5 of the Fourteenth Amendment.[204]

The question of fit between the remedial action and the alleged constitutional violation had long evaded coherent discussion. Several opinions now shed at least limited light on the issue. *United States v. Morrison*[205] required that the congruence and proportionality of a congressional remedial action depend on the measure's effectiveness in changing state conduct. *Board of Trustees v. Garrett*,[206] on the other hand, declared Title I of the Americans with Disabilities Act (ADA) incongruent and disproportional to the desired end because the remedy of rights granted by Congress in the ADA to employees with disabilities far exceeded the constitutional guarantees of the Fourteenth Amendment. It also emphasized that conduct by local government and the private sector was irrelevant to the inquiry whether a state had been violating the Constitution.[207]

Although the Supreme Court's methodology in this area of law represents only a recent foray into proportionality, the principle's adoption and application demonstrate how proportionality may be used to protect constitutional interests while still respecting the division of labor between state and federal levels of government and the sovereign interests inherent in our federal system. Proportionality allows courts to recognize the importance of the interests that Congress is attempting to protect from state intrusion, while at the same time giving appropriate consideration to the states' sovereign immunity. As the Supreme Court continues to flesh out this important area of law, it would serve the Court well to consciously consider the extent to which proportionality may help find an appropriate balance between individual and state interests.[208]

E. PROPORTIONALITY AS A TOOL TO DETECT VOTING RIGHTS AND EQUAL PROTECTION VIOLATIONS

The earlier sections of this part have focused on the implicit or explicit use of proportionality as a limiting principle on government discretion in regulating personal autonomy. This role gives proportionality the feel of an instrumental principle designated to facilitate the enforcement of citizens' due process and equal protection rights under the U.S. Constitution. This section discusses another use for proportionality that clothes the principle with a constitutional significance different from that in the areas described in earlier sections and chapters. Specifically, the Supreme Court has accepted proportionality in some areas of its equal protection and voting rights jurisprudence as one of the factors that inform the Court's decision in determining whether there has been a violation of a constitutional norm; disproportionality plays an evidentiary role. The two most widely recognized examples are public school desegregation and vote dilution. However, another aspect of voting rights, the one-person-one-vote rule, involves proportionality as a substantive right rather than an evidentiary tool; in addition, the standards used to enforce that rule incorporate several of the proportionality concepts we have identified.

1. Proportionality in Public School Desegregation

In a 1968 decision, *Green v. County School Board of New Kent County*,[209] the Court—displeased with the slow pace of desegregation allowed by the relaxed requirement established in *Brown v. Board of Education (Brown II)*,[210] which required public schools to desegregate "with all deliberate speed"—created an affirmative duty to integrate schools that were historically segregated. The freedom-of-choice plans deemed sufficient under *Brown II* were no longer acceptable if they were ineffective in achieving a "racially nondiscriminatory school system."[211] The Court said, "[t]he time for mere 'deliberate speed' has run out."[212] The time had come for school boards to bear the higher burden of "com[ing] forward with a plan that promises realistically to work, and promises realistically to work *now*."[213] To ensure the school boards complied with this order, the Court assumed "jurisdiction until it is clear that state-imposed segregation has been completely removed."[214]

The Court's opinion in *Green* seems to suggest that the effectiveness of school desegregation plans in achieving integration would be judged by numbers. Numbers and correlations of numbers played a particularly important role in two of the categories identified by the Court as relevant to the assessment of the school districts' compliance with the constitutional equal protection requirements: student assignments and teacher and principal assignments.[215] Proportionality was a logical tool for the Court to apply in the examination of numbers and correlations of numbers in these two categories, given its implicit predisposition to a requirement for some degree of proportionality between the racial makeup of the total number of students and staff and the assignments to various schools.[216]

It was not until 1971, however, that the Court expressly empowered district courts in *Swann v. Charlotte-Mecklenburg Board of Education*[217] to require racial proportionality, or racial balancing, as a remedy to previous segregation and as a tool to achieve integration. The Court was careful, however, to limit this decision with the caveat that the order's proportionality requirement was not a substantive constitutional right[218] but rather a "starting point in the process of shaping a remedy."[219] This suggests an instrumental approach to the principle's application. The Court also limited the use of proportionality to schools that were intentionally segregated by the state in the past[220] and disallowed its application to higher educational institutions.[221]

Proportionality was not limited to serving only a remedial role. According to *Swann*, it could also be used to detect equal protection violations in traditionally segregated school districts. The Court created a presumption that schools historically separated by race with a substantially disproportionate racial composition were in violation of their constitutional duty to create an integrated educational environment in public schools.[222] If the school district presented a desegregation plan under which some schools in a racially diverse district would continue to be attended predominantly by one race, the school district bore the burden to show that its disproportionate racial composition within the schools was not attributable to past discrimination.[223] This burden required the school district to show that "any current imbalance is not traceable, in a proximate way, to the prior violation."[224]

As time passes, however, the presumption of a constitutional violation in the presence of a racial imbalance may lose its force. The longer the time span between the initial action to achieve desegregation and the present, arguably, the less likely the current racial disproportionality in school attendance can be attributed to state conduct, absent proof of a school district's intent to segregate.[225] Indeed, demographic changes unrelated to state conduct—unsuccessfully presented as vestiges of public school segregation warranting remedial action from federal courts in *Pasadena Board of Education v. Spangler*[226]—have been the major recent contributor to racial imbalance in public schools. Thus, if the school district demonstrates "a history of good faith compliance," the causal link between a state's conduct and the racial imbalance becomes more attenuated, and the district court could fairly "accept the school board's representation that it has accepted the principle of racial equality and will not suffer intentional discrimination in the future."[227]

Courts may not create a presumption of an equal protection violation from racial imbalance in higher education.[228] The different approach is justified by the fact that students have a choice in which school to attend and cannot be forced to attend a certain institution.[229] Thus, the presence of a racial imbalance at a higher educational institution is not sufficient to shift the burden of proof to the state.[230] Rather, the burden shifts when the state is shown to have continued policies "rooted in its prior, officially segregated system that serve to maintain the racial identifiability of its universities."[231] When the burden thus shifts, the school must either dismantle the violating policies or show that it would be impossible to eliminate those policies without disadvantaging the school's educational needs.[232]

The Court's use of proportionality as a tool to detect constitutional violations with regard to race demonstrates the principle's utility in protecting important constitutional interests. That the Court turned to proportionality to help enforce equal protection rights—which, given the historical underpinnings of the equal protection clause of the Fourteenth Amendment, subject classifications based on race to the strictest judicial scrutiny—demonstrates the principle's ability to flex and fit different legal systems and standards. The variance in presumptions of unconstitutionality between public education and higher education also demonstrates that a finding of proportionality can be adapted to fit the needs of different contexts, even within the same legal system.

2. Proportionality in Voting Rights Cases

An examination of Supreme Court voting rights decisions reveals two situations in which the Court applies proportionality. First, proportionality is constitutionally required as a substantive right in the representation of individuals. Second, proportionality may be used as an evidentiary tool for detecting dilution of the voting strength of a racial class of voters in violation of Section 2 of the Voting Rights Act. Given that groups do not have a constitutional right to proportional representation, the latter use of proportionality is used as a rough baseline to determine whether group votes have been diluted.

a. "One Person, One Vote": Proportional Representation Among Voting Districts

The meaning of proportionality in the representation of individuals derives from the Supreme Court's interpretation of the constitutional command that representatives be chosen "by the People of the Several States" as requiring that "as nearly as practicable one man's vote in a congressional election is to be worth as much as another's."[233] To obtain this result, the Court established a constitutional requirement that congressional districts contain equal numbers of inhabitants.[234]

Based on the equal protection clause of the Fourteenth Amendment, the same requirement applies to state legislative districts.[235] Compliance with this principle requires states to revise their districts with a reasonable frequency, at a minimum every ten years.[236] It also requires that *both* houses of a bicameral state legislature be apportioned substantially on a population basis.[237]

The one-person-one-vote proportionality standard is strict for federal elections. The Constitution allows only the smallest deviation possible and only if it is necessary for the attainment of a legitimate state objective.[238] A party challenging a population difference must prove that the "population differences among districts could have been reduced or eliminated altogether by a good-faith effort to draw districts of equal population."[239] If the challenger fails to meet this burden, the contested districting plan will be affirmed.[240] If the plaintiff can show that the contested population differences were not a product of the state's good-faith effort to achieve equality, the state must prove that the differences were necessary to achieve a legitimate goal.[241] As long as the justifications are nondiscriminatory, the court may approve of a number of goals put forward by the state, including achieving compact districts, following municipal lines, preserving the essence of previous districts, and "avoiding contests between incumbent Representatives."[242]

To summarize, the population-based, substantive right to proportional representation is enforced with two of the proportionality principles this book examines. Deviations from proportional representation must be justified by a legitimate state interest (a standard akin to the German suitability requirement), and such deviations must be necessary to achieve the asserted interests (a version of alternative-means proportionality analysis).

b. Vote Dilution

Despite statutory provisions indicating that no group or class is entitled to proportional representation,[243] proportionality has also found its way into group voting rights as a factor that indicates an absence of vote dilution.

The basic preconditions for a vote dilution claim were established in *Thornburg v. Gingles*,[244] based on the statutory provisions of sections 2(a) and 2(b) of the Voting Rights Act (VRA).[245] Section 2(a) guarantees that neither race nor color can be used as a "voting qualification or prerequisite to voting."[246] Section 2(b) stipulates the following:

> A violation of [Section 2(a)] is established if, based on the totality of circumstances, it is shown that the political processes leading to nomination or election in the State or political subdivision are not equally open to participation by members of a class of citizens protected by subsection (a) of this section in that its members have less opportunity than other members of the electorate to participate in the political process and to elect representatives of their choice. The extent to which members of a protected class have been elected to office in the State or political subdivision is one circumstance which may be considered: *Provided*, That nothing in this section establishes a right to have members of a protected class elected in numbers equal to their proportion in the population.[247]

In light of these provisions, the *Gingles* Court required an initial showing for a successful vote dilution claim to include numerocity and compactness of the minority group sufficient to constitute a majority in a single-member district, political cohesion of the minority group, and white majority bloc voting in the contested district such that the minority group's preferred candidate will usually be defeated.[248] Once an initial showing is made, the absence or presence of vote dilution is determined on the basis of the totality of circumstances,[249] including previous elections that resulted in a proportional representation of the minority group.[250]

Proportionality in electoral success is only one of the factors to be considered.[251] Proportional representation of minority groups is not an unvarying indicator of the absence of vote dilution.[252] There are other, more subtle ways, argued the Court, in which minority group voting strength could be diluted without affecting proportionality.[253] Despite this language, some scholars argue that a showing of proportional representation in previous elections would make the burden on the minority group to prove vote dilution a very heavy one.[254]

It is clear that tension exists between considering proportionality in previous electoral success as a baseline for vote dilution and the specific prohibition against requiring proportional representation in Section 2(b) of the VRA, as well as the constitutional rejection of race-conscious districting.[255] Justice O'Connor very aptly described the essence of this tension in her *Gingles* concurrence:

> We know that Congress intended to allow vote dilution claims to be brought under § 2, but we also know that Congress did not intend to create a right to proportional representation for minority voters. There is an inherent tension between what Congress wished to do and what it wished to avoid, because any theory of vote dilution must necessarily rely to some extent on a measure of minority voting strength that makes some reference to the proportion between the minority group and the electorate at large.[256]

principles to invalidate rules or practices that place a substantial burden on the exercise of constitutionally protected trial rights.

When the government seeks to forcibly administer powerful medications to render defendants competent to stand trial or to make inmates easier to manage in jail or prison, the Supreme Court has imposed limitations that reflect both ends- and means-proportionality principles. Implicit means-proportionality principles are applied by courts when deciding whether a civil or regulatory measure is sufficiently punitive to trigger the substantive due process ban on punishment without criminal procedure safeguards; however, a finding of disproportionality merely serves an evidentiary function by implying an intent to inflict punishment.

Finally, ends- and means-proportionality analysis has sometimes been used to limit criminal procedure rights; in these cases, a finding of disproportionality favors the government, not the citizen. Numerous cases that require "standing," permit impeachment use, or otherwise limit the scope of the Fourth Amendment and other constitutionally required exclusionary rules are based on a finding that the benefits of more frequent exclusion of evidence are not worth the cost (ends proportionality) or that such exclusion is not needed to provide adequate deterrence (means proportionality). Ends proportionality is implicit in cases that deny Sixth Amendment rights to appointed counsel and jury trial in less serious cases; subconstitutional criminal procedure laws also often grant fewer procedural safeguards in such cases, apparently on the theory that the benefits of such safeguards are not worth the costs.

The next chapter examines implicit proportionality limits on the imposition of criminal liability. Various constitutional and subconstitutional rules, barring liability in the absence of "fair notice," reflect an implicit limiting retributive rationale: Persons who lack such notice are not sufficiently culpable to justify the imposition of criminal sanctions and stigma. Retributive principles and means and/or ends proportionality may also underlie constitutional prohibitions on "status" crimes and the requirement of proof beyond reasonable doubt. In subconstitutional criminal law, retributive and other proportionality limits are implicit in rules that bar or discourage strict liability. "Voluntary act" requirements reflect limiting retributive principles. Self-defense and other affirmative defenses of justification implicitly incorporate both ends- and means-proportionality principles; excuse defenses primarily incorporate limiting retributive proportionality. Retributive and ends-proportionality principles are implicit in criminal statutes that scale crime severity according to degrees of offender culpability and social harm.

The final chapter in this part explores proportionality as a limitation on criminal and quasi-criminal punishments. Unlike the topics in the two previous chapters, these are areas in which courts, state constitutional provisions, and scholars often explicitly speak of "proportionality" limits, but such limits have usually not been clearly defined. In cases that apply the Eighth Amendment's cruel-and-unusual-punishment and excessive fines clauses to the death penalty, lengthy prison terms, and civil or criminal forfeitures of property, the Supreme Court has invoked a standard of "gross disproportionality" to the offense being punished or the misconduct leading to the forfeiture. Death penalties and forfeitures are clearly limited by retributive principles, but it is less clear whether the Court intends to also put means- and/or ends-proportionality limits on these sanctions. Its standards for evaluating severe prison terms are even less clear; the Court has seemed to reject any independent retributive limits on such sentences and has failed to provide itself or lower courts with much guidance about when and why a long prison term should be found constitutionally excessive. A different set of rules, also based on the Eighth Amendment but not closely tied to the Court's sentencing cases, places some limits on harsh treatment of prisoners. The focus of these cases seems to be on unnecessary harshness, thus suggesting a form of means proportionality.

This chapter also examines state constitutional sentencing provisions, which courts have sometimes used to grant additional protections not required by the Eighth Amendment. Many examples of implicit retributive, ends-, and means-proportionality principles can be found in the cases construing these provisions. The chapter ends with a survey of proportionality principles in model codes and scholarly writings on sentencing and in sentencing laws and jurisprudence in the United States and other countries. Scholars expressly recognize all three types of proportionality, and these principles are often explicit or implicit in model codes, sentencing laws, and sentencing decisions.

When viewed separately, U.S. constitutional criminal procedure, criminal liability, and punishment rules show only halting, inconsistent, and often incoherent application of proportionality principles. But when these rules are viewed in the aggregate, along with the corroborating testimony of scholarly writings, model codes, and sentencing laws and decisions in the United States and abroad, it becomes clear that limiting retributive, ends-benefits, and alternative-means proportionality principles all enjoy broad support. In exercising their judicial review functions, courts should not hesitate to invoke these fundamental principles of justice. Courts should also state clearly which principle or principles they are applying, and adapt the principles to the particular context.

5 PROCEDURE

Implicit Proportionality Limits on Police Powers and Defendant Rights

THIS CHAPTER EXAMINES THE MANY examples of constitutional and subconstitutional criminal procedure rules that incorporate ends-benefits and/or alternative-means proportionality principles. The application of these principles is almost always implicit; courts rarely use the language of proportionality, and they do not separately analyze and clearly distinguish ends- and means-proportionality concepts. In each of the topic areas summarized here, we first identify the implicit proportionality principles being applied in the Court's decisions and then discuss how the policy analysis in these cases would be improved by their more explicit recognition and application.

Part A discusses Fourth Amendment standards that define "unreasonable" searches and seizures. In many of its decisions the Supreme Court has implicitly incorporated ends-proportionality principles in a multifactor balancing test under which the importance of asserted law enforcement or other government interests is weighed against the nature and degree of the resulting intrusion into privacy, physical liberty, and property. Occasionally the Court's balancing analysis has also implicitly applied means-proportionality principles and taken into account the availability of less intrusive ways of achieving the government's asserted purposes. In a few cases the Court has used a simpler version of balancing that is keyed to offense severity and offender risk. Under this (still implicit) offense- and offender-proportionality approach, the police have broader investigatory powers when they investigate more serious crimes; similarly, more serious intrusions into privacy, liberty, and/or property require a showing of more important government interests and thus can be used only to respond to serious offenses or apprehend dangerous suspects.

Part B discusses proportionality limits on pretrial detention and release conditions. The Eighth Amendment's excessive bail clause prohibits bail set at an amount higher than necessary to reasonably ensure the appearance of the accused at trial (alternative-means proportionality). Similarly, subconstitutional pretrial release and detention rules and statutes often define a range of increasingly restrictive release conditions and direct courts to choose the least restrictive option that will reasonably guarantee appearance and public safety. Constitutional and subconstitutional rules may also implicitly incorporate ends-proportionality principles by limiting bail in minor cases and requiring courts to consider offense seriousness as a factor in setting bail or other release conditions.

Part C examines a line of cases in which the Supreme Court has invalidated rules or practices that placed excessive burdens on the defendant's exercise of constitutionally protected criminal procedure rights. Sometimes these decisions have been based on the availability of less burdensome ways of achieving the state's asserted interests—a means-proportionality argument. In other cases the Court has seemed to invoke ends proportionality—the state's interests were not deemed to be of sufficient weight to justify the substantial burden on important rights. In still other cases the basis for the decisions is unclear but seems to reflect either ends proportionality or both ends and means proportionality.

Part D discusses constitutional limits on authorities' efforts to forcibly administer powerful medications in order to render an inmate easier to manage in jail or prison or to make a defendant competent to stand trial. The Supreme Court has placed both ends- and means-proportionality limits on these practices. The charged offense must be serious, the medication must be medically appropriate and effective, and there must be no less intrusive means of administering the drugs and achieving the desired effects.

Part E examines the use of proportionality principles in deciding when a nominally "civil" or "regulatory" measure is actually intended as "punishment" and is therefore subject to constitutionally required criminal procedure rules and limitations. The Court appears to be using a means-proportionality test here in asking whether the challenged measure is more severe than necessary to achieve the asserted nonpunitive, regulatory goal. However, the concern is not with disproportionality itself but rather with the inferred punitive intent—disproportionality serves an evidentiary function.

In the last two parts of this chapter the focus shifts from proportionality analysis as protector of rights to proportionality as a justification for limiting the scope of criminal procedure rights and remedies. Part F explores the many cases in which the Supreme Court has used implicit proportionality arguments to limit the scope of the exclusionary rules that enforce Fourth, Fifth, and Sixth amendment rights. The exclusionary remedy is not applied when the Court concludes that the cost of excluding the evidence in question would outweigh the additional enforcement benefits likely to result from exclusion (ends proportionality). Some justices have also argued that certain exclusionary remedies should be narrowly tailored—a form of means proportionality. In these contexts, a finding of ends and/or means disproportionality favors the government, not the citizen.

Part G examines implicit proportionality limits on pretrial, trial, and post-trial procedural rights. Sixth Amendment rights to appointed counsel and jury trial have been limited when the crime or the penalty is minor—a categoric ends-proportionality rule that is based in part on the assumption that for minor crimes the cost and administrative burdens of these safeguards outweigh their truth-seeking and other benefits. Here again, a finding of disproportionality favors the government. By the same reasoning, subconstitutional laws often grant fewer procedural rights in less serious cases, thus, in effect, "making the procedure fit the crime."

A. THE FOURTH AMENDMENT PROHIBITION OF UNREASONABLE SEARCHES AND SEIZURES

Ends- and means-proportionality principles are implicit in many of the Court's decisions defining the limits the Fourth Amendment places on government search-and-seizure powers. The language of proportionality has occasionally been explicitly invoked but without any clear or consistent definition.

1. Proportionality Principles Implicit in "Reasonableness Balancing"

In law enforcement and regulatory contexts in which special needs or other circumstances make the Fourth Amendment's warrant and probable cause standards impractical, the Supreme Court has used the amendment's more general prohibition of "unreasonable searches and seizures" to uphold a wide variety of warrantless (and often also suspicionless) intrusions. The Court has interpreted "reasonableness" as requiring a balancing of the strength of the government interests supporting the search or seizure against the nature and degree of the intrusion on the citizen's privacy, liberty, and/or property rights. Using this approach, the

Court and lower courts have upheld municipal building inspections; searches of regulated industries; investigatory stops, weapons frisks, and property detentions; automobile and jail inventories; immigration and drunk driving roadblocks; airport, subway, and other security measures; searches and drug testing of high school students, public employees, and convicts; and various extensions of police powers beyond the scope already justified by a warrant or an individualized suspicion.[1]

When courts invoke reasonableness balancing they examine a wide range of factors.[2] Some factors primarily reflect ends-benefits proportionality by directly or indirectly assessing the strength of the government's justifications for and interests served by the intrusion—the seriousness and immediacy of the harms the government sought to prevent and the degree of individualized or target-group suspicion. Other balancing factors primarily reflect alternative-means proportionality principles—the feasibility of applying individualized suspicion and warrant requirements in this context (versus the need to dispense with them) and the availability of less intrusive means to achieve the government's objective. However, the latter appears to be a fairly weak factor; at one time the Court seemed ready to adopt a least-intrusive means test in *Terry v. Ohio* ("stop and frisk") cases, but later cases expressly rejected this requirement not only under *Terry* but also in several other contexts.[3] Finally, some factors in the balance reflect both ends- and means-proportionality principles—assessments of the nature and degree of the intrusion (and of alternative means); considerations of the presence of a warrant, warrant substitute, or other limits on police discretion in conducting the intrusion; and the effectiveness of the government's challenged measures (and of alternative means to achieve these same purposes).

A number of scholars have articulated Fourth Amendment proportionality principles,[4] but majority opinions of the Supreme Court have never explicitly sought to justify the Court's reasonableness-balancing approach on proportionality grounds. However, several justices have cited proportionality principles in concurring or dissenting opinions. In *McDonald v. United States*,[5] Justice Jackson opined that warrantless entry to arrest for a minor offense would display "a shocking lack of all sense of proportion." And in *Atwater v. City of Lago Vista* Justice O'Connor invoked proportionality principles in her forceful dissent, critiquing the majority's refusal to engage in case-specific balancing and its approval of the custodial arrest of a woman for violation of a seat belt law punishable by only a $50 fine. Justice O'Connor argued that Atwater's arrest was disproportionate not only in relation to the minor nature of her offense (ends proportionality) but also relative to any legitimate need to take her into custody (means proportionality).[6] Justice O'Connor thus clearly approved of both ends- and means-proportionality principles, although she did not clearly identify and distinguish them.

Application of proportionality analysis, rather than the Court's multifactor balancing approach, would clarify the essential ends-benefits tradeoffs and might also encourage courts, in appropriate cases, to apply alternative-means analysis more frequently. In the *Atwater* case, for example, a better understanding of the distinct ends- and means-proportionality principles implicit in Justice O'Connor's dissent (and recognition of their widespread application) might have persuaded one of the five justices in the majority (most likely Justice Souter or Justice Kennedy) to invalidate the totally unnecessary, minor-offense arrest at issue in that case.

Another advantage of using explicit proportionality concepts is that they lend themselves more readily to the actual task courts face in these cases—setting appropriate and meaningful limits on excessive government measures. As the Introduction points out, proportionality principles are better suited to the process of judicial review than is a balancing metaphor since the latter suggests a specific, optimum solution. Courts have limited time, competence, and legitimacy to determine optimum solutions to complex, fact-specific, and fast-moving law enforcement problems. It is much easier and more appropriate for a reviewing court to say "This was clearly too much" than to say "This would have been the optimum." When courts review police search-and-seizure decisions after the fact and in the absence of previously defined decision rules (discussed later), the question is not what the optimum ends-benefits balance was at the time the decision was made or what the optimum choice among alternative means would have been but rather whether the measures used were so severe, relative to their purposes and/or to alternative means, that a court should find the search or seizure to be unreasonable.

However, proportionality analysis, like reasonableness balancing, is a standard that, because it depends on many factors assessed under the "totality of the circumstances," may be quite difficult for police and other officials to apply. These officials need practical, simplified decision rules. For this reason, the Supreme Court has often used balancing only to decide that further limits on or expansions of certain police powers are needed, after which it formulates a simpler set of rules to guide the exercise of these powers.[7] Yet judicial drafting of such decision rules is problematic: By what logic do courts translate from general standards to specific rules? And in doing this, how can they avoid the appearance of engaging in "judicial legislation"?

One solution to these problems would be for courts to simplify the first step in this process. At the policy-analysis stage, instead of engaging in vague, multifactor reasonableness balancing, courts could use a simplified version of proportionality, which would translate much more directly into a workable decision rule for officials. As discussed in the next section, the Court has in fact employed this approach in a few of its Fourth Amendment cases.

2. Simpler Proportionality Rules Based On Offense Severity and Offender Risk

In several cases the Supreme Court used implicit ends-proportionality principles keyed to offense severity and/or offender risk to limit the use of specified police measures. This approach (hereafter "offense-offender seriousness") is essentially a simplified version of reasonableness balancing, but the Court has not always invoked balancing in these cases, and the two approaches differ in important ways.

Reasonableness balancing and offense-offender seriousness both examine the nature and degree of the intrusion on privacy, physical liberty, or property that the search or seizure entails, but the offense-offender seriousness standard is much simpler on the "government need" side of the ledger. As noted in the previous section, reasonableness balancing examines a broad range of factors, including the immediacy of potential harms it seeks to prevent, degree of individualized or target-group suspicion, feasibility of applying individualized suspicion and warrant requirements, availability of less intrusive means to achieve the government's interest, presence of a warrant or other limits on police discretion, and effectiveness of the government's challenged measures and alternative measures. In contrast, the offense-offender seriousness approach focuses entirely on the severity of the suspected offense or the dangerousness of the offender. This narrower focus makes the offense-offender seriousness approach easier to apply and also facilitates direct translation into practical decision rules for police and other public officials. Most of these cases have in fact announced such a decision rule, based on offense severity and/or offender risk, and aimed at specified police measures.

In *Welsh v. Wisconsin*[8] the Court held—without mentioning reasonableness balancing—that the police could not make a warrantless, exigent-circumstances entry of a person's house to effect an arrest for a nonjailable first offense of drunk driving. The officers had probable cause to arrest and also reason to believe that delaying the arrest until a warrant was obtained would result in the loss of the crucial evidence of intoxication (blood alcohol levels steadily diminish over time in the absence of continued drinking). The Court noted that many courts view the seriousness of the offense as an important factor in assessing the reasonableness of a warrantless entry and concluded that "it is difficult to conceive of a warrantless home arrest that would not be unreasonable under the Fourth Amendment when the underlying offense is extremely minor."[9] It also quoted from an earlier decision in which Justice Jackson opined that warrantless entry in such a case would involve "a shocking lack of all sense of proportion."[10] The Court recognized that drunk driving poses major risks to persons and property but concluded that Wisconsin's decision to classify first-time violations as nonjailable, civil offenses is the best indication of the extent of the state's interest in making an arrest to enforce this law.[11]

In effect, the Court in *Welsh* held that the substantial intrusion of warrantless home entry was disproportionate in relation to the minor crime that intrusion sought to investigate. Yet the Court's emphasis on the warrantless nature of the entry and its citation of prior warrantless entry cases implied that the same physical acts would not have been viewed as disproportionate if the entry were based on an arrest warrant. Moreover, no subsequent case has extended *Welsh* to warrant-based entries to arrest. However, ends-proportionality principles still serve to justify the Court's narrow decision because warrantless entry is a greater intrusion than entry made with a warrant, and the former is also less likely to benefit the government. Warrantless entry is a greater intrusion subjectively because the homeowner has less assurance that the arrest is legal and that the officer's powers are limited. It is a greater intrusion objectively and also less likely to benefit the government because an arrest that lacks prior judicial review is more likely to lack probable cause and to intrude on innocent persons. A similarly limited, offense-severity proportionality principle underlies the common law rule (still recognized in some form by most states[12]) that forbids warrantless arrest for misdemeanors not committed within the presence of the arresting officer or citizen.

In several later cases, the Court used implicit offense-offender seriousness and ends-proportionality principles to limit other police measures. Although the Court in these cases invoked "reasonableness balancing" and did not cite its holding in *Welsh*, the reasoning of these decisions, as well as the decision rules adopted, was similar to the Court's approach in *Welsh*—the "government need" discussion focused almost entirely on the seriousness or dangerousness of the suspected offense or offender, and in most of these cases the Court, as it had in *Welsh*, fashioned a categoric decision rule limited to the particular police measure being challenged.

In *Tennessee v. Garner*,[13] the Court held that police may not use deadly force to stop and arrest a fleeing suspect unless there is probable cause to believe that the suspect poses a threat of serious physical harm to the officer or others or has committed a crime that involves the infliction or threatened infliction of serious physical harm. *Garner* reflects ends-benefit proportionality in that the Court expressly assumed it is better that a nondangerous suspect wanted for a nonviolent crime be allowed to flee than that the suspect be killed; death or risk of death to the suspect and/or to bystanders is disproportionate in relation to the public interest served by promptly apprehending such a suspect. Although the Court invoked reasonableness balancing, its focus on offender dangerousness and offense seriousness make the analysis much more like the approach of *Welsh*. Moreover, as in *Welsh*, the Court fashioned a practical decision rule keyed both to offense-offender seriousness and to the particular police measure at issue.

The decision in *Garner* was also based in part on a principle akin to means proportionality. The Court specified that deadly force must be necessary to prevent escape (nondeadly force must be used if it will be effective) and that, if feasible, some warning must be given (which, if it causes the suspect to submit, avoids the need to shoot); the Court further noted that a majority of American police departments forbid their officers to use deadly force against nonviolent suspects and concluded that "there is a substantial basis for doubting that the use of such force is an essential attribute of the arrest power in all felony cases."[14] In other words, nondeadly force (on the scene or in subsequent efforts to apprehend the suspect if he does initially escape) appears to be adequate to enforce the law against nonviolent suspects; the use of deadly force is unnecessary—and therefore means disproportionate—in relation to effective nondeadly means of apprehension.

Ends- and means-proportionality principles have also been implicitly invoked, along with explicit offense-offender seriousness criteria, to assess claims of excessive nondeadly force in making arrests, investigatory stops, and other seizures of the person. In *Graham v. Connor*[15] the Court held that three factors should be considered in such cases: "the severity of the crime at issue, whether the suspect poses an immediate threat to the safety of the officers or others, and whether he is actively resisting arrest or attempting to evade arrest by flight." The first and second factors reflect ends proportionality and offense-offender seriousness—as in *Garner*, the Court is saying that the force police use to effect a seizure may be excessive relative to the benefits to be achieved by the use of such force, as measured by the seriousness of the suspected crime or the suspect's dangerousness. The third *Graham* factor may reflect means proportionality: In the absence of active resistance or flight, the force used by the police may exceed what is necessary to safely effect the arrest.

In *United States v. Hensley*[16] the Court suggested another possible offense-offender seriousness proportionality limit on police powers. While holding that the *Terry v. Ohio* investigative stop procedure could be used to investigate a completed felony crime, the Court expressly declined to decide whether such stops may also be used for less serious, completed offenses. Several lower courts have adopted this ends-proportionality-based limitation on the *Terry* doctrine.[17] Moreover, in a variety of other contexts, lower courts have considered the seriousness of the offense to be an important factor in determining the reasonableness of a search or seizure, particularly very intrusive police measures.[18]

To summarize: *Welsh v. Wisconsin* and later cases that put offense-offender seriousness limits on specified police measures suggest a simpler and better way for courts to evaluate and limit such measures—better than the Court's vague, reasonableness balancing approach and perhaps also better than direct application of the ends- and means-proportionality principles that underlie reasonableness balancing. Offense-offender seriousness rules are easier for reviewing courts to apply, and, as these cases show, they also translate directly into workable and defensible decision rules for police and other public officials.

B. CONSTITUTIONAL AND SUBCONSTITUTIONAL LIMITS ON PRETRIAL DETENTION AND RELEASE ORDERS

Proportionality principles are implicit in federal and state constitutional texts and interpretive case law, as well as in statutes and rules governing pretrial release and detention. Alternative-means proportionality is widely recognized, but ends-benefits proportionality may also be implicit in some rules and decisions.

1. Federal and State Constitutional Excessive Bail Clauses

The prohibitions of "excessive" bail found in the Eighth Amendment and in many state constitutions clearly imply some sort of proportionality limit, but courts have had few occasions to interpret the meaning of these provisions. The sole U.S. Supreme Court ruling to date was in *Stack v. Boyle*,[19] where the Court, having stated that the purpose of bail is to ensure the presence of the accused at trial and other hearings, concluded that "[b]ail set at a figure higher than an amount reasonably calculated to fulfill this purpose is 'excessive' under the Eighth Amendment."[20] This language strongly implies a form of alternative-means proportionality: If a lower bail amount would suffice to achieve the government's interest, any higher bail is excessive.

2. Other Proportionality Limits on Pretrial Release and Detention Measures

Subconstitutional state and federal pretrial release rules also frequently incorporate alternative-means proportionality principles in provisions that regulate the use of various pretrial release alternatives. These laws define a range of increasingly restrictive release conditions and direct courts to choose the least restrictive option that will protect specified government interests. For example, the federal statute provides that defendants shall be released on an unsecured appearance bond or promise to appear unless the court finds "that such release will not reasonably assure the appearance of the person as required or will endanger the safety of any other person or the community"; when such a determination has been made, the court must then impose "the least restrictive further condition, or combination of conditions," from a list of fourteen options, that will "reasonably assure" appearance and safety.[21]

Some state constitutions, statutes, codes, and case law, as well as pretrial detention rules in foreign countries,[22] apply an offense- or expected-sentence-severity criterion as one factor and/or as an absolute upper limit on the amount of bail or the availability of pretrial detention. Some rules state that bail may not exceed a specified multiple of the maximum fine for the most serious offense charged; other rules preclude high bail or any bail requirement for specified minor crimes or offense categories.[23] Reviewing courts sometimes invalidate high bail amounts at least in part on the grounds that the amount is too high for the seriousness of the charged offenses.[24] Rules of this type might just represent an indirect measure of the risk of flight or further crime: Offenders who face more serious charges are presumed to have a stronger motive to flee and/or to be more dangerous. On this theory, proportionality to offense severity is not valued for its own sake but rather serves an evidentiary or proxy role.[25] However, to the extent that charged-offense severity is deemed directly relevant, such rules appear to reflect utilitarian ends-benefit proportionality principles; in less serious cases, the expense and hardship of high bail and pretrial detention are not justified by the state's interest in the prosecution. (Although offense severity is also relevant to limiting retributive proportionality principles, the latter do not seem to apply to measures that are not and constitutionally cannot be intended as punishment. See part E for a discussion of the "regulation" versus "punishment" distinction, as well as the general discussion in chapter 7 on retributive theory.)

The paradigmatic case under such an offense-based approach would be an offender charged with a minor crime who is deemed to be dangerous or to pose a substantial risk of flight—such an offender might commit other crimes or flee unless bail is set very high (hence, there is no means-proportionality problem), but the burdens of high bail or pretrial detention may outweigh the value to society of obtaining a conviction. Such cases are rarely reported, in part because pretrial release issues often become moot by the time appellate review can be obtained, but in several minor-crime cases, bail was reduced despite substantial evidence of offender danger and/or flight risk.[26]

Given the importance of pretrial release decisions—which may determine or render moot the ultimate resolution of the charges by trial or plea—it is surprising how little specific content the courts have given to federal and state constitutional and subconstitutional pretrial release and detention provisions. Courts might be encouraged to provide more frequent and useful guidance if they were to focus more specifically on the ways in which bail and other pretrial release decisions can be excessive. As the scattered examples discussed here suggest, these varieties of excessiveness correspond to alternative-means and possibly also ends-benefits proportionality.

C. CONSTITUTIONAL PROHIBITION OF EXCESSIVE BURDENS ON DEFENSE PROCEDURAL RIGHTS

In several cases the Supreme Court has invalidated rules or practices that placed a substantial burden on the defendant's exercise of constitutionally protected trial rights. Both the rationale and the scope of some of the rulings are unclear. Several decisions seem to be based on principles akin to means proportionality, whereas other decisions reflect implicit ends-proportionality principles or both means and ends proportionality.

In *United States v. Jackson*[27] the Court struck down a federal statute that permitted the death penalty to be imposed only when conviction is obtained by jury trial and the jury recommends death. In holding that this statute burdened the rights to plead not guilty and demand a jury trial and that the asserted state interest could be satisfied in less burdensome ways, the Court implicitly applied a means-proportionality requirement:

> The goal of limiting the death penalty to cases in which a jury recommends it is an entirely legitimate one. But that goal can be achieved without penalizing those defendants who plead not guilty and demand jury trial. In some States, for example, the choice between life imprisonment and capital punishment is left to a jury in every case—regardless of how the defendant's guilt has been determined.... Congress cannot impose such a penalty in a manner that needlessly penalizes the assertion of a constitutional right.

Another case based on implicit means-proportionality principles and explicitly using the language of proportionality is *Rock v. Arkansas.*[28] The Court held in *Rock* that limits on the defendant's right to testify at trial must be narrowly tailored and must not sweep more broadly than necessary to achieve legitimate government purposes. The Court noted that

> [o]f course, the right to present relevant testimony is not without limitation. The right "may, in appropriate cases, bow to accommodate other legitimate interests in the criminal trial process." But restrictions of a defendant's right to testify may not be arbitrary or disproportionate to

the purposes they are designed to serve. In applying its evidentiary rules a State must evaluate whether the interests served by a rule justify the limitation imposed on the defendant's constitutional right to testify [internal citations and footnote omitted].

Applying these standards, the Court struck down an Arkansas rule that placed an absolute ban on the use of hypnotically refreshed testimony. Because various less drastic procedural safeguards are available to deal with the potential unreliability of such testimony, Arkansas's rule was overbroad and unconstitutional.

In *United States v. Jackson (supra)*, the Court cited an earlier decision, *Griffin v. California*,[29] which had held that adverse comment by the trial judge or prosecutor on the defendant's failure to take the stand impermissibly burdened the privilege against compelled self-incrimination. But unlike *Jackson*, nothing in the language or procedural context of *Griffin* suggested a means-proportionality theory (i.e., one focused on alternatives to comment, available to the court and the prosecutor). Nor did the Court in *Griffin* signal an intent to rule broadly; it did not say that such comment lacks any probative value or that, regardless of probative value, any state action that burdens the defendant's testimonial choice is impermissible.

However, a narrower, ends-proportionality argument can justify the holding in *Griffin*; the probative value of the (comment-encouraged) inferences that might be drawn from the defendant's silence is low and is therefore outweighed by the burden that comment or the threat of comment places on the decision not to testify. Since the jury cannot know all of the reasons for the defendant's decision—some of which (e.g., the availability of impeaching prior convictions; the desire to shield a loved one or gang boss from liability) are consistent with innocence of the charged offense—the inference of guilt from defendant's silence is sometimes very weak. Subsequent cases appear to reinforce this view of *Griffin*. For example, in *Portuondo v. Agard*,[30] the Court distinguished *Griffin* and refused to condemn a prosecutor's argument to the jury that the defendant's presence at trial allowed him to tailor his testimony to that of prior witnesses. The Court concluded that such comment serves the central truth-seeking function of trial and does not impermissibly burden the right to be present at the trial.

An ends-proportionality analysis clearly underlay the Court's decision in *Brooks v. Tennessee*,[31] which struck down a state law that permitted the defendant to exercise his right to testify only if he took the stand at the outset of the defense case. The Court recognized the state's interest in preventing the defendant from shaping his testimony to conform with other defense witness testimony but held that the state law in question impermissibly burdened the right to testify (and also interfered with the effectiveness of counsel's assistance in exercising that right) by forcing the defendant to testify (or forego testifying) before he could determine whether taking the stand was in his best interest. The Court concluded: "Although the Tennessee statute does reflect a state interest in preventing testimonial influence, we do not regard that interest as sufficient to override the defendant's right to remain silent."[32] This language strongly suggests ends-proportionality analysis: The burden on the defendant's trial rights was found to be more important than the state's interests, which were supposedly served by imposing that burden.

Finally, the Supreme Court has implicitly invoked both means- and ends-proportionality principles in cases limiting in-court use of visible shackles. In *Deck v. Missouri*,[33] the Court held that the due process clause forbids the use of visible shackles in front of the jury during the penalty phase of a capital case, just as it forbids their use during the guilt phase of trials "unless that use is 'justified by an essential state interest'—such as the interest in courtroom security—specific to the defendant on trial." The "essential state interest" requirement is a categoric ends-proportionality rule (like "compelling" interest, in strict scrutiny analysis, discussed in chapter 3).

The constitutional standards regulating in-court shackling also incorporate means-proportionality principles. In *Deck supra*, the Court criticized the absence of any finding of a need for shackling and added: "Nor did [the judge] explain why, if shackles were necessary, he chose not to provide for shackles that the jury could not see—apparently the arrangement used at trial."[34] This language suggests a narrow-tailoring concept or even a least-restrictive-alternative requirement, akin to means proportionality.

These cases imply but do not clearly state their grounding in ends- and/or means-proportionality principles. The rationale and scope of these holdings— particularly *Griffin*—would have been clearer if the Court had made explicit reference to ends- and means-proportionality principles and had specified which aspects of each rule were governed by each principle.

D. CONSTITUTIONAL LIMITS ON FORCED MEDICATION OF INMATES AND DEFENDANTS AWAITING TRIAL

The Supreme Court has held that prison inmates and pretrial detainees have a due process liberty interest in avoiding forced medication with antipsychotic drugs designed to either make them easier to manage in jail or prison or render them competent to stand trial. The Court's decisions place both ends- and means-proportionality limits on these practices.

The latest of these cases, *Sell v. United States*,[35] involved the use of drugs designed to induce and maintain trial competency. The Court held that the Constitution permits the Government involuntarily to administer anti-psychotic drugs to a mentally ill defendant facing serious criminal charges in order to render that defendant competent to stand trial, but only if the treatment is medically appropriate, is substantially unlikely to have side effects that may undermine the fairness of the trial, and, taking account of less intrusive alternatives, is necessary significantly to further important governmental trial-related interests.[36]

The Court specified that a sufficiently important governmental interest exists where the offender is charged with a serious crime against person or property. However, trial and reviewing courts must also consider, as offsets to the government's substantial interest in timely prosecution, conviction, and punishment, whether the defendant has already been confined for a substantial period of time in a medical or mental health center and/or would be so confined if not rendered competent by forced medication. Either form of confinement would protect public safety and could satisfy a substantial portion of any future criminal sentence (via credit for time served awaiting trial), and any treatment received during such confinement might reduce the likelihood of the defendant's committing future crimes.

The *Sell* opinion further provides that forced medication requires a finding that less intrusive treatments are unlikely to achieve substantially the same results. Courts must also consider less intrusive means for administering the drugs (e.g., ordering the defendant to take the drugs, with threatened contempt sanctions, before forcibly administering them), and they must make certain that administration of the drugs is in the defendant's best medical interest in light of his medical condition, the potential side effects, and the likely effectiveness of the drugs in his case.

The *Sell* standards embody independent ends- and means-proportionality principles. Forced medication violates ends-proportionality principles if the loss of liberty and attendant medical risks outweigh the importance of the charges and the drugs' probable effectiveness in restoring competence and ensuring a fair trial. Such medication violates means proportionality if there are less intrusive ways to restore competency or administer the drugs. Moreover, forced medication might violate both of these proportionality principles if it were found not to significantly further the state's asserted interest.

In the first in this line of cases, *Washington v. Harper*,[37] involving the proposed medication of a dangerous prison inmate, the Court appeared to apply a somewhat looser standard, more akin to rational basis review, by asking whether the prison regulation was "reasonably related to legitimate penological interests." However, some proportionality analysis was implicit, and it is possible that the stricter standards adopted in later, trial-competency cases like *Sell* have modified

Harper. Of course, proportionality standards can and should be tailored to the specific context, and it seems likely that the Court will evaluate trial competency measures more strictly than measures designed to maintain prison and jail security.[38] The precise scope of the Court's rulings and the different standards applied in different contexts would be clearer if the Court were to explicitly recognize and separately apply the ends- and means-proportionality principles that underlie each of these decisions.

E. CONSTITUTIONAL STANDARDS FOR DISTINGUISHING CRIMINAL FROM CIVIL MEASURES

In a variety of contexts, courts must decide whether a nominally civil or regulatory measure is actually intended as punishment and is therefore subject to constitutionally required criminal procedure rules and limitations (an issue sometimes referred to as the "civil-criminal divide" or "boundary").[39] If a government measure is deemed to be a form of regulation, it can be imposed using much less demanding civil or administrative procedures—even if that measure imposes substantial monetary or custodial conditions (e.g., civil fines, pretrial detention of criminal defendants, involuntary civil commitment).[40] But if the measure is deemed to be punishment, its imposition without conviction and compliance with constitutionally required criminal procedures violates substantive due process.[41] Similar rules that distinguish between regulation and punishment determine whether a measure is subject to the ex post facto and double jeopardy clauses.[42]

In each of these contexts, proportionality is not sought in its own right but instead serves an evidentiary function—the excessiveness of a measure implies that the actual intent is to impose punishment. The notion of excessiveness applied in these cases seems to be a means proportionality concept by asking whether the measure is unnecessarily broad or unreasonably intrusive in light of its supposed nonpunitive purpose. Some scholars have suggested that a similar goal of flushing out illicit unconstitutional motivations underlies the narrow-tailoring requirement (also a form of means proportionality) under strict scrutiny analysis.[43]

However, only a few cases have invalidated government measures on this ground.[44] In recent years the Supreme Court has almost always found measures to be regulatory and has stressed that the excessiveness inquiry is only one of several factors courts should consider.[45] Moreover, in applying the excessiveness factor the Court has rejected a requirement of narrow tailoring—"a statute is not deemed punitive simply because it lacks a close or perfect fit with the nonpunitive aims it seeks to advance."[46] Of course, there are many degrees of means-proportionality analysis,[47] and the Court's rejection of narrow tailoring does not rule out less constraining forms. The focus in these cases was on the use of disproportionality to infer punitive intent, but the Court's strong language may also have been intended to signal an unwillingness to constitutionalize strict means proportionality as a direct limit on severe civil or regulatory measures, as some lower courts have done in the contexts of juvenile justice and involuntary civil commitment.[48]

F. PROPORTIONALITY LIMITS ON THE SCOPE OF CONSTITUTIONAL EXCLUSIONARY RULES

In criminal and quasi-criminal justice contexts, proportionality analysis is most often employed to safeguard individual rights and liberties from government overreaching. However, a finding of disproportionality sometimes favors the government. Several examples are discussed in this part (exclusionary rules) and in part G (proportionality-based limits on pretrial, trial, and posttrial procedural rights).

The Supreme Court has invoked a cost-benefit concept akin to ends proportionality to justify a variety of limits on the scope of exclusionary remedies for violations of constitutionally protected rights. The Court used this approach to admit evidence obtained in reasonable reliance on an invalid search warrant,[49] to limit the number of persons granted standing to contest police illegalities,[50] and to permit impeachment and other collateral use of evidence obtained in violation of the Fourth Amendment or the *Miranda* rule.[51] In each of these contexts the Court concluded that any added deterrence of police illegality obtained by applying or extending the exclusionary rule in the manner sought by the defendant is outweighed by the added cost of excluding reliable evidence.[52] As economists would say, the marginal cost of exclusion outweighs the marginal benefit.

A different ends-proportionality argument underlies another limitation on exclusionary remedies, the "attenuation" doctrine. In *Brown v. Illinois*,[53] the Court recognized four factors as relevant to whether the causal link between an illegal arrest and a subsequent confession would be deemed sufficiently attenuated to allow the confession to be admitted in the prosecution's case: whether *Miranda* warnings were given; the temporal proximity between the illegality and the confession; the presence or absence of intervening circumstances; "and *particularly*, the purpose and flagrancy" of the illegal arrest (emphasis added). Thus, it appears that the gravity of the police "offense" against the Constitution is the most important factor in determining the scope of the exclusionary rule—more egregious illegalities justify the exclusion of more remote evidentiary fruits.[54] The implicit reasoning is similar to one of Bentham's arguments in favor of punishments proportional to crime seriousness: The benefits of preventing more serious crimes justify the greater costs of more severe penalties.[55]

A similar, implicit ends-benefits proportionality principle may explain the narrower exclusionary remedies that many courts apply to subconstitutional rights violations.[56] The underlying ends-proportionality policy argument (rarely made explicit in these decisions) is that subconstitutional rights are less weighty and the benefit of enforcing these rights is outweighed by the cost of excluding relevant and reliable evidence.

As noted earlier, most decisions that limit the scope of constitutional exclusionary rules seem to reflect ends-benefits proportionality principles. However, a few could be viewed as applying an alternative-means proportionality concept. In *Harris v. New York*,[57] permitting impeachment use of evidence obtained in violation of the *Miranda* rule, the Court stated:

> The impeachment process here undoubtedly provided valuable aid to the jury in assessing petitioner's credibility, and the benefits of this process should not be lost, in our view, because of the speculative possibility that impermissible police conduct will be encouraged thereby. Assuming that the exclusionary rule has a deterrent effect on proscribed police conduct, *sufficient* deterrence flows when the evidence in question is made unavailable to the prosecution in its case in chief.[58]

Since the Court viewed the deterrence likely to be obtained from exclusion in the case in chief as sufficient to satisfy minimum constitutional requirements for an effective remedy, the analysis here is a form of means proportionality. Where exclusion of illegal evidence for impeachment adds no constitutionally required benefit, then a broader exclusionary rule that forbids such impeachment use would be excessive (means disproportionate) relative to a more narrowly tailored, constitutionally adequate remedy.

Similarly, several justices have recently articulated a narrow-tailoring, "no-more-than-necessary" test that reflects means-proportionality principles as a limitation on the *Miranda* rule and all remedies designed to enforce it. Justice Thomas's plurality opinion in *United States v. Patane* (joined by Chief Justice Rehnquist and Justice Scalia), repeatedly stresses the need to maintain "the closest possible fit between the Self-Incrimination Clause and any rule designed to protect it."[59] A means-proportionality principle applicable to judicially implied subsidiary rights designed to protect the Fifth Amendment privilege is also suggested in Justice Souter's concurring opinion in *Chavez v. Martínez*: "Is this new rule necessary in aid of the basic guarantee?"[60]

These narrow-tailoring opinions thus suggest a kind of proportionality analysis that differs substantially from the Court's cases evaluating the marginal costs and benefits of broader exclusionary remedies. Narrow tailoring implies means proportionality—the focus is on a comparison between alternative (broad versus narrow) exclusionary rules, and the assumption is that there is no actual or constitutionally required difference in the effectiveness of the broader and narrower rules. In contrast, the Court's cost-benefit decisions represent a form of ends-proportionality analysis. These cases assume that additional deterrence of illegalities may result from a broader exclusionary rule, and the cases thus focus on comparing that added benefit to the added cost of excluding probative evidence. The justices who have recently proposed a means-proportionality concept have not discussed how this approach compares to the Court's usual ends-proportionality analysis and why means-proportionality analysis is better.

Arguably, all of the cases that limit the scope of judicially created, constitutionally based exclusionary rules and subsidiary rights could be viewed as applications of means proportionality. On this view, each of these exclusionary rules and subsidiary rights has a constitutionally required minimum scope.[61] If the scope of a given exclusionary rule or implied right yields insufficient benefits in one or more constitutionally relevant ways—in particular, insufficient deterrence of violations or insufficiently frequent occasions for courts to clarify the meaning and scope of constitutional rights (the so-called teaching function of exclusionary rules[62])—then the exclusionary rule or implied right is not broad enough. If the scope of the rule or right or a proposed expansion either provides no additional benefits compared to a narrower rule or produces no benefits needed to provide a constitutionally adequate remedy or subsidiary right, then the existing or proposed rule or right is excessive in a means-proportionality sense, and a more narrowly tailored version is sufficient. Moreover, on this view, the social costs of excluding evidence or recognizing a subsidiary right are irrelevant if the scope of the exclusionary rule or subsidiary right in question is equal to or less than the minimum constitutional requirements. However, how are such minimum requirements determined? What is a sufficient exclusionary remedy or subsidiary right? An ends-proportionality approach avoids this problem by asking only whether the added benefits of a broader remedy or right are worth the added costs. But that approach raises a different problem: How can such seemingly incommensurate benefits and costs be objectively compared?

The Court and individual justices need to clarify which proportionality concepts they are using to determine the scope of exclusionary rules and subsidiary rights and why. In addition, some of the justices need to explain the very different approaches they have taken in various contexts. Conservative justices should explain why they are so willing to use proportionality concepts to favor the government (by limiting exclusionary remedies), whereas in other contexts they strongly oppose the use of these concepts to favor suspects, defendants, and other citizens. Liberal justices should explain why they take the opposite approach—favoring proportionality-type limits that benefit the individual citizen but opposing the use of similar concepts to favor the government.

G. PROPORTIONALITY OF PRETRIAL, TRIAL, AND POSTTRIAL PROCEDURAL RIGHTS TO OFFENSE SEVERITY

Many constitutional and subconstitutional procedural rights are not available or are narrower in scope for less serious crimes—what one might call "making the procedure fit the crime." Some of these limits are based on the historical or traditional meaning of the right in question, but to the extent that courts discuss policy arguments, the rationale is similar to that explicitly adopted by the Court, with respect to administrative due process, in *Mathews v. Eldridge*:[63] In minor cases the benefits of additional procedural safeguards (reduced risk of unfair or erroneous outcomes, multiplied by the severity of those outcomes) are outweighed by the costs and administrative burdens they incur. This is a form of ends-benefits proportionality and, as with the limits on exclusionary rules discussed in part F, a finding of disproportionality (of the costs and burdens of broader procedural rights, relative to the benefits as measured by crime severity) favors the government, not the citizen.

As is discussed in part A, a different offense-severity proportionality principle applies to police search-and-seizure powers: Less serious crimes give the police less power, and suspects have more rights. These seemingly contradictory offense-severity rules are explained by the differing interests involved. In both contexts, greater procedural protections are costly and tend to frustrate law enforcement and prosecution, which is a greater concern the more serious the offense. In the search-and-seizure context the burden on effective law enforcement and truth seeking is particularly great in that it may result in lost evidence (most of it very reliable physical evidence) and lost suspects. On the benefits side of the ledger, broader citizen rights provide greater protection for privacy, property, and physical liberty, but the value of this protection depends on the particular search or seizure and is not necessarily greater in the investigation of more serious crimes. At later stages of criminal procedure greater citizen rights may yield fewer convictions, but such rights help to avoid unfair or erroneous outcomes; that benefit is deemed to be more important than the procedural costs and lost convictions, and the net benefit of increased fairness and accuracy is greater the more serious the charges.

1. Limited Constitutional Procedure Rights in Minor Crime Cases

The Supreme Court has held that the Sixth Amendment jury trial right does not apply to crimes punishable with incarceration of six months or less.[64] A different but analogous rule limits the scope of the automatic Sixth Amendment right to appointed counsel at trial, recognized in *Gideon v. Wainwright*[65]—in misdemeanor cases the *Gideon* counsel right applies only if the actual sentence imposed includes some period of incarceration or at least a suspended custody term.[66]

The Court's limitation of the jury right (and in particular the scope of that limitation) is based in part on history: The "petty offense" jury right exception dates to the English common law era.[67] However, that limitation, as well as the limit on the *Gideon* appointed counsel right, also reflects a cost-benefit calculus akin to ends proportionality. In *Duncan v. Louisiana*[68] the Court stated that "[t]he possible consequences to defendants from convictions for petty offenses have been thought insufficient to outweigh the benefits to efficient law enforcement and simplified judicial administration resulting from the availability of speedy and inexpensive nonjury adjudications." And in *Scott v. Illinois*[69] the Court reasoned that broadly extending appointed counsel rights to misdemeanor cases would "impose unpredictable, but necessarily substantial costs on 50 quite diverse states."

Another example of a constitutional, petty offense rule appears in the text of the Fifth Amendment, which limits the right to grand jury indictment to persons charged with "a capital, or otherwise infamous crime." To the extent that these rights limitations are determined by judicial policy analysis rather than history or constitutional text, the limitations would be more coherent and consistent if the Court more explicitly examined the ends-benefits proportionality principles that underlie its decisions and explained why the same principle produces different limitations, depending on the particular right.

2. Offense-Severity Limits on Subconstitutional Procedural Rights

Similar offense-severity distinctions are found in state statutes and rules of criminal procedure, granting offenders charged with less serious violations fewer rights of appointed counsel, preliminary hearing review, defense discovery, jury trial, jury size, and time to file an appeal.[70] As with constitutional rights limitations, the offense-severity limits on subconstitutional rights would be more coherent and consistent if rule drafters explicitly examined the underlying ends-proportionality principles.

6   CRIMINAL LAW

Implicit Proportionality Limitations on Criminal Liability

NUMEROUS CONSTITUTIONAL AND SUBCONSTITUTIONAL LIMITATIONS on criminal liability embody one or more of the proportionality principles we have identified. Limiting retributive liability principles (no liability without individual culpability) underlie constitutional rules that prohibit punishment without fair notice that the conduct is criminal. Limiting retributive principles are also implicit in the prohibition of "status" crimes (e.g., being an addict). Such principles, as well as means and/or ends proportionality, may also underlie the requirement of proof beyond a reasonable doubt.

Proportionality principles are also reflected in numerous subconstitutional limitations on criminal liability. Limiting retributive principles and perhaps also ends or means proportionality underlie the rule of lenity and the abandonment of judicial power to recognize common law crimes (but not common law defenses). Rules barring or discouraging strict liability are based on limiting retributive principles and perhaps also ends or means proportionality. "Voluntary act" requirements reflect retributive limits on liability. Self-defense and other justification defenses incorporate independent means- and ends-proportionality principles. Affirmative defenses of excuse and partial excuse primarily embody limiting retributive principles. The scaling of offense severity according to offender culpability and harm reflects limiting retributive as well as ends-proportionality principles and in practice also means proportionality.

The following discussion first examines constitutionalized proportionality limits, then subconstitutional ones. We argue that much of the uncertainty and controversy surrounding some of these doctrines results from the failure to recognize and clearly articulate the application of underlying proportionality principles.

A. CONSTITUTIONAL LIMITATIONS ON CRIMINAL LIABILITY

A variety of federal constitutional doctrines reflect implicit retributive and perhaps also ends- and/or means-proportionality limits. These limits have been recognized under varying constitutional provisions (most are based on due process, but some on the Eighth Amendment), and courts have rarely noted their similar underlying rationales.[1]

1. Fair-Notice Requirements

Several constitutionalized limits on criminal liability are based in part on the idea that it is fundamentally unfair to impose the harsh penalties and stigma of the criminal law on persons who had no advance warning that their acts were criminal. The doctrines based on such "fair notice" concerns (sometimes expressed as "fair warning" or "legality" requirements) include the explicit textual prohibition of *ex post facto* statutes and other constitutional rules established in Supreme Court case law (e.g., the ban on retroactively applied judicial extensions of liability; the "void for vagueness" rule; the ban on prosecution following official assurances of legality; the constitutional prohibition on certain crimes of omission).

In *Bouie v. City of Columbia*[2] the Court held that unforeseeable and retroactive judicial extensions of liability pose the same fair-notice problems as the retroactive legislative enactments barred by the ex post facto clause. Under the Court's void-for-vagueness doctrine, vague statutes have been struck down because they fail to provide sufficient notice "to enable ordinary people to understand what conduct [the law] prohibits."[3] Conviction under statutes that approach but do not reach unconstitutional vagueness have been overturned when the defendants acted in reasonable reliance on official assurances or interpretations. For example, in *Cox v. Louisiana*[4] the defendant was charged with picketing "near" a courthouse after being told by a sheriff and a mayor that he and other demonstrators could meet across the street. In *Lambert v. California*[5] the Court relied on due process, fair-notice principles to reverse a conviction under a municipal felon registration law, holding that the defendant's conduct was "wholly passive—mere failure to register"; unlike other registration laws and regulatory crimes of omission, violation of this law was "unaccompanied by any activity whatever" other than mere presence in the city. The Court therefore held that persons could not constitutionally be convicted under that law absent proof of knowledge of the duty to register or the probability of such knowledge.

However, in what sense are criminal liability and punishment unfair in the cases covered by these doctrines? Fairness, like proportionality, requires a normative frame of reference, and courts have rarely related fair-notice rationales to purposes of punishment or any other normative principles. The simplest and most compelling explanation for these constitutional limits is the limiting retributive principle that criminal liability may not be imposed without a showing of individual culpability and that, where advance notice is lacking, the actor did not freely choose to violate the law and thus is not sufficiently culpable.[6] As the Court said in *Lambert*, conduct should not be punished if it "would not be blameworthy in the average member of the community."[7] In some of these cases the charged acts might be deemed immoral for reasons unrelated to positive law; nevertheless, they are not immoral in a legal sense, and there is a constitutionally unacceptable risk of punishing persons who are morally, as well as legally, innocent.

As discussed more fully in part B, one could also argue that criminal liability without fair notice violates utilitarian proportionality principles, but such arguments have not thus far been cited in Supreme Court and lower-court decisions that implement the constitutional limitations discussed earlier.

2. Status Crimes

In *Robinson v. California*,[8] the Supreme Court held that a California statute making it a crime to "be addicted to the use of narcotics" inflicted cruel and unusual punishment. The decision seems to have been based more on retributive than on utilitarian proportionality limits;[9] even if it were cost effective to punish people for drug addiction, it is unfair because they cannot help having what may be a lifelong condition, even during periods of sobriety. The Court in *Robinson* focused on the defendant's limited culpability, viewing addiction as an "illness which may be contracted innocently or involuntarily";[10] the Court compared the statute to one that criminalizes the condition of being "mentally ill, or a leper, or ... afflicted with a venereal disease" or "having a common cold" and concluded that "[e]ven one day in prison would be a cruel and unusual punishment for [such a] 'crime.'"[11]

Since much the same could be said for punishing the inevitable symptoms of drug addiction, some observers predicted that the Court would eventually adopt a constitutionalized "voluntary act" requirement that would prohibit punishment of addicts for the "symptoms" of possession and use of narcotics.[12] However, this broad reading of *Robinson* was disavowed in *Powell v. Texas*,[13] where the Court upheld the conviction of a chronic alcoholic for being found drunk in a public place. The Court rejected the defendant's arguments that he could not stop himself from getting drunk and then going out or remaining in public and that punishing him for these acts amounted to punishing him for his disease of alcoholism. The plurality and two concurring opinions in *Powell* emphasized that the defendant was being punished not for a mere status or disease or even for the act of becoming drunk but rather for the act of being or remaining in public (while drunk). None of these opinions appeared concerned with whether Powell really had the ability to keep himself from going out or remaining in public once he became drunk. *Powell* thus suggested that the constitutional defect in *Robinson* was the punishment of mere status or propensity and that an act may constitutionally be punished even if it is involuntary.

Nevertheless, five justices in *Powell* (the four dissenters plus Justice White, concurring) stated that *Robinson* prohibits conviction not just for a diseaselike status (e.g., drug addiction, chronic alcoholism) but also for the immediate and inevitable consequences of such a status (e.g., possessing drugs; being under the influence of drugs or alcohol; being homeless and under the influence in public).[14] None of those justices is still on the Court; however, subsequent lower-court decisions have adopted a narrow extension of *Robinson* in holding that criminal liability may not be imposed on homeless persons for engaging in the necessary activities of life (eating, sleeping) while in public spaces.[15] The Eighth Amendment analysis in these cases appears to be based on a limiting retributive principle that prohibits criminalization of an involuntary status and acts necessarily resulting from that status. An alternative basis given for some of these rulings is that the challenged enforcement policies unduly burdened the right of interstate travel and were neither narrowly tailored nor supported by a compelling state interest.[16] (The means- and ends-proportionality principles implicit in such strict scrutiny analysis are discussed in chapter 3.) It seems curious, however, that courts inclined to invoke such principles would apply them to the right to travel rather than the rights to life and liberty, which are more centrally implicated. One can certainly argue that criminal conviction of involuntarily homeless persons for engaging in necessary life activities violates ends and/or means proportionality; the inability of these persons to avoid such violations results in law enforcement benefits that are minimal (violating ends proportionality) or nonexistent (adding no benefit, thus violating means proportionality). (See further discussion of involuntary acts in part B.)

Some states, in basing their decisions jointly or solely on state constitutional provisions, have recognized constitutional limits on strict and vicarious liability. These cases usually involve employers' liability for their workers' acts (e.g., selling liquor to minors), based solely on a defendant's status as an employer, owner, or licensee.[17] Most of the cases seem to be grounded in limiting retributive principles, but some employ a balancing test akin to ends proportionality and/or a necessity principle akin to means proportionality.[18]

3. The Requirement of Proof Beyond a Reasonable Doubt

The due process requirement of proof beyond a reasonable doubt of all elements of the charged offense (and the closely related presumption of innocence principle) can be justified under limiting retributive liability principles, as well as alternative-means and perhaps also ends-benefits proportionality. The reasonable doubt standard reflects a policy judgment that it is better to err on the side of finding no criminal liability—that too few convictions are better than too many and that, as Blackstone said, it is better that ten guilty people escape punishment than that one innocent person should be convicted and punished. The limiting retributive rationale for this rule is that it is more important to prevent undeserved liability than to ensure that all deserving offenders are punished.[19]

As for alternative-means proportionality, this principle states a preference for less intrusive measures provided they are equally effective. A strong version of that principle requires that the least intrusive measure be chosen unless it is shown to be less effective. Thus, all three principles—the reasonable doubt rule, the limiting retributive liability principle, and a strong version of alternative-means proportionality—express a preference for less intrusive measures and are more concerned about excessive criminal liability than insufficient liability.

The reasonable doubt rule might also draw support from ends-benefits proportionality principles. In the case that constitutionalized this rule, *In re Winship*, the Court seemed concerned to demonstrate that the net benefits are worthwhile even though the rule prevents the conviction of some guilty offenders:[20]

> [U]se of the reasonable-doubt standard is indispensable to command the respect and confidence of the community in applications of the criminal law. It is critical that the moral force of the criminal law not be diluted by a standard of proof that leaves people in doubt whether innocent men are being condemned. It is also important in our free society that every individual going about his ordinary affairs have confidence that his government cannot adjudge him guilty of a criminal offense without convincing a proper factfinder of his guilt with utmost certainty.

4. Summary

The constitutional fair-notice, status-crimes, and reasonable-doubt limitations on the imposition of criminal liability all seem to be based primarily on retributive principles, but utilitarian ends- and means-proportionality principles may also serve to justify some of these limitations. Courts should make these underlying normative principles explicit instead of speaking in vague terms about "fairness." An express recognition of limiting retributive limits would promote more consistent application of these principles not only in this context but also for other constitutional doctrines that, expressly or implicitly, invoke notions of blame and culpability—in particular, doctrines that limit punitive damages (chapter 4) and forfeitures and sentencing (chapter 7). To the extent that utilitarian proportionality principles apply to constitutional liability-limiting rules, the role of these principles should be clarified and related to doctrines discussed throughout this book, incorporating similar constitutionalized ends- and means-proportionality limits.

A clearer statement of underlying normative principles might also help to explain why criminal liability is more closely limited in some ways than in others. For instance, why are constitutionalized "cognitive" liability requirements seemingly much stricter than "volitional" requirements? In contrast to the numerous fair-notice rules discussed earlier, the Supreme Court strongly resisted volitional limits in *Powell v. Texas*, and lower courts have only occasionally recognized them. Similarly, whether constitutionalized liability limits are retributive or utilitarian, courts should explain why similarly strict limits are not placed on excessive punishment once an offender has been found liable (see chapter 7). The liability-versus-punishment distinction cannot be based simply on the value of protecting totally innocent persons; the reasonable doubt rule (and to a lesser extent, all of the constitutional liability rules discussed previously) also apply to those who are clearly guilty of one or more crimes, thereby protecting them from being found liable for additional or more serious crimes.

B. SUBCONSTITUTIONAL LIMITS ON CRIMINAL LIABILITY

Many examples of implicit and occasionally explicit limiting retributive and ends- and/or means-proportionality principles appear in subconstitutional limits on criminal liability and in scholarly writings on criminal law jurisprudence. One of the most influential scholars of criminal law jurisprudence, H. L. A. Hart, distinguished between the "general justifying aim" of the criminal law, which he viewed as utilitarian (primarily efficient crime control), and the principles applied to the distribution of punishment in individual cases, which are retributive as well as utilitarian.[21] Hart's retributive principles of distribution applied both to liability issues (who may be punished) and to severity issues (how hard they may be punished; the latter issue is discussed in chapter 7). On the liability question Hart stipulated that only those who are blameworthy may be punished. This is a form of limiting retributivism, although Hart did not employ that term. Another leading scholar, Herbert Packer, similarly insisted that a finding of moral responsibility (blameworthiness or culpability) is a necessary (but not sufficient) condition for criminal liability and punishment.[22] As shown below, Hart's and Packer's views find broad support in state and federal criminal statutes and cases.

1. Fair-Notice Rules

The rule of lenity (also known as the rule that criminal statutes are strictly construed in favor of defendants) is in some respects a subconstitutional version of the fair-notice doctrines discussed in part A.[23] The limiting retributive rationale for the rule is that, if there are multiple interpretations of the scope of a statute, it would be unfair to adopt a broader interpretation than the defendant may have reasonably anticipated—his culpability is lessened or eliminated if he could not have known that his acts would later be determined to fall within the criminal prohibition. The rule of lenity may also find support in ends- and/or means-proportionality principles; if it is uncertain whether broader liability will provide benefits sufficient to justify the greater costs and burdens (ends proportionality) or indeed any additional benefits (means proportionality), courts should err on the side of imposing too little rather than too much liability.

A commonly cited alternative rationale for the rule of lenity is based more on notions of the separation of powers and legislative primacy: Legislatures, not courts, should decide when criminal liability will be expanded because this is essentially a moral judgment, and legislators are more directly politically accountable[24] (they may also have greater access to the comprehensive data and policy analysis needed to make wise criminalization decisions). However, one could make the same arguments in favor of a legislative monopoly on decisions to contract the scope of criminal liability, yet the rule of lenity not only does not apply to such decisions but actually encourages courts to make them. Thus, the bias in favor of narrower rather than broader criminal liability must be based on other grounds, and the retributive and utilitarian proportionality principles cited earlier seem to be the best choices.

Similarly conflicting rationales appear to underlie the policy, which has been adopted in almost every U.S. state, of abolishing common law crimes and imposing liability only when offenses are declared and defined by statute. Again, this policy is potentially biased in favor of defendants since courts in most of these jurisdictions retain the authority to recognize or expand common law defenses.[25] As with lenity, a preference for statutory over judicial creation and expansion of crimes can be justified under limiting retributive (fair-notice) principles, and perhaps also by utilitarian ends and means proportionality. Persons who could not have known their conduct would later be deemed criminal are less blameworthy, and they may also be less dangerous and in need of deterrence and restraint; moreover, punishing such persons is unlikely to deter others (it is difficult to make an effective example of someone who did not choose to do wrong). Punishment that adds no additional crime-control benefit is unnecessary, thus violating means proportionality. If only meager added benefits result, they may be outweighed by the stigma and harshness of punishment, thereby violating ends proportionality.

2. Limits on Strict Liability

As noted earlier, many leading scholars have insisted that the imposition of criminal liability requires proof of culpability (moral blameworthiness). Thus, these scholars have objected to criminal laws that expressly or by interpretation impose strict (or "absolute") liability by eliminating, for one or more major elements of the crime, any requirement of proof of criminal purpose, knowledge, or other culpable mental state. The drafters of the American Law Institute's Model Penal Code likewise rejected strict liability for nonpetty offenses. As the commentary to the code explains:[26]

> [I]f practical enforcement precludes litigation of the culpability of alleged deviation from legal requirements, the enforcers cannot rightly demand the use of penal sanctions for the purpose. Crime does and should mean condemnation and no court should have to pass that judgment unless it can declare that the defendant's act was culpable. This is too fundamental to be compromised. The law goes far enough if it permits the imposition of a monetary penalty in cases where strict liability has been imposed.

Accordingly, the code specified that, except for petty infractions punishable by only a fine or civil penalty, the prosecution must prove at least criminal negligence with respect to each material element of the crime.[27]

The insistence that all those convicted be culpable suggests a grounding in limiting retributive principles,[28] but the requirement to prove at least criminal negligence can also be justified on utilitarian proportionality grounds. The ends-proportionality argument is that the crime-control purposes of punishment are not served when the actor is not even negligent (because the person is not sufficiently dangerous or deterrable to justify the costs and burdens of criminal conviction); moreover, punishing such persons diminishes the stigma of criminal penalties generally, thus reducing the behavior-shaping and crime-control benefits of convictions obtained in other cases.[29] The means-proportionality argument is that conviction for a strict liability crime adds *no* net crime-control benefit that would not already be achieved by enforcement of other (non-strict-liability) criminal laws or by the use of measures outside of the criminal law.

Some states have enacted the American Law Institute's Model Penal Code approach described earlier, and a few courts have found that strict liability violates state constitutional provisions.[30] In other states strict liability for jailable offenses is not absolutely forbidden, but courts presume a legislative intent to require proof of a culpable mental state unless the legislature has stated otherwise. For example, a New York statute[31] provides that at least criminal negligence is required for all material elements of all offenses (including traffic offenses) unless the statute clearly indicates a legislative intent to impose strict liability. In Minnesota, a presumption against strict liability was created by the courts rather than by statute.[32] Also, in a widely cited 1952 case, *Morrissette v. United States*,[33] the U.S. Supreme Court held that, for crimes derived from common law larceny, courts should presume a legislative choice to carry over the common law element of intent to steal another's property (negated in *Morrissette* by the defendant's belief that the property he took had been abandoned), except where Congress has made clear its desire to eliminate the intent requirement.

In a number of later cases the Court read a requirement of proof of mental culpability into federal criminal statutes when it cited the presumption against strict liability, concerns about statutory overbreadth, and/or vague statutory language. In *United States v. U.S. Gypsum Co.*,[34] the Court stated that crimes with no intent element have a "generally disfavored status" and held that a criminal antitrust violation requires a showing that the defendant at least acted knowingly. In *Liparota v. United States*,[35] the Court held that, in criminal prosecutions under the federal food stamp program, the government must prove that the defendant knew his actions were unauthorized or illegal. It noted that without this requirement the statute would "criminalize a broad range of apparently innocent conduct."[36] Similar concerns with overbreadth and lack of fair notice led the Court to interpret the requirement of willfulness in complex federal regulatory statutes to mean that the defendant must be shown to have known he was acting illegally.[37]

In *Staples v. United States*,[38] the Court held that a statute prohibiting possession of an unregistered machine gun required proof, as an element of the crime, that the defendant knew the gun could fire automatically. In addition, *U.S. v. X-Citement Video*[39] held that, although the term "knowingly" would grammatically apply only to the element of transporting child pornography, the statute should be construed to apply that mental culpability requirement to all elements of the crime, including the age of the depicted performers and the sexually explicit nature of the material. In the aggregate, these cases imply a general presumption of legislative intent not to impose strict liability for serious federal offenses.[40]

3. The Voluntary Act Requirement

Although the Supreme Court has declined to recognize a constitutionalized voluntary act requirement (see discussion of status crimes in part A), such a requirement is found in most state laws and in the American Law Institute's Model Penal Code.[41] This requirement is based on a limiting retributive theory:[42] A person is not morally blameworthy for a bodily movement that is the product of epilepsy, sleep, unconsciousness, or other unwilled process. (However, as illustrated by the famous case of *People v. Decina*,[43] such a person can sometimes be blamed for a prior voluntary and culpable act: in *Decina*, an epileptic's decision to drive a car knowing that a seizure could occur at any time.)

4. Affirmative Defenses

Many traditional affirmative defenses of justification (the defendant's criminal act was "the right thing to do" under the circumstances) incorporate both means- and ends-proportionality principles, and a violation of either one results in denial of a complete defense.[44] In the law of self-defense, for example, alternative-means proportionality (usually referred to as the principle of necessity) requires that defensive force not be excessive relative to available alternative defensive measures. For instance, a person who is attacked cannot kill to avoid being killed if the threat could also be avoided by nondeadly means such as superior strength (or, in many jurisdictions, safe retreat from the threat). Ends-benefits proportionality in self-defense (which is often explicitly referred to as a "proportionality" rule)[45] requires that defensive force must not be excessive relative to the threatened harm; for example, one cannot kill an attacker to avoid receiving a minor battery even if the killing is "necessary" (because no other effective means of prevention is available). Similar proportionality principles apply under the defense of necessity (or choice of evils): The criminal act must reasonably appear likely to prevent a greater harm (ends proportionality); in addition, the act must appear to be necessary (means proportionality) in that a less serious crime or a noncriminal act would not prevent the threatened harm.[46]

The ends- and means-proportionality principles in justification defenses are used to assess whether the defendant's acts were excessive. Thus, in this context, as was true of several criminal procedure rules discussed in chapter 5, a finding of ends or means disproportionality favors the government, not the citizen. However, implicit ends-proportionality principles are also favoring defendants here; they help to explain why justification defenses are and should be recognized. For example, denying the general necessity defense and thus holding defendants liable whose criminal acts avoided greater harms that could not otherwise be prevented would violate ends proportionality because, along with the costs and burdens of obtaining convictions, criminal liability would discourage acts that produce more socially desirable results.

In some cases of justification, however, it is not so clear that the prohibited act has avoided greater harm; in those instances, the justification defense must also rely on limiting retributive proportionality—the defendant is not sufficiently blameworthy. For example, when an innocent (but well-armed) nonaggressor is attacked by a drunken mob and kills them one by one as each approaches, it is difficult to say that the large number of resulting deaths is a lesser harm even if one discounts the value of the attackers' lives because of their unprovoked aggression. Nevertheless, we can still conclude that the shooter is not culpable (his right to defend himself is absolute,[47] and/or his resort to deadly force was not even criminally negligent), and he therefore should not be held liable.

Other traditional criminal law doctrines provide a complete or partial defense to criminal liability based on a theory of excuse. These defenses include duress, insanity, involuntary intoxication, infancy, and the entrapment defense (at least under the subjective, "no-predisposition" standard used in most jurisdictions), as well as the partial excuses (reducing murder to manslaughter) of provocation and unreasonable mistake (also known as "imperfect" self-defense).[48] In the cases where such defenses apply, the defendant has "done the wrong thing" (unlike the justification defenses discussed earlier), but due to the defendant's disturbed mental state and/or coercive external circumstances, the defendant is not viewed as criminally blameworthy (or, for partial excuses, not fully blameworthy).[49]

The focus on reduced culpability in excuse defenses implies that the primary rationale for them is a theory of limiting retributivism. However, in some of these cases one could argue that utilitarian proportionality also provides support for the defense: If such persons are not very deterrable and not generally dangerous, the costs and burdens of convicting them (or of convicting them of a more serious crime) outweigh the crime-control benefits (ends proportionality). If such benefits are deemed to be nonexistent, so that non-criminal-law measures or lesser criminal penalties will achieve equally good results, then means-proportionality principles support the use of these alternatives. For example, if physical restraint (incapacitation) of dangerous, insane offenders is the only benefit of convicting and imprisoning them, this can be achieved just as well by the alternative of civil commitment.

5. Scaling of Crime Severity and Penalty Ranges

In all contemporary American jurisdictions the structures of criminal statutes and codes defining criminal liability reflect, albeit crudely, both retributive and utilitarian proportionality principles.[50] Crimes are grouped into felony, misdemeanor, and petty offense classifications and sometimes also by degrees within each of these broad classes. These crime classifications and assigned penalty ranges (as well as the degree of social stigma and the other collateral consequences of conviction that flow from these statutory provisions) clearly reflect a scaling of offense seriousness based on retributive values (harms caused or risked, and culpability as measured by intent or other mental states). However, for most crimes as a matter of formal law and for all crimes as a matter of law enforcement practice, these rules mainly impose upper limits on the offense levels and sanctions imposed; mandatory minimum penalties, though common, are still the exception; prosecutorial charging decisions are unregulated by law; and charging leniency is common, especially in the plea bargains that determine most convictions. Statutory crime classifications thus embody a limiting retributive theory, which, like the reasonable doubt rule, gives greater weight to avoiding excessive severity than excessive leniency. Stronger limits on severity than on leniency may also reflect means-proportionality principles—a preference for less severe measures unless a need for greater severity is shown.

Penalties and collateral consequences that are scaled in proportion to social harms are also consistent with ends-benefits proportionality principles. The degrees of social harm that help to determine crime classifications serve as a proxy for the benefits of punishment, and the penalty range and collateral consequences invoked by each crime class are a proxy for punishment costs and burdens. Punishment costs and burdens are thus scaled to the likely benefits; in addition, would-be offenders are given a statutory incentive to "prefer" less harmful offenses.

The details of these retributive and utilitarian theories are examined in chapter 7, part F, which discusses proportionality in writings on sentencing theory. The fact that similar arguments apply to offense classifications, as well as the severity of sentences imposed, underscores a point made in part A: There can be no sharp distinction between theories of criminal liability and criminal punishment—the same principles justify and limit severity in both contexts.

6. Summary

The implicit rationales for the subconstitutional liability rules discussed here appear to be primarily retributive, although one could also cite utilitarian ends- and means-proportionality principles in support of most of these rules. Courts, legislatures, and other public officials should explicitly recognize the proportionality principles that underlie each rule in order to improve the coherence, consistency, and fairness of law making, law enforcement, and law interpretation by these officials. For example, recognition of the primary role of retributive limits on criminal liability might lead to the conclusion that, contrary to the Model Penal Code and the law in most states, a defense of excusing necessity should be recognized for cases of coercive nonhuman threats; such a defense should be parallel with and at least as broad as the duress defense provided for crimes coerced by human threat. The classic example is a driver whose brakes unexpectedly fail and who drives straight ahead despite the high probability of killing an innocent person in the road rather than steering off the road and over a cliff, which has a high probability of causing his own death.[51] Such a person is simply not culpable and, under broadly recognized limiting retributive proportionality principles, he should not be held criminally liable.

Where multiple proportionality principles apply to an issue of criminal liability, we believe they should be applied independently—the retributive, means-, and ends-proportionality concepts each guard against distinct forms of excess, and criminal liability should not be imposed in violation of any of them. However, we also believe that retributive proportionality is the most important of these principles and that different branches of government should apply the principles differently.

Since the broadest consensus appears to support the importance of limiting retributive values (they are implicit in almost all of the rules discussed here, as well as those in part A) and because a violation of such values constitutes the essence of unfairness and governmental oppression, retributive limits on criminal liability should be viewed as primary; they should be the first principles to be examined in each case, and such limits should trump utilitarian arguments for a broader scope of liability. Legislatures should try never to impose criminal liability without sufficient culpability as measured by the broadly adopted rules we have discussed, namely, at least criminally negligent, voluntary conduct as to both crime elements and affirmative defenses, after fair notice of criminal prohibition, and with the degree of liability not exceeding the degree of culpability. Where such culpability exists, legislatures should then aim to respect both means and ends proportionality; the extent of liability (and costs of enforcement) should be proportionate to the likely public benefits and not excessive when compared to noncriminal measures or a lesser degree of criminal liability. Furthermore, since assessments of culpability and the benefits of liability are uncertain, the legislature should, if in doubt, err on the side of imposing too little rather than too much liability—just as courts and juries do when they apply the reasonable doubt standard and the rule of lenity.

In interpreting criminal laws, judicial and executive branch officials should adopt a strong presumption that the legislature does not intend to impose liability without sufficient culpability. Where sufficient culpability appears to exist or the legislature has made clear its intent to not require it, these officials should also presume that the legislature does not intend to impose liability in circumstances where it would violate ends or means proportionality. However, this should be a weaker (easier to overcome) presumption than that with regard to required culpability, and it should accord more deference to legislative decisions to criminalize certain conduct. Greater deference to legislative judgments in making utilitarian assessments is appropriate in light of the lesser degree of consensus about utilitarian limits on criminal liability and also because of important differences in the nature and application of retributive and utilitarian proportionality concepts. As noted earlier, retributive limits are matters of fairness and the limits of coercive state power, and courts have an important role to play in ensuring fairness and safeguarding individual liberty. Furthermore, utilitarian assessments often require collection and analysis of complex empirical data on the likely costs and benefits of proposed and alternative measures, and legislatures are better equipped to do this. Finally, when courts and other officials are uncertain whether liability in a given case would violate retributive, ends, and/or means proportionality, they should—as they do under the reasonable doubt standard and the rule of lenity—err on the side of imposing too little rather than too much liability.

7 PUNISHMENT

Explicit and Implicit Proportionality Limits on Sanction Severity

THIS CHAPTER EXAMINES PROPORTIONALITY PRINCIPLES found in constitutional and subconstitutional sentencing law and theory. It also discusses constitutional severity limits on the treatment of prisoners and on the quasi-criminal penalty of civil or criminal forfeiture. When courts and scholars explicitly invoke proportionality in these contexts, the usual reference is to retributive punishment goals. However, utilitarian philosophers also strongly advocate proportionality in punishment, using both ends-benefits and alternative-means concepts. Moreover, the court opinions discussed here reveal many implicit examples of these two utilitarian principles.

In each topic area we first identify the explicit and implicit proportionality principles that courts and/or writers apply and then explain how policy analysis in these contexts would be improved by more precise definition and application of these principles. Parts A through D examine Eighth Amendment limitations on the death penalty, the length of prison terms, the treatment of prisoners, and the use of civil and criminal forfeiture. Part E surveys state constitutional provisions and cases that limit excessive punishment. Part F examines proportionality principles found in subconstitutional sentencing theory, law, and practice, as well as in foreign sentencing laws.

The most important finding that emerges from a review of these topics is that the Supreme Court applies very different proportionality standards in various contexts. Death penalty eligibility and the permissible size of fines and forfeitures are subject to limiting retributive constraints that appear to trump crime-control goals. As earlier chapters have explained, independent, constitutionally required retributive limits have also been imposed on punitive damages (chapter 4) and on findings of criminal liability (chapter 6). But the length of prison terms is not similarly constrained. One could argue, of course, that important differences between these contexts justify various levels of protection; however, these differences cut in both directions.[1] Moreover, the Court's constitutional standards governing lengthy prison sentences are incoherent and are not tied to any clear meaning of proportionality. Another set of standards, poorly integrated with other branches of the Court's Eighth Amendment jurisprudence, applies to the treatment of prisoners. State constitutions are sometimes used to grant additional protection, and in some states proportionality standards are quite different from those based on the Eighth Amendment. But in general, state courts have been cautious, even when broader state protection could be justified by textual differences between state and federal guarantees.

In all of these contexts, one can find many examples of principles akin to limiting retributive, ends, and/or means proportionality, but these principles have rarely been clearly articulated. In contrast, all three proportionality principles find strong support in scholarly writings on sentencing theory, in the structure and sometimes the explicit rationales of U.S. sentencing laws, and in sentencing laws and decisions in foreign countries. These well-developed subconstitutional principles corroborate the poorly articulated and weakly applied versions found in constitutional decisions.

Courts should make explicit use of these proportionality principles when called upon to interpret Eighth Amendment standards and particularly when they interpret state constitutional provisions that limit sanction severity. We urge lawyers, judges, and academics to resist the assumption that legal standards that prescribe the constitutional limits on punishments are settled and unlikely to change. To facilitate open-mindedness in these matters—on federal, as well as state, constitutional standards and of course also with respect to subconstitutional sanction issues—we examine the Court's decisions in some detail, including well-considered dissenting views.

Since many of the U.S. constitutional doctrines discussed here are based on interpretations of the Eighth Amendment that are of quite recent vintage (beginning with death penalty cases in the 1970s), we first provide a brief review of the Court's earlier pronouncements on the scope and meaning of that amendment. Aside from a few nineteenth-century decisions that upheld capital punishment,[2] the first major Eighth Amendment case in the Supreme Court was *Weems v. United States* (1910).[3] That case involved a Philippine penalty of fifteen years of hard labor in chains, combined with permanent loss of civil rights. Although the sentence was invalidated as much for its unusual nature (relative to common law traditions) as for its disproportionality to the conviction offense (falsifying a public record), *Weems* explicitly stated that the Eighth Amendment requires punishments to be "graduated and proportioned to offense."[4] In *Trop v. Dulles* (1958),[5] a four-judge plurality applied Eighth Amendment proportionality limits to the penalty of divestment of citizenship, noting that "the words of the Amendment are not precise, and...their scope is not static. The Amendment must draw its meaning from the evolving standards of decency that mark the progress of a maturing society." Finally, two cases decided in the 1960s applied the Eighth Amendment to criminalization decisions rather than sentencing. These cases, *Robinson v. California*[6] and *Powell v. Texas*[7] are discussed in chapter 6, part A. They have rarely been cited in the Court's other Eighth Amendment cases, whereas the "evolving standards" concept from *Trop* and the central focus on sentencing proportionality first identified in *Weems* have frequently been cited.

A. EIGHTH AMENDMENT LIMITS ON DEATH PENALTY ELIGIBILITY AND EXECUTION METHODS

1. Eligibility for the Death Penalty

In *Coker v. Georgia*[8] the Supreme Court stated that the Eighth Amendment prohibits "not only those punishments that are 'barbaric' but also those that are 'excessive' in relation to the crime committed.... A punishment is 'excessive' and unconstitutional if it (1) makes no measurable contribution to acceptable goals of punishment and hence is nothing more than the purposeless and needless imposition of pain and suffering; or (2) is grossly out of proportion to the severity of the crime." Although the *Coker* opinion adds that a punishment might be held unconstitutional on either ground, the Court usually relies on both. It has, however, occasionally ruled out death solely on the second ground (*Coker* is an example).

As to the first standard, the Court has repeatedly said that the two recognized goals served by the death penalty are retribution and deterrence of capital crimes.[9] The punishment theory underlying the second standard (gross disproportionality) must be retribution since the Court's cases focus on harm and culpability (these traditional retributive factors are discussed further in part F).[10]

The first *Coker* standard (no measurable contribution to acceptable punishment goals) is ambiguous. This standard might invoke only the minimum constitutional requirement of a rational basis for state action.[11] In the United States, this would not usually be thought of as a question of proportionality, although it is in Europe.[12] In any case, given the number of cases in which the Court has struck down penalties based in part on the first *Coker* standard and the importance the Court clearly attaches to Eighth Amendment review of death penalties, the Court must intend a somewhat stricter standard than rational basis.

Alternatively, the first standard could implicitly incorporate means- and/or ends-proportionality concepts. The means-proportionality argument is that the death penalty is unnecessary and therefore excessive relative to the next-most-severe alternative penalty (life in prison, with or without parole) whenever death adds no additional deterrent or other social benefits.[13] This interpretation finds some support in the Court's earliest death penalty standards[14] and in its decisions invalidating the death penalty for certain felony accomplices, persons with mental retardation, and offenders under eighteen years of age at the time of the crime.[15] In each of these cases, although the Court expressed doubt that the specified group of offenders was at all deterred by the threat of capital punishment, it did not assert that there was no deterrent effect (which would be a no-rational-basis argument). If the Court meant to concede the possibility of some deterrent effect, its decisions could be justified by a means-proportionality argument—the minimal deterrence these offenders would experience from the threat of receiving the death penalty is no greater than that provided by the threat of a lesser penalty (in particular, life imprisonment). In some cases, the Court has come close to explicitly endorsing this alternative-means rationale. In *Roper v. Simmons* the Court said that, "[t]o the extent the juvenile death penalty might have residual deterrent effect, it is worth noting that the punishment of life imprisonment without the possibility of parole is itself a severe sanction, in particular for a young person."[16]

The ends-proportionality version of the first *Coker* standard would be that the death penalty—a sanction unique in its severity—is excessive relative to its meager deterrent benefits. But since no one expects such offenders to escape severe sanctions, the real ends-benefits issue is whether the *added* deterrent benefits of execution, compared to life imprisonment, justify the added severity. This theory finds little support in death penalty cases, however, and it also conflicts with the specific terms of the first *Coker* standard—ends-proportionality analysis would not ask whether a penalty makes "*no* measurable contribution" to acceptable punishment goals but rather whether it makes an *insufficient* contribution.

The Court's somewhat amorphous and always controversial death penalty eligibility jurisprudence would greatly benefit from more precise proportionality analysis. The Court ought to confirm and explicitly state that the second *Coker* standard is based on limiting retributive principles, and it should specify the retributive factors that are constitutionally relevant. The Court should also clarify the theory or theories underlying the first *Coker* standard. Under a theory of alternative-means proportionality, the death penalty would be unconstitutional where it adds no benefit (relative to constitutionally recognized punishment purposes) in comparison with life imprisonment. An ends-proportionality theory would assume that capital punishment adds some benefit and would ask whether that benefit justifies the added sanction severity.

2. Execution Methods

In recent years there have been numerous constitutional challenges to the procedures used to carry out the most common method of execution, lethal injection.[17] The principle objection to these procedures is that the three drugs that are almost universally employed, and the procedures used to inject them, risk causing severe pain to offenders who are still conscious. In evaluating this objection, courts appear to assume that the Eighth Amendment categorically prohibits modern execution methods known to involve extreme pain (just as it prohibits painful ancient methods such as burning at the stake) without regard to the offender's desert, net benefits achieved, or possible alternative ways of causing death—such methods are banned simply because it is wrong to ever treat a person in a barbaric way. Some courts have further assumed that the Eighth Amendment also bars methods that involve a risk of inflicting severe pain that is both substantial and unnecessary in light of feasible modifications of injection procedures.[18]

The prohibition of avoidable risk of severe pain is a form of means-proportionality analysis that is consistent with the "purposeless and needless" language of *Coker v. Georgia* and that also finds support in the small number of Supreme Court decisions involving execution methods[19]

In *Baze v. Rees*[20] the Supreme Court upheld Kentucky's use of the three-drug procedure. However, five of the seven opinions (written or joined by seven of the nine justices) agreed that, at least under some circumstances, the Eighth Amendment bans procedures involving a risk of substantial and unnecessary pain. The least protective version of this test is contained in Justice Roberts's plurality opinion, joined by Justices Kennedy and Alito; that test would invalidate a method of execution if the state, "without a legitimate penological justification," refused to adopt an alternative procedure that is shown to be "feasible, readily implemented, and in fact [able to] significantly reduce a substantial risk of severe pain."[21]

B. EIGHTH AMENDMENT LIMITS ON THE DURATION OF PRISON TERMS

Proportionality principles have been applied, but very poorly defined, in the Supreme Court's cases evaluating lengthy prison sentences. A three-factor test announced in *Solem v. Helm*[22] and still at least loosely applied by a majority of the Court directs courts to (1) compare the sentence to the gravity of the offense and then to compare (2) sentences imposed for other crimes in the same jurisdiction and (3) sentences imposed for the same crime in other jurisdictions. The *Solem* Court's analysis of the first factor clearly incorporated limiting retributive principles, and those principles, as well as means and ends proportionality, may be implicit in the second and third factors. However, the Court needs to more clearly explain what kinds of proportionality each factor measures. It should also clarify the modifications it has made to the *Solem* standards in later cases.

The remainder of this part first summarizes the Court's prison-duration cases, including those decided before *Solem*. It then reviews the explicit and implicit proportionality principles applied in these cases and discusses the ways in which the Court's application of these principles would be improved by more explicit and precise application of the analytic categories this book describes.

1. A Review of the Court's Prison Duration Cases

Since 1980 the Supreme Court has decided six cases in which the duration of a prison sentence was attacked on Eighth Amendment grounds. All six cases were 5–4 decisions in form or substance (the concurring justice in *Hutto v. Davis, infra,* agreed with the three dissenters but felt bound by precedent). In only one of these cases did the Court rule in favor of the offender.

In *Rummel v. Estelle,*[23] the Court upheld a life sentence with parole eligibility after ten to twelve years[24] under a Texas recidivist (three-strikes) statute. Rummel's criminal record consisted of three nonviolent property crimes. His most recent offense was obtaining money (about $121) by false pretenses (failing to honor his promise to repair an air conditioner after accepting payment for the job). His two earlier convictions involved fraudulent use of a credit card and passing a forged check; the total property loss for all three crimes was $229. Justice Rehnquist's majority opinion asserted that the Court's death penalty cases applying proportionality principles "are of limited assistance" in deciding a case like *Rummel* "[b]ecause a sentence of death differs in kind from any sentence of imprisonment, no matter how long."[25] Justice Rehnquist also stated that Eighth Amendment decisions "should not be, or appear to be, merely the subjective views of individual

Justices" and "should be informed by objective factors to the maximum possible extent."[26] He concluded that any distinctions between prison terms of different durations "are indeed 'subjective,' and therefore properly within the province of legislatures, not courts,"[27] thus implying that the Eighth Amendment imposes almost no proportionality limits on lengthy prison sentences.

In an opinion by Justice Powell, the four dissenting justices argued that Rummel's sentence should be invalidated under a version of the three-pronged proportionality standard adopted three years later in *Solem v. Helm*. Justice Powell did not discuss how proportionality analysis relates to sentencing purposes, but he briefly invoked a concept akin to means proportionality, noting that the state of Texas "has not attempted to justify the sentence as necessary either to deter other persons or to isolate a potentially violent individual."[28]

Two years later, in *Hutto v. Davis*,[29] the Court again seemed to recognize few if any Eighth Amendment limits on prison terms. The defendant had been given a sentence of forty years (two consecutive twenty-year terms) and a $20,000 fine for two drug offenses (possession with intent to distribute and distribution) involving a total of about nine ounces of marijuana. (There was no indication in any of the Supreme Court or lower court opinions as to when Davis would have become eligible for parole.) The trial judge made the terms consecutive because Davis had previously been convicted of selling LSD, and the current offenses were committed while he was on bail pending appeal from that conviction. However, there were also mitigating circumstances: The record included a letter from the prosecutor, agreeing that the forty-year sentence was a "gross injustice" in light of much lighter sentences given other drug offenders and pointing out that subsequent legislation had reduced the maximum penalty for Davis's offenses from forty to ten years.[30] In a *per curiam* opinion, the Court affirmed Davis's sentence, relying on *Rummel*. The Court specifically disapproved of a four-factor test applied by the lower court, based on the Fourth Circuit's decision in *Hart v. Coiner*.[31] Those four factors, which were quite similar to the three-factor test later adopted by the Court in *Solem, infra*, included (1) the nature of the conviction offense, especially whether it involved violence; (2) the legislative purposes underlying the sentence imposed and whether they could be achieved through a significantly less severe penalty; (3) the punishment given similar offenders in other states; and (4) punishments given to other offenders in the sentencing state. The principal difference between the *Hart* and *Solem* standards was the second *Hart* factor, which incorporates alternative-means proportionality principles.

Solem v. Helm,[32] decided one year after *Hutto*, was the first case in which the Supreme Court attempted to define what makes a lengthy prison term unconstitutional. It remains the only case in which the Court has found such a sentence to be in violation of the Eighth Amendment. Jerry Helm received a sentence of life

without possibility of parole under a South Dakota "four-strikes" recidivist statute. He actually had six prior felony convictions—three for third-degree burglary
and one each for obtaining money under false pretenses, grand larceny, and felony
(third-offense) drunk driving. His most recent (seventh) felony offense was issu-
ing a no-account check for $100.

Justice Powell's majority opinion in *Solem* traced the history of proportionality rules, beginning with Magna Carta provisions that required fines to
be graded according to offense seriousness. Powell concluded that the proportionality principle is well established in Anglo-American law and in the Court's
prior cases. Moreover, he maintained, neither the history nor the language of the
Eighth Amendment suggests any distinction between types of punishments—all
of the amendment's clauses (bail, fines, cruel and unusual punishments) forbid
excessiveness, and "it would be anomalous indeed" if fines and the death penalty
were subject to proportionality analysis but not the "intermediate punishment of
imprisonment."[33] Powell conceded that death penalty cases are of limited value
in assessing prison sentences; that reversals of such sentences on proportionality
grounds will be "exceedingly rare";[34] that reviewing courts should grant substantial deference to legislative judgments; and that proportionality review "should
be guided by objective factors."[35] Powell found three such factors in the Court's
prior cases: "First, we look to the gravity of the offense and the harshness of the
penalty.... Second, it may be helpful to compare the sentences imposed on other
criminals in the same jurisdiction. If more serious crimes are subject to the same
penalty, or to less serious penalties, that is some indication that the punishment at
issue may be excessive.... Third, courts may find it useful to compare the sentences
imposed for commission of the same crime in other jurisdictions."[36]

As to the first factor, Justice Powell explicitly rejected the Court's earlier fears
about judicial subjectivity. He argued that courts are competent to objectively
assess degrees of offense gravity and punishment severity, and he noted that judges
are required, in a variety of contexts, to draw similar lines along a continuum.[37] He
suggested that offense gravity should be assessed in terms of the harm caused or
threatened to victims and society, as well as the offender's culpability (including
the defendant's degree of intent (*mens rea*) and motives). The latter criteria are
closely related to traditional elements of retributive punishment theory (discussed
in part F). However, except for several brief comments,[38] Justice Powell did not
explicitly discuss sentencing purposes or explain how they are related to any of his
three factors.

Applying these criteria, Powell noted first that Helm's current and prior
offenses were all minor and nonviolent and that his sentence was the most severe
authorized by South Dakota at the time. Powell conceded that states are justified
in punishing recidivists more severely but added in a footnote: "We must focus

on the principal felony—the felony that triggers the life sentence—since Helm already has paid the penalty for each of his prior offenses."[39] As for the second factor listed earlier, Powell argued that Helm had been treated at least as severely as many South Dakota criminals who had committed much more serious crimes. Under the third factor, Powell concluded that Helm had been punished more severely than he would have been in any other state.

Seven years later, in *Harmelin v. Michigan*,[40] the Court modified the *Solem* standards and upheld a mandatory sentence of life without parole imposed on a first offender convicted of possessing 672 grams of cocaine.[41] Harmelin contested both the severity of his sentence and its mandatory nature. Five justices voted to uphold the sentence in two opinions written by Justices Scalia and Kennedy. Most of Justice Scalia's opinion for the Court was joined only by Justice Rehnquist. Scalia argued that *Solem* was wrongly decided—that the Eighth Amendment contains no proportionality guarantee and that proportionality review is inherently subjective and too narrowly tied to retributive punishment theory, involves judgments best left to the legislature, and is inconsistent with federalism. Part IV of Scalia's opinion, joined by Justices Rehnquist, O'Connor, Kennedy, and Souter, concluded that mandatory penalties, even severe ones, "may be cruel, but they are not unusual in the constitutional sense, having been employed in various forms throughout our Nation's history."[42] Scalia distinguished the Court's cases requiring an individualized determination that capital punishment is appropriate because "death is different" (quoting *Rummel*).[43]

Justice Kennedy's concurring opinion, joined by Justices O'Connor and Souter, concluded that the Court's prior Eighth Amendment cases recognize a "narrow" proportionality principle based on five underlying assumptions:[44] (1) Fixing prison terms for specific crimes requires fundamental choices about sentencing purposes that are primarily for the legislature, not the courts; (2) the Eighth Amendment "does not mandate any one penological theory"; (3) "marked divergences" both in penal theories and in prison terms "are the inevitable, often beneficial result of the federal structure"; (4) proportionality review should, as much as possible, be informed by "objective factors," the "most prominent" of which is "the objective line between capital punishment and imprisonment for a term of years" (because courts "lack clear objective standards to distinguish between sentences for different terms of years"); and therefore (5) "the Eighth Amendment does not require strict proportionality between crime and sentence. Rather, the Amendment forbids only extreme sentences that are 'grossly disproportionate' to the crime."

Justice Kennedy also announced a revised version of the three-factor *Solem* test: Intra- and interjurisdictional comparative assessments (*Solem* factors 2 and 3) "are appropriate only in the rare case in which a threshold comparison of the crime committed and the sentence imposed [*Solem* factor 1] leads to an inference of gross disproportionality."[45] Kennedy concluded that the latter standard was not met in Harmelin's case. His crime was much more serious than Solem's $100 bad check; the amount of cocaine Harmelin possessed (more than 1.5 pounds) might produce as many as sixty-five thousand doses, threatening "grave harm to society" in terms of the effects on users, crimes committed by users, and violent crimes committed "as part of the drug business or culture."[46] Therefore, Michigan legislators "could with reason conclude" that Harmelin's crime "is momentous enough to warrant the deterrence and retribution of a life sentence without parole."[47]

Justices White, Marshall, Blackmun, and Stevens dissented in two opinions. Justice White argued that proportionality principles have long historical roots and have been read into all of the clauses of the Eighth Amendment; that the cruel and unusual punishment clause makes no distinction among types of punishments; that the *Solem* factors have worked well; that the second and third factors are actually more objective than the first and strongly support a finding of disproportionality in Harmelin's case; and that Justice Kennedy's application of the first *Solem* factor is both too subjective and too narrow because it focuses mainly on the harm threatened by this amount of drugs and not enough on critical culpability issues such as intent and motive. Justice White further noted that Harmelin was never charged with or convicted of distribution or even intent to distribute.

Justice Stevens also wrote a dissent, objecting that mandatory sentences of death or life without parole conclusively presume that all eligible defendants are incorrigible and that society's interests in deterrence and retribution outweigh any considerations of rehabilitation. Stevens argued that such a presumption is irrational;[48] if some covered offenders are not incorrigible, treating them all as if they are is unnecessarily severe.

The culpability factors emphasized by Justice White strongly imply a theory of limiting retributive proportionality. Justice Stevens's objection that the mandatory penalty is overbroad because not all eligible offenders are incorrigible implicitly invoked means proportionality. However, neither justice (nor any of the other justices who wrote opinions in *Harmelin*) provided a clear definition of Eighth Amendment proportionality. Justice Scalia seemed to believe that this concept is inherently tied to retributive sentencing goals and that "it becomes difficult to even speak intelligently of 'proportionality,' once deterrence and rehabilitation are given significant weight."[49] Justice Kennedy explicitly stated that all traditional punishment purposes are valid, including retribution, deterrence, incapacitation, and rehabilitation, since "[t]he Eighth Amendment does not mandate any one penological theory."[50] One reading of Kennedy's opinion would be that the Eighth Amendment is violated only if a sentence is "disproportionate" relative to *all* of the state's asserted punishment purposes. But Justice Scalia objected (as he did even more forcefully in *Ewing*, discussed next) that proportionality has no meaning relative to nonretributive goals such as deterrence, incapacitation, and rehabilitation. None of the other justices responded to Scalia's critique or suggested a non-retributive theory of proportionality. As we have shown throughout this book, utilitarian ends- and means-proportionality principles are well suited to this task.

Ewing v. California[51] is, at the time of this writing, the Court's most recent prison-duration case interpreting the Eighth Amendment. The Court upheld a sentence of twenty-five years to life, imposed under California's unusually severe three-strikes law, and further modified the *Solem-Harmelin* standards. Gary Ewing had been convicted of shoplifting three golf clubs worth $399 each, and over the previous twenty years he had incurred more than a dozen convictions for theft, burglary, robbery, battery, possession of a firearm, and possession of drug paraphernalia. As in *Harmelin*, five justices voted to uphold the sentence. Justice O'Connor's plurality opinion, joined by Justices Rehnquist and Kennedy, adopted the narrow proportionality principle articulated in Justice Kennedy's *Harmelin* concurrence, including each of Kennedy's five underlying principles summarized earlier, along with his further proviso that the second and third *Solem* factors need be considered only in rare cases in which the first factor raises a "threshold" inference of gross disproportionality.

Applying Kennedy's approach, O'Connor concluded that a comparison of Ewing's sentence with his current and past offenses raised no such inference. O'Connor noted that the purposes of the three-strikes law are to deter repeat offenders and incapacitate those who have not been deterred, and she cited evidence suggesting that the law had furthered both goals.[52] In assessing the gravity of Ewing's conviction offense (stealing three golf clubs), O'Connor argued that this was more serious than Helm's crime and that it was constitutionally irrelevant that Ewing's theft offense could, if both the prosecutor and the court agreed, be treated as a misdemeanor rather than a felony. O'Connor further argued (in what appears to be an important modification of the *Solem-Harmelin* standards) that, in order to accord proper deference to the state's choice of punishment goals, the gravity of Ewing's "offense" should include not just his conviction offense but also his extensive prior record.[53]

Justices Scalia and Thomas, concurring, argued that the *Solem* proportionality tests are unworkable and that no such requirement should be recognized under the Eighth Amendment. Justice Scalia repeated points he had made in his *Harmelin* opinion—that the Eighth Amendment was aimed only at excluding certain modes of punishment; that the proportionality concept is inherently tied to retributive goals; that since the Kennedy and O'Connor plurality opinions in *Harmelin* and *Ewing* do not require states to adopt retribution or any other penological theory (and specifically approve deterrent and incapacitative purposes), the concept of proportionality cannot be intelligently applied; and that if proportionality review means that "all punishment should reasonably pursue the multiple purposes of punishment," then the Court would not be "applying law but evaluating policy."[54]

Justices Stevens and Breyer wrote dissenting opinions, each joined by the other and by Justices Souter and Ginsburg. Justice Stevens argued that the Eighth Amendment sets proportionality limits for all forms of punishment; that such limits have also been applied to bail and to punitive damages awards; that sentencing judges have long employed proportionality principles to guide their discretion; and that the Eighth Amendment "expresses a broad and basic proportionality principle that takes into account all of the justifications for penal sanctions."[55]

Justice Breyer's dissent appeared to accept Justice O'Connor's view that prior record is relevant to the "gravity of the offense," but Breyer maintained that the focus still ought to be on the conviction offense.[56] He also made an implicit means-proportionality argument in noting the absence of evidence that shoplifting is difficult to detect or that lengthy prison terms are necessary to deter this crime. Taking all of this into account—Ewing's sentence,[57] his conviction offense, and his prior record—Breyer concluded that a threshold inference of gross disproportionality had been raised, particularly since, as he argued, there is no point in having a "threshold" test unless it is easier to meet than the ultimate test.

Justice Breyer then turned to intra- and interjurisidictional comparisons (noting, as Justice White had, dissenting in *Harmelin*, that such comparisons make proportionality review more objective). He concluded that these comparisons validated his threshold determination: "Outside of California's three-strikes context, Ewing's recidivist sentence is virtually unique in its harshness for his offense of conviction, and by a considerable degree...at a minimum, 2 to 3 times the length of sentences that other jurisdictions would impose in similar circumstances."[58] Nor could Breyer find any important practical administrative justifications for the California statute that might justify such harsh results. At this point Breyer made another implicit means-proportionality argument, questioning the need for the statute to sweep so broadly. The goal of the legislature was to deter and incapacitate felons who commit "serious" and "violent" crimes (including many violent and drug crimes, but excluding all property crimes, no matter how high the loss); but, as Ewing's case illustrates, the statute provided that any felony, including many property crimes that would not constitute first or second strikes, could qualify as a third strike. Thus, Breyer concluded, "Ewing's 25 year term amounts to overkill."[59]

In a companion case to *Ewing, Lockyer v. Andrade*,[60] the Court held that the Court of Appeals had erred in granting federal habeas corpus relief and overturning a California three-strikes sentence. On its facts, *Andrade* presented a much stronger basis for a finding of Eighth Amendment disproportionality. Andrade's fifty-year minimum sentence was twice as long as Ewing's, and his conviction offenses were less serious—two counts of misdemeanor theft (shoplifting of nine videotapes worth about $150, taken from two stores), which were charged as felonies because of Andrade's previous property crimes. His prior record was also less serious (unlike Ewing, Andrade had no previous violent or weapons convictions), and his current and prior property offenses were all driven by his need to buy heroin to feed his addiction. However, the Eighth Amendment holding in *Andrade* was blurred by the procedural context. Under the Antiterrorism and Effective Death Penalty Act of 1996 ("AEDPA"), a federal court may grant habeas relief only if the state court's decision is "contrary to, or involved an unreasonable application of, clearly established Federal law" as determined by the Supreme Court.[61] Thus, as Justice O'Connor's majority opinion explicitly noted, the Court's decision upholding Andrade's sentence was not a ruling that his sentence complied with the Eighth Amendment. The Court was holding only that habeas relief should not have been granted because the state appellate court's decision affirming Andrade's sentence was not so erroneous as to meet the AEDPA review standard.

Justice Souter's dissenting opinion, joined by Justices Stevens, Ginsburg, and Breyer, argued that the state court's decision was not only erroneous but also sufficiently unreasonable to justify habeas relief. Souter viewed the *Andrade* facts as indistinguishable from *Solem* (particularly if one deems a fifty-year minimum sentence as equivalent to life without parole for a thirty-seven-year-old offender). Souter also found Andrade's sentence irrational when measured against the state's asserted purpose, which, according to the state's briefs, was incapacitation of high-risk offenders. Souter argued that the three-strikes statute represents a legislative finding that the danger such an offender posed requires a minimum sentence of twenty-five years, but Andrade received two consecutive twenty-five-year-minimum terms. In Souter's view, it is irrational to assume that the defendant could "somehow become twice as dangerous to society when he stole the second handful of videotapes."[62] This is essentially a means-proportionality argument—a fifty-year sentence is much more severe than needed to respond to the added danger that can be inferred from a second episode of shoplifting. Once again, however, neither Souter nor any of the other justices defined their Eighth Amendment proportionality principles.

2. Critique of the Court's Prison-Sentence Proportionality Review Standards

The three-factor test from *Solem v. Helm*, as modified in *Harmelin* and *Ewing*, remains the Supreme Court's only attempt to give precise content to the Eighth Amendment's proportionality limitations on severe prison sentences. What kinds of proportionality are implicit in these standards? The first *Solem* factor, which assesses the gravity of the defendant's crime in relation to the sentence, appears to focus on retributive elements—the harm caused by the offense and the defendant's culpability (intent and motive). But if, as the *Ewing* plurality opinion asserts, the defendant's prior convictions are also relevant to the "gravity" of his offense and the state's goals of deterrence and incapacitation of recidivists are relevant as well, then even the first *Solem* factor must also include nonretributive proportionality principles, and the most plausible formulations of such principles correspond to ends and/or means proportionality. As we noted earlier, several dissenting justices have made implicit means proportionality arguments over the years, apparently in relation to the overall "gross disproportionality" standard most closely associated with the first *Solem* factor.[63]

As for the second *Solem* factor (i.e., comparing sentences for other crimes in the same state), both retributive and utilitarian ends proportionality may be relevant. If much more serious crimes often receive the same or lower penalties, this implies that the defendant has received punishment in excess of his deserts and/or sentence burdens unjustified by the social harms prevented (ends disproportionality). (Means disproportionality would not be implied since the minimum degree of adequate punishment to achieve utilitarian crime-control purposes is not necessarily correlated with crime seriousness.) Under the third *Solem* factor (i.e., comparing sentences imposed for the same crime in other states), all three forms of proportionality may be relevant. If similar offenders in other states receive much less severe penalties, this implies retributive disproportionality (sentences in the home state exceed desert), and/or ends disproportionality (sentence burdens are not justified by social harms), and/or means disproportionality (lower penalties would likely be adequate in the home state if they are widely deemed adequate in other states; if very unusual circumstances in the home state are believed to render lower penalties inadequate, the burden should be on the state to show why this is so).

Although retributive and ends- and/or means-proportionality principles are implicit in a number of the Court's decisions, these principles need to be made explicit and more carefully applied. Doing so might have changed the result in some of these cases by sharpening the analysis of retributive values and showing how proportionality principles can be used to evaluate excessiveness relative to nonretributive sentencing purposes. A better understanding of the distinction between strict ("defining") and more flexible ("limiting") retributive proportionality theories (discussed more fully in part F) might have made it easier for the Court to recognize independent retributive limits on the severity of prison terms under the Eighth Amendment. Justice Kennedy's assertions in *Harmelin*, adopted by Justice O'Connor's plurality opinion in *Ewing*, that the Eighth Amendment "does not mandate...any one penological theory" and does not require "strict proportionality" may have been based on the erroneous assumption that retributive theory is an all-or-nothing proposition. The theory of limiting retributivism permits substantial scope for the operation of traditional crime-control purposes, which these justices clearly wished to preserve.

Given the importance of these nonretributive, crime-control goals, explicit recognition and application of nonretributive (ends and means) proportionality principles would also have been helpful in these cases, particularly if the Court is unwilling to impose limiting retributive constraints on crime-control goals. Justice Scalia was clearly right in saying that nonretributive punishment goals cannot be assessed with retributive proportionality principles. However, he was wrong in assuming that there are no suitable nonretributive proportionality principles. As we have shown throughout this book, utilitarian ends- and means-proportionality principles are well established in many areas of constitutional law; such principles can and should be used to evaluate excessiveness relative to nonretributive punishment goals. The Court's implicit use of both of these principles, when defining the contemporary meaning of the Fourth Amendment's ban on "unreasonable searches and seizures" (see chapter 5), is particularly instructive. Why should utilitarian proportionality principles be applied under the Fourth Amendment but not the Eighth?

One interpretation of the Court's most recent holdings is that a sentence violates the Eighth Amendment only if it is grossly disproportionate in relation to *all* traditional sentencing purposes invoked by the state. However, the better view is that some degree of retributive proportionality should be an independent constitutional requirement in every case, placing upper limits on crime-control measures even if such measures do not violate utilitarian (ends and means) proportionality principles.[64] When multiple proportionality principles have been recognized in other areas of constitutional law, they usually operate independently—a violation of any of the principles suffices for a finding of unconstitutionality. An example is the two-pronged standard of strict scrutiny (discussed in chapter 3).

It is particularly important to recognize independent retributive limits on the length of prison sentences. Upper retributive proportionality limits reflect fundamental human rights principles of fairness and protection from abuses of government power,[65] and such limits have been applied as a matter of federal constitutional law in a number of other contexts, including the death penalty (part A), fines and forfeitures (part D), punitive damages awards (chapter 4), and issues of criminal liability (chapter 6). No coherent and convincing rationale explains why independent retributive limits apply in all of the latter contexts but not to lengthy prison terms. Such sentences are often the practical equivalent of a death sentence, and they are usually much more severe than punitive damages, fines, and forfeitures. Nor can stricter retributive limits on criminal liability be justified by a special concern to protect totally innocent persons; the reasonable doubt rule (and to a lesser extent, all of the constitutional liability rules discussed in chapter 6) also applies to persons who are clearly guilty of one or more crimes, thereby protecting them from being found liable for additional or more serious crimes.

If courts are unwilling to recognize constitutionally required upper retributive limits, at least the ends- and means-proportionality principles should receive independent application since each represents a distinct and important form of utilitarian excessiveness. A sentence supported by utilitarian purposes should be held unconstitutional if it grossly violates ends proportionality (because the sentence's burdens greatly exceed the likely crime-control benefits) *or* if it grossly violates means proportionality (because a much less severe sentence would be adequate to achieve the state's asserted crime-control purposes).

Returning to the facts of the Supreme Court's six modern prison-duration cases (including the one pro-defendant decision, *Solem v. Helm*, which some may believe to have been cast in doubt by later cases), how would each be analyzed under limiting retributive and ends- and means-proportionality principles?[66] Clearly, an independent upper retributive limit would have strengthened the case for a finding of unconstitutional disproportionality in some of these cases or at least would have helped to establish threshold disproportionality under the first *Solem-Harmelin-Ewing* factor, thus permitting consideration of intra- and interjurisdictional comparisons (*Solem* factors 2 and 3). In terms of the two dimensions of traditional retributive theory discussed in part F—actual or threatened harm and personal culpability—there is a clear imbalance between the minor conviction offenses and the severe penalties imposed in most of these cases. William Rummel got a life sentence (with no guarantee of parole when he became eligible after 10 years in prison) for a $121 false-pretenses crime amounting to breach of contract; Roger Davis got a 40-year sentence (parole eligibility unknown) for possessing six ounces of marijuana and selling another three; Jerry Helm got life without parole for a $100 bad check; Gary Ewing got 25 years to life for shoplifting three golf clubs; and Leandro Andrade got 50 years to life for shoplifting nine videotapes.

Analysis of the four habitual-offender cases (*Rummel, Solem v. Helm, Ewing,* and *Andrade*) from a retributive proportionality perspective is complicated by the lack of scholarly consensus on how to weigh prior record. Some scholars claim prior record has no bearing on the deserved sentence, whereas others assert that such a record modestly increases desert (see further discussion in part F). However, even on the latter view, the prior-record enhancements given to these four offenders can hardly be characterized as modest; all three received sentences far more severe than what they would have deserved without a prior record—sentences comparable to those given to offenders committing the most serious crimes. In addition, the current and prior crimes of at least two of these offenders, Helm and Andrade, were related to their chemical dependency, further lowering their volitional capacity and thus their culpability.

Application of independent utilitarian ends- and means-proportionality principles might also change the analysis in some of these cases, thereby providing at least a sounder basis to find threshold gross disproportionality that permits intra- and interjurisdictional comparisons. Even accounting for prior record and assuming that repeat offenders will continue to commit similar crimes, the crime-control benefits of lengthy incarceration may be greatly exceeded by the substantial human and financial costs of extended imprisonment (ends proportionality), and such benefits may be just as well achieved by much less severe penalties (means proportionality). As noted earlier, the latter (means proportionality) arguments are implicit in several dissenting opinions in these cases. Older and infirm offenders such as Ewing and Andrade are likely to have entered or be nearing the point in their lives when their pace of criminal conduct greatly diminishes, thus steadily lowering the offender-specific preventive benefits of prison while steadily raising the cost (especially for medical care). Even before offender risk subsides, specific deterrence of chemically dependent offenders like Helm and Andrade is doubtful,[67] while treatment in prison or even in the community will often prevent their future crimes just as effectively as lengthy incarceration. The crime-control benefits of lengthy incarceration must also be discounted by the possible significant disutilities of penalties that are grossly disproportionate to the conviction offense. Such disutilities include lost or even reverse deterrence (offenders have no incentive to avoid more serious crimes and may be tempted to assault witnesses or arresting officers); distortion of societal norms of relative crime seriousness; and/or diminished public and offender respect for laws and penalties.[68]

Retributive and utilitarian proportionality principles are difficult to apply to a very serious drug case like *Harmelin*. The majority in that case noted that the drugs he possessed might yield as many as sixty-five thousand doses, making his sentence arguably consistent with one element of retributive proportionality (harm) and also with ends proportionality—severe social harms justify severe penalties. However, Harmelin was charged only with possession, yet his life-without-parole sentence treated him the same as if he had been charged and convicted of sale or intent to sell. Harmelin's sentence was thus excessive relative to his culpability and the greater culpability of offenders who are proven to have sold or intended to sell yet receive penalties no more severe. This argument should be sufficient to establish threshold disproportionality, which would then be strongly supported by intra- and interjurisdictional analysis. Interjurisdictional comparison also supports an argument based on means disproportionality—the much lower sentences imposed in almost all other jurisdictions imply that a less severe penalty would achieve equally good results.

The defendant in *Harmelin* also contested the mandatory nature of his penalty. This argument was summarily rejected by Justice Scalia, who was joined on this point by four other justices. But unlike Justice Scalia, the other four justices who approved of Michigan's mandatory penalty accepted some Eighth Amendment proportionality limits. Two of these justices (Kennedy and Souter) remain on the Court, and the other two have been replaced by Justices Alito and Roberts. In the future, one of these justices—or more likely, a state court interpreting one of the state constitutional excessive-penalty prohibitions discussed in part E—might be persuaded to take another look at the problems posed by the *interaction* between severity and lack of case-specific sentencing discretion. A strong case can be made that severe mandatory penalties are inherently excessive relative to desert; even if many of the eligible offenders deserve the mandatory penalty, it is very unlikely that *every* eligible offender does.[69] Similar inherent overbreadth arguments can be made on utilitarian grounds, particularly with respect to means proportionality: When a group of offenders is subjected to a severe mandatory penalty with no possibility of parole release, it is almost certain that, in at least some of these cases, such a penalty is unnecessary to achieve adequate deterrence, incapacitation, and other valid utilitarian goals.[70] To the extent that the life-without-parole penalty in Harmelin's case (or in *Solem, supra*) was designed to incapacitate dangerous offenders, the absence of any parole release option likewise violates means proportionality—it is virtually certain that some offenders sentenced under this law will cease to be dangerous at some point before they die.

To summarize, in all six of the Court's modern prison-duration cases more precise application of limiting retributive and utilitarian ends- and means-proportionality principles would provide strong arguments in favor of a finding of gross disproportionality at least as a threshold matter, thus permitting application of the more objective and more defendant-friendly second and third *Solem* standards.

C. EIGHTH AMENDMENT LIMITS ON THE TREATMENT OF PRISONERS

The Supreme Court has held that Eighth Amendment limits apply not only to measures that are intended as punishment for crimes (discussed in parts A, B, and D) but also to certain unacceptable treatment of convicted prisoners[71] that is not part of their formal prison or jail sentence.[72] Inmates have used the Eighth Amendment to challenge denial of medical care; failure to provide protection from other inmates, guards, or suicide risk; various other harsh prison conditions; severe disciplinary measures imposed for violation of prison and jail rules; and excessive force used by prison and jail guards.[73]

Because convicted prisoners are deemed fit subjects for harsh treatment and because the operation of jails and prisons is difficult and dangerous, courts adopt a deferential attitude. Nevertheless, numerous Supreme Court and lower court cases have found that inmates proved or sufficiently alleged an Eighth Amendment violation. Very few cases expressly mention proportionality, but implicit proportionality principles often appear in the reasoning of these decisions—even though neither of the standards currently applied in prisoners' rights cases mentions or implies such principles. We argue that courts should explicitly invoke proportionality principles in some of these cases—those involving claims of excessive force or discipline—because the essence of these cases, like those involving severe sentences, is the question whether the challenged measures are excessive relative to the inmates' desert and/or to proper purposes and available alternatives.

In *Estelle v. Gamble*[74] the Supreme Court stated that the Eighth Amendment is violated by the "unnecessary and wanton infliction of pain" on inmates, involving measures "totally without penological justification," and that these issues are assessed in light of "the evolving standards of decency that mark the progress of a maturing society." Most of this language was taken from a death penalty case, *Gregg v. Georgia*,[75] but subsequent prisoners' rights cases have rarely relied so directly on Eighth Amendment sentencing standards. Some lower court cases from the 1970s used the "unnecessary and wanton" standard or a generalized Eighth Amendment "necessity" principle to find certain inmate restraint measures unconstitutional because they were much more severe or lasted much longer than necessary.[76] The emphasis on necessity in these early cases strongly suggests a version of means-proportionality analysis. In addition, a few 1970s cases appear to have applied limiting retributive principles in finding challenged prison disciplinary measures to be excessive relative to the seriousness of the infractions being punished.[77]

In later prisoners' rights cases the Supreme Court developed two sets of standards specifically designed for inmate mistreatment claims. Each includes both an objective and a subjective component; neither strongly emphasizes proportionality.[78] Inmates' claims of inadequate medical care, absence of protection from assault or suicide, harsh prison conditions or handling, and severe disciplinary measures require a showing of prison officials' "deliberate indifference" to inmates' health or safety, a standard akin to "recklessness" in the criminal law.[79] In *Rhodes v. Chapman*[80] the Court held that the objective component for such claims requires deprivation of "the minimal civilized measure of life's necessities" and added that many unpleasant or even harsh prison conditions will fail to meet this standard (harsh treatment is deemed to be a legitimate part of the penalty). In a later case the Court stated that the objective component requires deprivation of an "identifiable human need such as food, warmth, or exercise" and that the deprivation must lack penological justification.[81]

A different subjective standard applies to claims of excessive force by prison officials in restoring order or subduing an unruly inmate. According to the

Court, a more deferential standard is appropriate because the state must balance competing interests—safeguarding the inmate versus protecting other inmates and noninmates—and officials must often act quickly.[82] The subjective standard for these cases is that the officials acted "maliciously and sadistically for the very purpose of causing harm."[83] On the other hand, the objective component in this context is lower because, when the "malicious and sadistic" standard is met, "contemporary standards of decency always are violated.... This is true whether or not significant injury is evident," provided the injury is not de minimis.[84]

The current standards summarized here are unsatisfactory. It is not clear why a separate subjective element is required in this context, given that Eighth Amendment limits on sentencing and forfeitures do not include any such element. This element may have been designed to transform administrative measures into "punishment" subject to the cruel and unusual punishment clause; however, a subjective element also applies to prison disciplinary measures that are clearly intended as (further) punishment. Alternatively, perhaps subjective standards are used to emphasize the need to defer to decisions by prison officials and to intervene only when these officials act culpably. Nonetheless, this rationale does not explain why the objective standards applied to the treatment of prisoners also differ from those applied to sentences and forfeitures. Explicit proportionality analysis seems particularly appropriate when evaluating claims of alleged excessive force used to subdue or transport an inmate or of unduly severe disciplinary measures since the essence of these claims is excessiveness (not deprivation).[85]

Notwithstanding the formal standards currently applied, many examples of implicit means-proportionality principles appear in recent Supreme Court and lower court cases. In *Hope v. Pelzer*[86] the Supreme Court found an Eighth Amendment violation when an inmate who had been disruptive at a chain gang work site was taken back to the prison and painfully handcuffed for seven hours to a tall "hitching post" without adequate water, unprotected from sunburn on his shirtless body, and with no bathroom breaks. Citing the lack of any continuing emergency situation or safety concerns, the Court found that this treatment violated the inmate's dignity and imposed "wanton and unnecessary pain." In *Delaney v. DeTella*,[87] involving confinement in a tiny segregation cell for six months with no out-of-cell exercise, the Seventh Circuit found that periodic exercise is an essential human need and that no legitimate concerns (such as the inmate's extreme dangerousness) justified such extended and total denial of exercise. In other words, such denial was unnecessary.

Similarly, in *Anderson-Bey v. District of Columbia*,[88] the District Court found the allegations sufficient to state a claim because the very tight handcuffs placed on the plaintiffs for their all-day transport to another prison imposed more pain than was necessary to maintain security. In *Trammel v. Keane*, the Second Circuit used proportionality language, as well as implicit means-proportionality analysis, to conclude that, in light of an inmate's many disciplinary violations, the admittedly severe measures taken in his case were warranted by the need to strongly deter and reform him and "directly and proportionately targeted [his] misconduct."[89] The measures were deemed necessary and thus not excessive relative to less severe alternatives.

Implicit proportionality principles have also been applied indirectly as evidentiary tools. In *Hudson v. McMillian*,[90] the Supreme Court stated that the following factors are relevant in applying the "malicious and sadistic" standard: (1) the extent of the injury suffered; (2) the need for the application of force; (3) the relationship between the need and the amount of force used; (4) the threat reasonably perceived by the responsible officials; and (5) any efforts made to temper the severity of a forceful response. These factors seem to reflect both means- and ends-proportionality concepts by examining the need for and narrow tailoring of the force, as well as the injury suffered, compared with the threat reasonably perceived; the analysis closely resembles Fourth Amendment excessive force principles (discussed in chapter 5, part A). However, at least in theory, these principles appear to have inferential value only in the Court's Eighth Amendment excessive force cases; indeed, the Court has specifically rejected any direct application of reasonableness or means-proportionality concepts.[91]

To summarize, courts often emphasize the "unnecessary" or "gratuitous" use of force or discipline, but under the Court's two-pronged standards, proportionality principles are almost always implicit and are sometimes deemed relevant only as a way to infer improper intent. Since the gist of many of these claims is excessiveness, ⁺ would sharpen and improve analysis if courts explicitly invoked proportionality principles, which could still be tailored to reflect context-specific needs.

Broader application of proportionality principles in favor of inmates in these cases also seems very appropriate in light of the explicit imposition of means- and ends-proportionality principles *against* inmates—to limit the remedies available in prisoners' rights suits. The Prison Litigation Reform Act of 1995[92] requires claims for relief to be "narrowly drawn" (i.e., to be only as broad or as long lasting as necessary to correct the particular violation shown for the particular inmates bringing the suit), while giving "substantial weight to any adverse impact on public safety or the operation of a criminal justice system caused by the relief."

D. EIGHTH AMENDMENT LIMITS ON FINES AND FORFEITURES

Prohibitions on excessive fines can be traced to the Magna Carta (1215)[93] and were expressly included in the English Bill of Rights (1689), founding-era state bills of rights, and the Eighth Amendment.[94] However, the Supreme Court did not have occasion to interpret the Eighth Amendment provision until the end of the twentieth century and then only in the context of civil and criminal forfeitures, not cases involving actual fines (which at this writing have never come before the Court). The forfeiture cases are discussed in the following section, and lower court fine and penalty cases are taken up after that. Limiting retributive proportionality principles are fairly well defined in the Supreme Court and lower court cases, but as in the sentencing cases discussed previously, courts have failed to recognize and articulate proportionality principles suitable for defining constitutional excessiveness relative to the nonretributive (deterrent) purposes served by fines, forfeitures, and civil penalties.

1. The Supreme Court's Civil and Criminal Forfeiture Cases

The Court's forfeiture cases were foreshadowed by its ruling in *Browning-Ferris Industries v. Kelco Disposal*.[95] *Browning-Ferris* held that the Eighth Amendment excessive fines clause is inapplicable to punitive damages awards obtained by private litigants because the clause applies "primarily, and perhaps exclusively, to criminal prosecutions and punishments"; the clause thus cannot apply in a civil suit, at least "when the government neither has prosecuted the action nor has any right to receive a share of the damages awarded." However, the government does "prosecute" forfeiture actions and receives the money or property forfeited, and such actions have punitive, as well as remedial, purposes, so it was no great surprise when, several years later, in *United States v. Alexander*,[96] the Court held that an *in personam* criminal forfeiture of the defendant's entire business might constitute an excessive fine.

The amendment's application to civil, *in rem* forfeitures raises additional problems since those actions are, at least in form, directed at property rather than persons and do not require the property's owner to be criminally convicted, prosecuted, or even chargeable. But in *Austin v. United States*,[97] the Court held that the key issue is not whether a forfeiture is classified as civil/*in rem* or criminal/*in personam* but rather whether the measure constitutes "punishment" at least in part and is not purely "remedial." The Court further held that a measure imposes punishment if it serves retributive or deterrent purposes, whereas a purely remedial measure is designed to compensate the government for enforcement costs and/or lost revenues. The Court thus decided that the *in rem* civil forfeiture of the defendant's mobile home and auto body shop after he pleaded guilty to distributing cocaine could be an excessive fine, but it remanded the case without attempting to define standards for determination of the excessiveness issue.

In *United States v. Bajakajian*,[98] the Court did provide such a standard and used it in an *in personam* criminal forfeiture case to hold that the excessive fines clause would be violated by full forfeiture of $357,144 in cash (the defendant apparently acquired the cash legally but failed to report it when attempting to take it out of the country). Justice Thomas's majority opinion applied a standard of "gross disproportionality" to the gravity of the offense the forfeiture is designed to punish, citing *Solem v. Helm* but not the more recent case of *Harmelin v. Michigan* (both cases are discussed in part B). Applying this standard, Justice Thomas stressed several aspects of Bajakajian's offense: (1) the technical nature of the crime (nonreporting of a cash transport that itself was perfectly legal); (2) the trial court's finding that the crime was unrelated to any other illegal activities; (3) the fact that defendant did not fall into any of the groups targeted by the statute (money launderers, drug traffickers, tax evaders); (4) the defendant's recommended sentence under the sentencing guidelines (six months' incarceration and a $5,000 fine), which the Court viewed as a better measure of the defendant's culpability relative to other violators of this statute than the much higher statutory maximum penalties; and (5) the minimal harm to the government caused by defendant's nonreporting.

The harm and culpability factors stressed in *Bajakajian* correspond to the two traditional elements of blameworthiness, thus suggesting a grounding in limiting retributive proportionality.[99] But as noted earlier, forfeitures may constitute punishment if they serve deterrent, as well as retributive, purposes. Thus, unless the Court is going to impose retributive limits on deterrent purposes (which it has refused to do in the context of prison sentences; see part B), the Court needs to develop and apply standards of utilitarian "excessiveness." One commentator has suggested that some forfeitures impose burdens out of proportion to the law enforcement benefits achieved and are also excessive in their unnecessary severity and overinclusiveness.[100] These two forms of excessiveness correspond to ends- and means-proportionality principles. Courts should openly recognize and further develop these principles.

Subsequent forfeiture cases in federal and state courts have usually distinguished *Bajakajian* and upheld the forfeiture,[101] but a few cases have found an excessive fines violation.[102]

2. Fines and Punitive Civil Penalty Cases in the Lower Courts

Lower courts both before and after *Bajakajian* have occasionally found criminal fines or punitive civil penalties[103] to be unconstitutionally excessive. Some of these cases are based additionally or solely on state constitutional provisions (discussed more fully in part E). In applying the federal "gross disproportionality" standard from *Bajakajian*, some lower courts[104] have invoked the three proportionality factors from *Solem v. Helm* since that case (but not the three factors) was cited in *Bajakajian*.

Some cases decided prior to *Bajakajian* suggested one or more nonretributive proportionality principles, and at least some of these holdings survive after *Bajakajian*, at least as a matter of state constitutional law. Here is a sampling of those decisions.

People v. Malone[105] held that a $100,000 fine (the statutory maximum) imposed for an offense involving $400 of property damage violated Colorado and federal excessive fines provisions. The Court held that relevant factors include not only the severity of the conviction offense but also the defendant's "character and background" and his ability to pay the fine; as to the latter, the court concluded that a fine is excessive if it is "disproportionate to the defendant's [financial] circumstances." The character and background factors may suggest potential (but unspecified) nonretributive proportionality principles. The ability-to-pay factor identifies either a new form of excessiveness or one indirectly related to ends or means proportionality—the uncollectible portion of the fine provides either no additional benefit (means) or insufficient additional (symbolic?) benefits to justify the added public and private burdens (ends).

In *People v. Antolovich*,[106] a statutory-maximum fine of $25,000 was held to violate the Michigan Constitution's excessive fines clause where the fine was imposed for delivery of one gram of cocaine for no profit and not as part of a pattern of criminal behavior by an offender with a history of steady employment and no prior record. The court stated that, in considering whether a fine is excessive, "due regard must be had [1] to the object designed to be accomplished, [2] to the importance and magnitude of the public interest sought to be protected, [3] to the circumstances and nature of the act for which it is imposed, [4] to the preventive effect upon the commission of the particular kind of crime, and [5] in some instances to the ability of accused to pay."[107] The second and fourth factors appear to reflect implicit ends-proportionality principles. The court focused on the first factor and concluded that the purpose of authorizing fines up to $25,000 ("to stifle the allure of potentially enormous profits from illegal drug trafficking") did not require imposition of that amount in this case (an implicit means-proportionality argument).

Commonwealth v. Heggenstaller[108] held that a $6,550 fine imposed for unpaid telephone charges ($1.25 per month, totaling $28.75) violated the Pennsylvania excessive fines clause. The court's sole criterion of excessiveness suggests an implicit means-proportionality principle—"[a] fine should be sufficient enough to discourage the conduct."

3. Summary

The infrequent and inconsistent application of the Supreme Court's excessive fines standards suggests that the Court and lower courts need to clarify the apparent limiting retributive theory of "gross disproportionality" and also to specify whether and how disproportionality is to be measured relative to nonretributive purposes. Litigants should also challenge some of the question-begging arguments in these cases; for instance, when extremely high statutory maximum fines are cited in support of forfeitures, actual fines, or penalties, counsel should argue the excessiveness of those maxima.[109]

E. STATE CONSTITUTIONAL LIMITS ON EXCESSIVE PUNISHMENT

Most state constitutions contain prohibitions of excessive punishments. Some use language identical to the Eighth Amendment excessive fines and cruel-and-unusual clauses, but many textual variants exist, including prohibition of cruel *or* (not *and*) unusual punishment, cruel punishment alone, and disproportionate punishment.

In interpreting their own constitutions, state courts have an especially important limiting role to play since they face no problems of federalism and fewer issues of democratic legitimacy (because they are elected or otherwise more directly politically accountable than federal judges). In addition, when the wording of a state constitution is different from that of the Eighth Amendment, state courts have more leeway to adopt a different interpretation, particularly when the state text explicitly requires proportionality or generalized excessiveness analysis. Of course, elected state judges may be reluctant to appear too "pro-criminal" when called upon to check the excesses of the executive and legislative branches, but the same is true when elected judges interpret other criminal law and procedure rules that protect criminal suspects and defendants. Moreover, even a cursory examination of state law excessive-punishment rulings reveals numerous decisions that find prison sentences unconstitutionally excessive.

The following discussion first surveys the variety of state constitutional texts related to excessive punishments and the case law interpreting these provisions. It then examines in more detail the decisions in Illinois, a state with particularly well-developed state constitutional sentencing jurisprudence. Most of the state cases appear to be applying a version of the federal standards under *Solem v. Helm*, which, as discussed in part B, do not clearly specify what theories of proportionality are being applied. In some states, however, the constitutional texts and/or judicial interpretations have produced clear examples of the use of limiting retributive principles and occasionally ends and/or means proportionality. The focus of the following discussions is on prison sentences. State excessive fines cases were discussed in part D.

1. State Constitutional Texts and Interpretive Case Law

All fifty states have constitutional provisions related to sentencing. Every state, with the exception of Connecticut and Vermont, has a provision that specifically limits severe punishments of all kinds. But those two states have provisions that limit severe fines, and Vermont courts interpret that state's "proportioned" fines clause to apply to all types of penalties.[110] The forty-nine states with all-penalties provisions fall into five categories:

1. Ten states have constitutions that either explicitly or by interpretation require proportionate penalties. The eight with explicit provisions are Indiana, Maine, Nebraska, New Hampshire, Oregon, Rhode Island, Vermont, and West Virginia. Of these states, all but Vermont also have constitutional provisions that fall into one of the following four categories. In addition, Illinois has a provision that requires punishment "according to the seriousness of the offense" and that is commonly referred to as the "proportionate-penalties clause" (see further discussion in the following section on Illinois constitutional sentencing cases). And in Washington the Supreme Court has interpreted that state's constitutional ban on cruel penalties in light of proportionality principles recognized in state statutes.[111]
2. Nineteen state constitutions prohibit cruel *or* unusual penalties, including two states, Maine and New Hampshire, with proportionate-penalty clauses (category 1 above). The other seventeen states are Alabama, Arkansas, California, Hawaii, Kansas, Louisiana, Massachusetts, Michigan, Minnesota, Mississippi, Nevada, North Carolina, North Dakota, Oklahoma, South Carolina, Texas, and Wyoming.
3. Six state constitutions prohibit cruel penalties (omitting the "unusual" element), including one state, Rhode Island, with a proportionate-penalty clause. The other five states are Delaware, Kentucky, Pennsylvania, South Dakota, and Washington.
4. Twenty-two state constitutions prohibit cruel and unusual penalties, including eight states with a proportionate-penalty clause and/or one of the provisions in the next category. Those states are Alaska, Georgia, Indiana, Nebraska, Oregon, Tennessee, Utah, and West Virginia.
5. At least nine states, all of whom are included in one of the first four categories, have additional state constitutional provisions related to excessive penalties or treatment. Five states (Indiana, Oregon, Tennessee, Utah, and Wyoming) prohibit "unnecessary rigor" in the treatment of persons arrested or held in custody;[112] Georgia prohibits

such persons from being "abused"; Louisiana's constitution prohibits "euthanasia, [ ] torture, or [ ] cruel, excessive, or unusual punishment"; South Carolina prohibits "corporal," as well as cruel or unusual, punishment; and Alaska recognizes that inmates have a right to rehabilitation pursuant to a state constitutional provision that requires all criminal administration to be based on "the principle of reformation" (as well as on public protection, community condemnation, victims rights, and restitution).[113]

Cases that construe these state constitutional provisions are as varied as the provisions themselves and do not always track differences in constitutional text. Some courts cite such differences as grounds for recognizing broader state constitutional protection, whereas other courts ignore textual differences and apply federal constitutional standards. Courts in states from the first two categories (those with proportionate-penalty clauses or clauses that prohibit cruel *or* unusual punishment) are somewhat more likely to grant broader protection, but many states in each category do not do so. The reluctance of state courts to grant broader protection against excessive penalties under state constitutions is surprising given the much greater frequency with which state courts recognize expanded criminal procedure rights in other contexts. For example, many courts have given citizens greater protection from searches and seizures under state provisions worded similarly or even identically to the Fourth Amendment.[114]

Whether or not the state constitution is worded differently or is deemed more protective, numerous cases across a diverse group of states have invalidated sentencing provisions or specific sentences under state constitutional law.[115] Although most courts merely apply the *Solem v. Helm* framework, some state courts have developed more precise proportionality analysis or stated principles. The several Illinois proportionality tests are discussed in a later section. The following are examples of decisions from other states.

The California Supreme Court has strongly implied a focus on limiting retributive proportionality. *In re Rodriguez*[116] held that, under the state's cruel-or-unusual clause, "the measure of the constitutionality of punishment for crime is individual culpability."

In *Conner v. State*,[117] the Indiana Supreme Court held that the state's proportionate-penalties clause grants more protection than the Eighth Amendment. The court further held that the defendant's six-year sentence for selling a harmless substance represented to be marijuana was unconstitutionally disproportionate because it was twice as severe as the three-year maximum penalty applicable to the sale of real marijuana. The court therefore vacated the sentence and remanded with instructions to impose a sentence of no more than three years.

The Kentucky Supreme Court, in applying that state's ban on "cruel punishment" in *Workman v. Commonwealth*,[118] invalidated sentences of life without parole given to two fourteen-year-old rape offenders. The court's decision was based in part on the principle, akin to alternative-means proportionality, that a punishment is unconstitutionally excessive if it "go[es] beyond what is necessary to achieve the aim of the public intent as expressed in the legislative act [or] ... exceeds any legitimate penal aim."

In *State v. Hayes*,[119] the Louisiana Court of Appeal vacated a mandatory sentence of life without parole under that state's cruel or unusual punishment clause (but without emphasizing the differences between state and federal constitutional texts). The court found the sentence constitutionally excessive, citing the following facts: Hayes's current offense involved theft of approximately $1,000 from his employer; he admitted the crime and returned $693 still in his possession; he had a second job, and that employer thought highly of Hayes and believed he could be rehabilitated; his prior crimes were mostly minor property offenses; his one "crime of violence" (required to impose the life sentence) was a strong-armed robbery and theft of a bicycle committed when Hayes was a juvenile; and the presentence report recommended a sentence of ten years. The general standards invoked in *Hayes* were that penalties must be "meaningfully tailored to the culpability of the offender, the gravity of the offense, and the circumstances of the case" and must not be "disproportionate to the harm done" or "shock[ ] one's sense of justice."[120] This language suggests the application of both implicit limiting retributive principles and ends proportionality. Ends- and/or means-proportionality principles were also implicit in the court's statement that the trial court's sentence "imposes an undue burden on the taxpayers of the state" in a case where "a severe sentence, for example, between twenty and forty years, would have met all of the societal goals of incarceration."[121]

In *People v. Bullock*,[122] the mandatory life-without-parole penalty upheld by the Supreme Court in *Harmelin v. Michigan* (discussed in part B) was found to violate the Michigan Constitution in part because that state's constitution forbids cruel *or* unusual punishments. The Michigan Supreme Court implicitly adopted a retributive theory, stressing the defendant's limited culpability in the absence of any proof of sale or intent to sell. And contrary to Justice Kennedy's analysis in *Harmelin*, the Michigan court refused to hold the defendant responsible for the potential harms that might have been caused if the large quantity of drugs he possessed had been converted into individual doses. Proportionate punishment under the Michigan Constitution "must be tailored to the defendant's personal responsibility and moral guilt"; anyone who obtained some of these drugs and caused harm "can and should be held individually responsible" for such harm.

Utilitarian proportionality principles are also clearly implied by the word-ing of several state constitutional texts. The five state constitutions that prohibit "unnecessary rigor" in the treatment of persons in custody have thereby recognized an implicit means-proportionality limitation. In addition, ends-proportionality principles are endorsed in Article 18 of the New Hampshire Constitution (part 1), which states: "All penalties ought to be proportioned to the nature of the offense. No wise legislature will affix the same punishment to the crimes of theft, forg-ery, and the like, which they do to those of murder and treason. Where the same undistinguishing severity is exerted against all offenses, the people are led to forget the real distinction in the crimes themselves, and to commit the most flagrant with as little compunction as they do the lightest offenses...." The fear that the people will "forget the real distinction" of crimes and commit greater crimes with no greater "compunction" invokes the norm-reinforcing and marginal deterrent values of penalties proportionate to social harm, both of which are implicit ends-proportionality arguments (see further discussion in part F).

2. Illinois Constitutional Sentencing Cases

Article I, Section 11 of the Illinois Constitution declares that "[a]ll penalties shall be determined...according to the seriousness of the offense." The Illinois Supreme Court has concluded that no change in meaning was intended in 1970 when this language was substituted for the provision in the prior (1870) constitu-tion, which called for penalties to be "proportioned to the nature of the offense."[123] Like its predecessor, the current provision is commonly known as the state's proportionate-penalties clause. A penalty violates the proportionate-penalties clause if either of the following tests is met: (1) the penalty "is a cruel or degrading punishment not known to the common law, or is a degrading punishment which had become obsolete in the State prior to the adoption of its constitution, or is so wholly disproportioned to the offense committed as to shock the moral sense of the community";[124] or (2) the offense has a higher penalty than another offense with identical substantive elements.[125]

Neither of these tests bears a close resemblance to any of the factors recog-nized by the U.S. Supreme Court in *Solem v. Helm*; the first test is both narrower and broader than the first *Solem* factor, and neither of the Illinois tests involves comparisons to penalties in other jurisdictions (the third *Solem* factor). Further-more, unlike the modified *Solem* standards adopted by the plurality opinion in *Ewing*, the Illinois constitutional provision and interpretive case law focus entirely on the defendant's current "offense," without consideration of the seriousness of the defendant's prior record.

Several of the proportionality concepts identified in this book may be implicit in the Illinois standards. The final clause of the first Illinois test appears to be based on a limiting retributive theory; the language used ("so wholly disproportioned" as to "shock the moral sense of the community") suggests a criterion based on blameworthiness, and the Illinois Supreme Court has emphasized offender culpability when interpreting this standard.[126]

The second Illinois test may be based more on notions of due process (lack of rational basis; concerns about abuse of prosecutorial discretion) than on proportionality, but it could incorporate all three of the proportionality principles we have identified. If crimes with identical substantive elements receive different penalties, there is a great risk that offenders who receive the more severe penalty have been punished in excess of their deserts (limiting retributive proportionality) and/or that the benefits achieved by the more severe penalty are not worth the greater burdens on defendants (ends benefits), and/or that the greater penalty is not needed to achieve all of the relevant sentencing purposes (alternative means).

For many years the Illinois Supreme Court recognized a third type of state constitutional disproportionality, applicable when two or more offenses have "related" legislative purposes and where "conduct that creates a less serious threat to the public health and safety is punished more harshly."[127] This so-called cross-comparison test involved a more limited form of intrajurisdictional comparison than the second *Solem* factor: Only offenses that reflected related legislative purposes were compared, and the relative severity of crimes was explicitly tied to the social harms caused by each crime. The focus on harm suggested a theory of utilitarian ends-proportionality (which, unlike retributive proportionality, does not give substantial weight to offender culpability; see discussion in part F).

After two decades of experience with the cross-comparison proportionality test, which had been increasingly applied in recent years, the Illinois Supreme Court abandoned that test in *People v. Sharpe*.[128] The court concluded that judicial application of both prongs of this standard ("related" legislative purposes and "less serious threat to the public health and safety") was unworkable and invaded the legislative prerogative to define criminal punishments. The court worried that reviewing courts could not know all of the purposes the legislature had in mind, whether it viewed certain harms or conduct as more serious and what factors it took into account in setting the penalty—in particular, whether greater sentence severity was justified by factors other than social harm, such as recent increases in the frequency of a crime. Perhaps another, unstated reason that cross-comparison review seemed too "legislative" is that most of the cases that invoked this standard were in essence facial attacks on statutory penalties by means of a pretrial motion to dismiss rather than "as applied" attacks on a particular sentence imposed.

The *Sharpe* opinion also cited an earlier decision, *People v. McDonald*,[129] which purported to hold that the proportionate-penalties clause has the same meaning as the Eighth Amendment's cruel and unusual punishment clause. However, *McDonald* was a death penalty case that involved the narrow issue of what mitigating factors defendants have a constitutional right to ask the jury to consider. Moreover, any broad reading of the *McDonald* court's truncation of the scope of the Illinois Constitution would render the broader state constitutional text superfluous and would also be inconsistent with the other two Illinois proportionality tests discussed earlier (especially the "identical elements" test)—both of which the *Sharpe* court reaffirmed.

Curiously, although the *Sharpe* court seemed eager to cut back on the scope of judicial proportionality review, it nevertheless chose not only to retain the two other state proportionality tests but also to revive a due process standard (whether the penalty is "reasonably designed to remedy the particular evil that the legislature was targeting") that preceded the emergence of the cross-comparison test. And while the court stressed that lower courts should not continue to apply the latter in the guise of due process analysis, it seemed to approve of an earlier case in which a due process violation was found on the basis of a comparison of the lower penalty provided for a crime that the legislature clearly considered more serious.[130]

Thus, while the *Sharpe* court rejected a standard that focused entirely on a comparison of seriousness and penalties for different crimes, it did not and probably could not prevent courts from making such comparisons in the course of applying two of the three remaining state constitutional excessive-penalty standards ("shocks the moral sense of the community" and due process). Of course, notwithstanding the *Sharpe* court's strenuous objections to cross-comparison proportionality review, Illinois courts must apply federal constitutional law and thus must continue to compare the seriousness and penalties for other crimes under the second *Solem* standard (which, under *Harmelin* and *Ewing*, becomes applicable once there is a threshold finding of gross disproportionality). Under *Solem-Harmelin-Ewing* and the two state standards, courts will probably continue to compare the purposes, seriousness, and assigned penalties of different crimes despite the *Sharpe* court's concerns about such judicial assessments.

In addition to its limited practical effect, *Sharpe* is a very disappointing and poorly reasoned decision. The court overstated the problems of *People v. Wisslead*,[131] the 1983 case that adopted the cross-comparison test. Moreover, the *Sharpe* opinion's policy arguments, summarized earlier, prove too much (being inconsistent with the three remaining forms of proportionality review). That opinion also failed to consider less drastic solutions to problems that had arisen in post-*Wisslead* case law. Most of that case law was a response to a mass of overlapping and often complex sentencing laws—a development that not only helps explain many of the inconsistencies in the application of cross-comparison proportionality review but also underscores the importance of such review.

The Sharpe court should have disapproved of the reasoning (but not necessarily the results) of some of the post-*Wisslead* cases and should have considered modifying rather than abandoning the cross-comparison standard. That standard should have been restated to require some sort of clear or substantial disproportionality in the treatment of the offenses being compared and perhaps to encourage more frequent "as applied" review in lieu of pretrial facial challenges that invalidate a penalty under all circumstances. Cross-comparison review could also have been limited to closely related crimes, as it is in Oregon.[132] The *Sharpe* court should also have considered revising the overall structure of proportionate-penalties-clause jurisprudence. For instance, the three types of state disproportionality—like the second and third *Solem* prongs—could be viewed not as separate final tests but rather as ways of demonstrating a single, overall standard of unconstitutional excessiveness. In any case, the overall or several standards should have been more clearly defined in terms of retributive and/or utilitarian proportionality principles.

In short, the waxing and waning of the Illinois cross-comparison test underscores not only the difficulty but also the importance of proportionality review. The lesson for other states is not that such review is impossible but rather that it must be done carefully and be based on clear principles. State courts of last resort must also show patience, political courage, and respect for the difficulties faced by lower courts. The *Sharpe* decision reflected none of these virtues.

F. PROPORTIONALITY PRINCIPLES IN SUBCONSTITUTIONAL SENTENCING THEORY, LAW, AND PRACTICE

The state and federal constitutional proportionality rules discussed in parts A thorough E expressly or implicitly reflect well-established principles of law and philosophy. In this part we present a brief survey of the ways in which these principles have been defined and applied in writings on sentencing theory (first section), U.S. subconstitutional sentencing law and practice (second section), and sentencing laws and decisions in other countries (third section).

1. Sentencing Theory

Although some scholars agree with the Supreme Court justices who have asserted that the concept of proportionality applies only under a retributive theory of punishment,[133] many others have recognized one or more nonretributive proportionality concepts, some of which have been proposed as possible constitutional limitations.[134] The following discussion reviews the ways in which both retributive and nonretributive proportionality principles have been or could be applied to limit unreasonably severe penalties. We begin by clarifying the meaning of retributive proportionality, noting two very different versions of retributive theory (only one of which is appropriate for constitutional analysis). We then discuss proportionality concepts in nonretributive sentencing theories.

a. Retributive Proportionality

The English-language literature on retributive punishment theories is extensive.[135] For present purposes, the most important and widely accepted principles of these theories are the following.

First, retributive (or "just deserts") theory, unlike utilitarian or other "consequentialist" theories, considers only defendants' past actions, not their probable future conduct or the effects the punishment might have on crime rates. Second, retributive theory examines the blameworthiness of the defendant's actions and focuses primarily on the offense being sentenced. Some retributive scholars believe that the current offense is the only relevant consideration and that any prior convictions are irrelevant; other scholars hold that prior crimes modestly increase an offender's blameworthiness.[136] Third, the offender's blameworthiness for an offense is generally assessed according to two elements: the nature and seriousness of the harm foreseeably caused or threatened by the crime and the offender's culpability in committing the crime (in particular, the offender's degree of intent (*mens rea*), motives, role in the offense, and mental illness or other diminished capacity).

Finally, there are two very different theories about the role that retributive values should play in sentencing. These two approaches have sometimes been referred to as "defining" and "limiting" retributivism.[137] According to the first theory, principles of just deserts should define the degree of punishment severity as precisely as possible; offenders should receive their just deserts, no more and no less. This theory, as elaborated by writers such as Andrew von Hirsch, permits crime-control, budgetary, or other nonretributive values to affect both the overall scale of punishment severity (absolute amounts, as determined by the most and the least severe penalties) and the choice among penalties deemed to be equal in severity, but it insists on fairly strict ordinal proportionality in the relative severity of penalties imposed on different offenders.[138] Since defining retributivism leaves little room for the operation of nonretributive values and goals, it is clearly too narrow an approach for federal constitutional purposes; the Supreme Court has held that the Eighth Amendment permits states to pursue a variety of sentencing goals.

The other theory, limiting retributivism, allows all traditional punishment purposes to play a role but places outer limits both on who may be punished (only those who are blameworthy)[139] and how hard they may be punished (within a range of penalties that would be widely viewed as neither unfairly severe nor unduly lenient). This theory is most often associated with the writings of Norval Morris, who viewed retributive assessments as imprecise and therefore posited a range of "not undeserved" penalties.[140] Other writers have proposed flexible retributive limits on different grounds, emphasizing the special importance of avoiding unfairly severe penalties. For example, philosopher K.G. Armstrong states that justice grants "the *right* to punish offenders up to some limit, but one is not necessarily and invariably *obliged* to punish to the limit of justice.... For a variety of reasons (amongst them the hope of reforming the criminal) the appropriate authority may choose to punish a man less than it is entitled to, but it is never just to punish a man more than he deserves" (emphasis in original).[141]

As revealed in the cases discussed earlier in this chapter, limiting retributivism appears to be the approach the Supreme Court has applied when it has invoked retributive principles. This approach, which emphasizes limits on excessive measures, is consistent with both the text of the Eighth Amendment and the role of constitutional guarantees as protectors of human rights and bulwarks against unfairness and abuse of governmental power.

b. Nonretributive Proportionality

Nonretributive (utilitarian or consequentialist) purposes of punishment focus on the future: What effect will the proposed sentence have on the offender, on would-be offenders, and/or on society and at what cost?[142] The traditional nonretributive purposes include special (or individual or specific) deterrence, incapacitation, and rehabilitation of this offender (because he is thought likely to commit further crimes), as well as general deterrence of would-be violators (both through fear of receiving similar punishment and by the educative or norm-reinforcing effects that penalties have on views about the relative harmfulness and wrongness of different crimes).[143]

In light of these nonretributive punishment goals, a penalty can be disproportionate (or excessive) in two distinct and independent ways that correspond to ends-benefits and alternative-means proportionality: (1) the costs and burdens of the sentence (or the added costs and burdens compared to a lesser penalty) may outweigh the likely benefits (or added benefits) produced by the sentence; and (2) the sentence may be disproportionate (that is, unnecessary and therefore excessive) when compared to other, less costly or burdensome means of achieving the same goals. Each of these utilitarian proportionality principles has ancient roots.

1) Ends-Proportionality Principles

The eighteenth-century philosopher Cesare Beccaria[144] argued in favor of criminal penalties that are proportional to the seriousness of the offense, as measured by the harm done to society. In the early nineteenth century, Jeremy Bentham made several specific utilitarian arguments that favored punishments proportional to the seriousness of the offense. From the point of view of public resource allocation, "the greater an offence is, the greater reason there is to hazard a severe punishment for the chance of preventing it."[145] Similarly, from the point of view of the suffering imposed on the offender, Bentham argued that "the evil of the punishment [should not exceed] the evil of the offence."[146] He also noted the marginal deterrent value of penalties proportionate to offense severity: Offenders should "have a motive to stop at the lesser" crime.[147]

The utilitarian ends-proportionality principle has some elements in common with retributive proportionality—in particular, both principles require proportionality relative to offense severity. However, the two theories operate quite differently. First, retributive theory considers the harm caused or threatened by the defendant's crimes and considers it just to punish in proportion to that harm; utilitarian theory also argues for punishment in proportion to the harm of the defendant's crimes but only when this will prevent future similar crimes by this offender (through special deterrence, incapacitation, and/or rehabilitation) or will prevent such crimes by others (through general deterrence and norm reinforcement). Moreover, utilitarian theory considers not only the harm associated with a particular act similar to the defendant's but also the aggregate harm caused by all such actions and the difficulty of detecting and deterring these actions.[148] Second, retributive theory punishes in direct proportion not just to the actual or threatened harms associated with the offender's crime but also to his culpability (e.g., intent, motive, role in the offense, diminished capacity). For utilitarians, such culpability factors are relevant only to the extent that they are related to the likely future benefits of punishment (e.g., the dangerousness and deterrability of this offender or others).

Finally, in choosing the proper sentence for a particular offender or group of similar offenders, retributive theory disregards the crime-control benefits, as well as the collateral consequences of imposing punishment; proportionate sanctions are deemed inherently valuable. Utilitarian theory considers not only the actual crime-control or other benefits produced by sanctions but also, as an offset against those benefits, any undesirable collateral consequences of the sanction.[149] One such consequence would be "reverse deterrence" (for instance, if a severe three-strikes law encourages felons to kill arresting officers or potential witnesses). Other possible undesirable consequences of penalties that are grossly or frequently disproportionate to the conviction offense include undermining the public's sense of the relative gravity of different crimes, as well as public loss of respect for and willingness to obey and cooperate with criminal justice authorities. As philosopher H.L.A. Hart has said, "[If] the relative severity of penalties diverges sharply from this rough scale [of proportionality], there is a risk of either confusing common morality or flouting it and bringing the law into contempt."[150]

2) Means-Proportionality Limits on Sentence Severity

This principle recognizes basic utilitarian efficiency values: Among equally effective means to achieve a given end, those that are less costly or burdensome should be preferred. In the punishment context, Norval Morris calls this the principle of parsimony.[151] Cesare Beccaria argued that punishment must be not only proportionate to the crime but also "necessary, the least possible in the circumstances."[152] Jeremy Bentham similarly held that punishment itself is an evil and should be used as sparingly as possible; a measure should not be used if "the same end may be obtained by means more mild."[153] Numerous modern authors and model code drafters have endorsed this principle in some form,[154] and as previous parts of this chapter have shown, unnecessarily-excessive-means arguments appear in numerous statutes and court opinions.

3) Distinguishing Ends- and Means-Proportionality Assessments

Although ends- and means-proportionality assessments are conceptually distinct, some cases might seem to incorporate elements of both. The two proportionality concepts evaluate the excessiveness of a measure in very different ways—relative to the likely benefits and to alternative means of achieving those benefits—but some ends-proportionality assessments also involve comparisons to alternative means. If an allegedly excessive measure adds some additional net benefit but also extra net costs or burdens relative to an alternative measure, the ends-benefits proportionality question is whether the greater costs or burdens of the challenged measure (compared to the alternative measure) exceed (or grossly exceed) the likely added benefits of the challenged measure.

For example, if a court were to conclude that, in a given category of cases, the death penalty adds some constitutionally recognized net benefit that would not be achieved by the alternative of life without parole, the court would then need to ask whether the added costs and burdens of capital punishment in such cases (grossly) exceed the added benefits. On the other hand, if the court concluded that the death penalty adds *no* net benefit that could not be achieved by means of less severe penalties, it would then need to engage in alternative-means analysis, and the question would be whether life without parole (or another effective alternative penalty) is *so much* less severe that the death penalty should be deemed (grossly) disproportionate.

4) Differences Between Public Policy and Constitutional Proportionality Analysis

Utilitarian proportionality principles are defined and applied differently in varying legal contexts and for different purposes. One of the most important distinctions has to do with which kinds of costs and burdens of a government measure are weighed against either the expected benefits or alternative means. For public officials and policy makers the public costs of a measure are very important elements in proportionality analysis: Measures should not cost (including public, as well as privately borne, costs and burdens) more than the benefits they are expected to produce or more than effective alternative measures.

However, when defining a defendant's constitutional right not to be subjected to an excessive sentence, the crime-control and other benefits of the sentence should probably be weighed only against the burdens the sentence imposes on the defendant (ends proportionality), and alternative measures should be examined only in terms of their relative burdens on the defendant (means proportionality). The constitutional argument is that it is fundamentally unfair to impose severe burdens that greatly outweigh the expected public benefits or to impose such burdens when effective alternative measures are much less burdensome. As a matter of sound public policy, it is also unwise, but probably not fundamentally unfair to the defendant, to impose a sentence that costs taxpayers more than the expected benefits are worth or more than an effective alternative.

Another difference between public policy and constitutional proportionality analysis relates to the inherent limits of constitutional limit setting. Public policy may strive for as close a fit as possible between costs and benefits and as efficient a choice as possible among alternative means. However, when courts seek to enforce constitutional proportionality limits on sentencing, they should intervene only if the burdens on the defendant are clearly excessive relative to the benefits or if equally effective alternative sanctions or other measures are clearly less burdensome.[155] These inherent limits on judicial review decisions are reflected (but to an excessive degree) in the Supreme Court's requirements of "gross disproportionality" under the Eighth Amendment.

On the other hand, the appropriate deference courts should pay to policy decisions and case-specific assessments made by legislatures, executive officials, and lower courts must not be used as an excuse for total abdication of judicial responsibility to protect defendants from abuse of governmental power. The limiting retributive and utilitarian proportionality principles described earlier are well established in Anglo-American jurisprudence, and courts should not hesitate to apply them. Nor should they be deterred by the seeming subjectivity of these standards, reflecting the inherent limits of judicial review. A standard of "clear" or "gross" excessiveness, relative to retributive, ends-, and/or means-proportionality principles, is no more subjective than other standards commonly applied by reviewing courts, such as "reasonableness," "compelling state interest," "fair notice," and "abuse of discretion."

2. Sentencing Law and Practice in the United States

In practice and sometimes also in theory, all modern sentencing systems explicitly or implicitly incorporate versions of the limiting retributive and ends-proportionality principles discussed earlier. Many American systems also explicitly recognize the means-proportionality concept of sentencing parsimony.

In so-called indeterminate sentencing systems, which are still the most common sentencing regimes in the United States,[156] the statutory maximum sentence and occasional minimum-sentence requirements set upper and lower limits on sanction severity based solely on the offense of conviction (and in some cases prior convictions). Most of these systems lack an explicit rationale for the statutory maxima and minima, but since these limits are set solely on the basis of offense severity and prior offending, it appears that they reflect (albeit very crudely) retributive and ends-proportionality scaling of sanctions. Within the wide ranges these systems provide, judges and parole boards may tailor the sentence to reflect case-specific utilitarian (crime-control) purposes, as well as case-specific retributive assessments. The survival of so many indeterminate sentencing regimes, despite the widespread loss of faith in the rehabilitative goals that originally justified these systems, is probably due both to institutional inertia and vested interest and to the current popularity of incapacitation and other risk-management theories that, like rehabilitation, are assumed to require substantial case-level discretion. But at least part of the durability of these regimes, despite decades of sustained attack by sentencing theorists and reformers, may be due to the widespread support for a hybrid, limiting-retributive-based approach—one that recognizes desert-based upper and lower limits on sanction severity, within which other sentencing purposes may play a substantial role.

A minority of American jurisdictions have at least partially replaced the indeterminate model with sentencing guidelines or statutory determinate sentencing systems.[157] Guidelines and determinate sentencing systems vary dramatically, but they all involve recommended, proportionally scaled sentencing ranges—sometimes substantially narrower than the previous statutory ranges—based on the offender's conviction offense and prior record. Several state guidelines systems explicitly base the recommended sentences on principles of desert, but all state and federal guidelines systems at least implicitly reflect a limiting retributive model; some also explicitly recognize the principle of parsimony.[158]

The Minnesota Sentencing Guidelines, in effect since 1980, provide a particularly strong example of a successful guidelines-based limiting retributive system in operation, one that incorporates an explicit just deserts basis for sanction scaling, reduced but (especially in practice) still quite substantial sentencing ranges, and an explicit recognition of the parsimony principle. The sentencing regime that has evolved in Minnesota bears a strong resemblance to Norval Morris's limiting retributive model.[159]

3. Foreign Sentencing Laws and Decisions

Each of the three proportionality principles we have identified enjoys widespread support in foreign and international sentencing laws. Although U.S. constitutional requirements must be defined in terms of American legal, political, cultural, and historical traditions, the Supreme Court has occasionally found additional support for its decisions in the laws of other nations and under the terms of international human rights conventions.[160] The following is a brief sampling of foreign and international law proportionality requirements in sentencing.

Recent comparative sentencing scholarship reveals broad support for retributive and means-proportionality principles. There is general agreement among Western nations as to the definition of various crime-control punishment purposes, the most important aggravating and mitigating culpability and harm factors, and the overarching importance of the principles of offense-proportionality and parsimony (as noted earlier, the latter is a form of means proportionality).[161] Proportionality appears to be defined in terms more consistent with limiting than defining retributivism—there is much greater emphasis on avoiding disproportionately severe sentences than unduly lenient ones, and courts are granted considerable flexibility in mitigating penalties and choosing among sanction types.

Sentencing proportionality is also explicitly recognized in international criminal prosecutions. The Statute of the International Criminal Court[162] grants defense and prosecution rights to appeal a sentence on grounds that it is disproportionate to the crime and directs trial courts to take into account factors such as the gravity of the crime and the individual circumstances of the convicted person.

Some excellent examples of constitutional sentencing proportionality requirements can be found in high court decisions from other common law countries. Applying the general proportionality requirements of the Canadian Charter of Rights and Freedoms, the Canadian Supreme Court held in *Smith v. the Queen*[163] that a mandatory seven-year-minimum sentence for importing narcotics violated the charter. In reaching this conclusion, the court appeared to apply limiting retributive, ends-benefits, and alternative-means proportionality standards.

Section 12 of the charter bans "cruel and unusual treatment or punishment." The *Smith* court appears to have assumed that Section 12 imposes a retributive standard and held the mandatory minimum penalty invalid under that standard; since the minimum penalty applied regardless of the drug type or quantity and the offender's purposes or other characteristics, "it is inevitable that, in some cases, a verdict of guilt will lead to the imposition of a term of imprisonment which will be grossly disproportionate" to what the offender deserves.[164]

However, that finding was only the first step in the proportionality analysis. Section 1 of the charter provides that charter rights may be subject to such "reasonable limits as may be demonstrably justified in a free and democratic society." The court in *Smith* found that deterring drug importation was a goal "of sufficient importance to warrant overriding the retributive limits of Section 12 (essentially, an ends-proportionality test).[165] However, the court further held that the means chosen to pursue this goal were unnecessarily severe. Section 1 requires that, to override charter rights, the means chosen should impair those rights as little as possible, and the court held that the mandatory minimum statute in question failed this minimum impairment requirement—"We do not need to sentence the small offenders to seven years in prison in order to deter the serious offender."[166]

Other examples of the application of multiple, independent constitutional sentencing proportionality standards appear in foreign cases that involve dangerous offenders. High courts in Canada, England, and South Africa have upheld lengthy indeterminate prison terms imposed on such offenders only where the conviction offense is very serious (retributive and/or ends proportionality) and provided further that there are provisions for periodic review of the offender's dangerousness so that his detention continues no longer than is necessary to protect the public (means proportionality).[167]

CONCLUSION

ALL WESTERN NATIONS FACE A tension between the need for administrative and penal regulation and the maintenance of individual rights and autonomy. Principles of proportionality have been widely used in other countries to assist courts in reconciling these competing interests and preserving the rule of law, but proportionality principles have been substantially underutilized in the United States.

We have examined the operation of these principles in the law of war, in common law damages rules and antitrust remedies, in foreign jurisdictions, and in various standards of judicial review in American constitutional, statutory, and common law. Explicit and implicit proportionality principles have been applied in many different contexts and take a wide variety of forms, but they all have in common the fundamental value judgment that intrusive government and private actions should not be demonstrably excessive relative to their moral and practical justifications. Our primary emphasis is on the use of proportionality principles as an instrumental method of reviewing excessive government measures. We argue that more precise and consistent definition and application of proportionality principles will permit U.S. courts to better serve their vital roles as guardians of individual liberties and will make judicial review more rigorous, more transparent, and more disciplined.

Explicit principles of proportionality have been only occasionally adopted by U.S. courts. They have never been clearly defined or harmonized. Thus, punitive damages awards must be "reasonable and proportionate"; a standard of "rough proportionality" applies to land-use conditions; federal legislation enacted to enforce rights protected by the Fourteenth Amendment is reviewed for "congruence and proportionality"; and a "gross disproportionality" standard is used when individuals challenge severe criminal penalties and forfeitures of property.

The underdeveloped state of proportionality jurisprudence in the United States is not due to competition from any superior set of principles; there is currently no general theory of what factors or normative concepts permit courts to invalidate a government action on the grounds of excessiveness. Different factors and norms are cited in different legal contexts. Claims, for example, that legislative or executive measures unduly impinge on individual civil rights are subject to varying levels of judicial "scrutiny" (strict, intermediate, rational basis, and variants of each of these); searches and seizures are reviewed under a "reasonableness" standard; and limitations on the imposition of criminal liability are most often based on concepts of "fair notice."

The most widely applied of these standards, invoking varying levels of scrutiny, does not provide a satisfactory basis for a general theory of judicial review because its polar categories (rational basis and strict scrutiny) are inflexible rules, the choice of which is almost always outcome determinative; such rigid rules give judges too little discretion and tend to break down in practice.[1] Moreover, the factors deemed relevant in applying each of these levels of scrutiny assume a purely utilitarian normative framework and consider only the asserted state interests and the degree to which measures are tailored to achieve them. Nonutilitarian concerns, in particular fairness and degrees of individual fault, are excluded.

As a result of these differing and poorly articulated proportionality and other standards, courts are not consistent in carrying out their reviewing functions and face persistent criticisms that their decisions are unprincipled, too "activist," or not active enough.

A closer analysis of the multiple existing standards of judicial review, however, reveals more consistent patterns and a small number of proportionality concepts that are implicit in review standards across many areas of the law. In this book we have identified three basic ways in which government and private measures have been found to be disproportionate: (1) relative to fault (limiting retributive proportionality as to liability or sanction severity); (2) relative to the likely practical benefits of the measure (ends-benefits proportionality); and (3) relative to other ways of achieving the same purposes (alternative-means proportionality). We have examined the many forms these three basic legal proportionality concepts have taken in varying legal contexts and the different ways in which courts have formulated standards of judicial review that embody them. We have sought to categorize, harmonize, and more clearly define both the existing judicial review standards and their underlying proportionality concepts. We conclude that proportionality has all of the prerequisites to serve an instrumental role in checking excessive government action.

The widespread use of proportionality principles in American, foreign, and international law reflects their deep moral and philosophical roots. The variety of ways in which these principles have been formulated also shows that they can be applied to many different legal contexts by providing highly adaptable and useful analytic tools whenever courts and other policy makers are called upon to decide whether a governmental or private measure is excessive. Each principle can be tailored to fit the particular context. In some situations, for example, the high value placed on individual rights at stake justifies a strict version of means proportionality, equal to or approaching a "least restrictive means" requirement. In other contexts, the lesser value of rights and/or very high value of government interests at stake calls for a looser version, for example, requiring the government to choose another effective means only if it is substantially less burdensome (or the chosen means is grossly more burdensome). Courts may also accommodate contextual differences by varying burden-of-proof allocations.

Proportionality principles would be even more useful if their ubiquity, variable forms, and common features were more widely recognized and the principles were defined more clearly. This would permit borrowing of useful formulations developed in other legal contexts and encourage more frequent, more precise, and more consistent application of these principles, thereby improving not only the decisions courts must make but also the way in which those decisions are received and acted upon. Courts must protect citizens from excessive governmental measure without doing either too much or too little. They must also clearly and consistently explain their decisions to uphold or strike down challenged government measures so that these decisions are accepted by citizens and officials and can provide clear guidance for future government action and the resolution of any further challenges. Existing standards of review often fail to meet any of these criteria.

The proportionality principles we have identified incorporate all of the essential features of a unified standard of judicial review that effectively reconciles state and individual interests. As a threshold matter, the German principle of suitability, like the American rational basis test, will invalidate government actions that serve no legitimate public interest. If that test is not met, the challenged measure is invalid with no need to consider more complex proportionality tests. If the suitability test is met and the measure is a form of punishment or other penalty, then limiting retributive liability and severity principles are applied. These principles reflect the fundamental, nonutilitarian value judgment that it is unfair and unacceptable for the state to impose severe punitive measures in the absence of individual culpability or in excess of an individual's degree of culpability. Finally, if the suitability test and retributive limits are satisfied, courts should apply some version of the alternative-means and ends-benefits proportionality principles. These tests, which apply independently, reflect widely shared utilitarian values: A government measure should not be demonstrably more burdensome than necessary to achieve its asserted purposes, nor should the burdens of the measure be excessive in comparison to its probable benefits (given the importance of the asserted purposes, the measure's likely success in achieving those objectives and any negative collateral consequences).

Proportionality principles may be recognized under federal or state constitutional law or as a matter of common law or legislative policy. As our survey of U.S. law demonstrates, there is nothing novel about federal constitutional proportionality review. Moreover, there is no reason that the Supreme Court and lower courts should not explicitly endorse such review in a variety of contexts. Some may object that the principle of proportionality was not mentioned in the Constitution. Of course, neither was "strict scrutiny" or "the evolving standards of decency." The Framers recognized that the Constitution cannot provide for every detail; they also acknowledged that the Constitution's broad provisions are subject to legal rules of interpretation that derive from *common sense* and that the construction of a particular provision must be natural and reasonable.[2] The widespread implicit application of the proportionality principles we have identified shows that they reflect fundamental values in our culture and legal order. It was natural and reasonable for courts to draw upon these principles when interpreting due process, reasonableness, and other constitutional provisions formulated in broad terms. The time has come for courts to recognize such principles explicitly.

There is even more reason to recognize proportionality principles when state courts interpret state constitutional provisions and when courts and legislators deal with issues of nonconstitutional law. These decisions confront no issues of federalism and, since state and local officials are either elected or appointed by elected state or local officials, there are fewer issues of democratic legitimacy than when courts engage in federal constitutional review.

The proposed introduction of explicit proportionality principles will not eliminate judicial deference to the government's factual findings, nor should it. But such deference must not be blind; courts must defer only to well-detailed findings that justify the adopted measure in light of the desired result and available alternative measures. Nor will the use of these proportionality principles eliminate strict scrutiny analysis; that doctrine (which, as we have shown, implicitly incorporates ends- and means-proportionality principles) will be preserved for the matters to which it currently applies. A strong, rulelike presumption of invalidity will continue to protect core fundamental rights and suspect classes from regulatory intrusion. This is in accord with the special treatment of core fundamental rights in jurisdictions such as Germany,[3] which are strongly committed to the application of proportionality principles. In addition, proportionality principles are not needed and will not apply when government measures violate absolute values, such as those that prohibit extremely painful or degrading treatments under all circumstances.

Proportionality will thus operate in matters that are currently governed by rational basis or intermediate scrutiny or that have not been assigned to any of the Court's scrutiny levels (this includes most of the matters discussed in part II and all of the criminal justice matters discussed in part III). Proportionality principles will more effectively safeguard currently underprotected matters of individual autonomy in order to prevent the application of clearly undeserved measures, to lessen regulatory overinclusiveness, and to ensure that the burdens of government measures do not substantially outweigh the likely benefits. Because these features make proportionality analysis substantially superior to the existing systems of constitutional review in the United States, we propose that it be adopted as a general standard of review.

NOTES

INTRODUCTION

1. The concept of the rule of law has many formulations that are classified into formal and substantive theories. Brian Z. Tamanaha, On the Rule of Law: History, Politics, Theory 91 (Cambrige Univ. Press 2004). The central concept of the formal theory of the rule of law is formal legality: All government action is based on general, prospective, clear, and certain rules (idem). Substantive theories, in addition to formal legality, impose substantive restrictions on legal rules (idem). The "thickest" substantive theory of the rule of law, called the "social welfare" theory, promotes "substantive equality, welfare, and preservation of community" (idem). As such, a universal model of the rule of law exists not as a solid concept but as a combination of three "themes" necessary for any theory of the rule of law to function: government limited by law, formal legality, and rule of law, not people (idem at 114–26). In most modern liberal democracies, the concept of the rule of law—despite some tension between democracy and individual rights, mainly because the latter may be curtailed by democratic process and thus are threatened by it—assumes an interaction of formal legality, democracy, and individual rights (idem at 104–108, 110). Welfare states go even further by combining the rule of law with distributive equality—two values that are not mutually exclusive—to provide all of their citizens with an equal start (idem at 120).

The universal model of the rule of law would necessarily include a proportionality tool. Proportionality would be required for the rule of law theories that
include a notion of individual rights and/or distributive equality to provide a
mechanism to rationally limit government discretion. *See* idem ("Rule of law systems can also accommodate doing justice in an individual case, so long as the
[formal] rules of law are departed from to achieve justice infrequently, under
compelling circumstances."). *See also* Vicki C. Jackson, *Being Proportional about
Proportionality*, 21 CONST. COMMENT. 803 (2004) (book review) (describing the
way in which proportionality is becoming a term of art in constitutional law).

2. Formal legality requires "generality, clarity, public promulgation, stability over
time, consistency between the rules and the actual conduct of legal actors, and
prohibitions against retroactivity, against contradictions, and against requiring the impossible." TAMANAHA, *supra* note 1, at 93 (citing LON L. FULLER, THE
MORALITY OF LAW ch. 2 (2d rev. ed., Yale Univ. Press 1969)).

3. This goal is consistent with the substantive understanding of the rule of law.
TAMANAHA, *supra* note 1, at 91.

4. *See generally* DAVID M. BEATTY, THE ULTIMATE RULE OF LAW (Oxford Univ. Press
2004) (advocating for the application of the principle of proportionality as the
standard of review; also discussing the principle's history in the United States).

5. *See, e.g.,* Timmons v. Twin Cities Area New Party, 520 U.S. 351, 358 (1997) (holding
that regulations that impose severe burdens on associational rights protected by
the First Amendment must pass strict scrutiny). However, as noted in text, *infra*,
enumerated "liberty" rights receive relatively little constitutional protection once
a person has been found guilty of a criminal offense.

6. *See* Washington v. Glucksberg, 521 U.S. 702, 720–21 (1997).

7. *See* Roger P. Alford, *In Search of a Theory for Constitutional Comparativism*, 52
UCLA L. REV. 639, 660 (2005) (stating that the natural law theory of individual
autonomy is generally discredited as a constitutional theory).

8. *See* Lawrence v. Texas, 539 U.S. 558, 578 (2003) ("[The] right to liberty under the
Due Process Clause gives [homosexuals] the full right to engage in their conduct
without intervention of the government. 'It is a promise of the Constitution that
there is a realm of personal liberty which the government may not enter'" (quoting Planned Parenthood of Southeastern Pa. v. Casey, 505 U.S. 833, 847 (1992)).
This has not prevented constitutional scholars from interpreting the Court's reference to "implicit ordered liberty" as an indicator of its implicit acceptance of the
principles of natural human rights:

> Indeed, *Lawrence* suggests that natural law theory has continued cur-
> rency in constitutional jurisprudence. Liberty is defined in its broad-
> est "transcendent dimensions" to include "freedom of thought,
> belief, expression, and certain intimate conduct" (*Lawrence*, 539 U.S.
> at 562). *Lawrence* offers a theory of constitutional anthropology that
> endows personhood with the freedom to define "one's own concept of

existence, of meaning, of the universe, and of the mystery of human life." *Lawrence*, 539 U.S. at 574. "[M]ore than any other decision in the Supreme Court's history" *Lawrence* also "presuppose[s] and advance[s] an explicitly equality-based...theory of substantive liberty." Laurence H. Tribe, *Lawrence v. Texas, The "Fundamental Right" That Dare Not Speak Its Name*, 117 HARV. L. REV. 1893, 1898 (2004). It all but embraces a Millean libertarianism that counsels against state attempts to impose relational boundaries absent injury to persons or protected institutions. *Lawrence*, 539 U.S. at 567; idem at 599 (Scalia, J., dissenting); Tribe, *supra* at 1938 & n.174.

Alford, *supra* note 7, at 671–72 (alterations in original).

9. *See, e.g.,* Griswold v. Connecticut, 381 U.S. 479, 519–20 (1965) (Black, J., dissenting).

10. "The enumeration in the Constitution, of certain rights, shall not be construed to deny or disparage others retained by the people." U.S. CONST. amend. IX.

11. *See* Roe v. Wade, 410 U.S. 113, 152–53 (1973) (listing the decisions in which the Court or individual justices found the constitutional roots of the fundamental rights—in this case, the right to privacy—by using a variety of constitutional provisions or theories, including finding the roots of the right of privacy in the First Amendment (*see* Stanley v. Georgia, 394 U.S. 557, 564 (1969)); in the Fourth and Fifth amendments (*see, e.g.,* Terry v. Ohio, 392 U.S. 1, 8–9 (1968)); in the penumbras of the Bill of Rights (*Griswold*, 381 U.S. at 484–85); and showing that the only reference to the Ninth Amendment for support in establishing an unenumerated right may be found in the concurrence of Justice Goldberg in *Griswold*, 381 U.S. at 486 (Goldberg, J., concurring)). *See also* Justice Douglas's statement in his dissent in *Olff v. East Side Union High School District* that the word "liberty," while not defined in the Constitution, contains the fundamental rights retained by the people under the Ninth Amendment (404 U.S. 1042, 1044 (1972) (Douglas, J., dissenting)) (quoting *Griswold*, 381 U.S. at 484). In his concurrence in *Griswold*, Justice Goldberg pointed out the fallacy of this concern, explaining that the Ninth Amendment is not to be used as an independent source of fundamental rights but rather that it textually demonstrates that there are unenumerated rights protected by the Constitution, determined on the basis of "'traditions and (collective) conscience of our people'" to be so fundamental that they "cannot be denied without violating those 'fundamental principles of liberty and justice which lie at the base of all our civil and political institutions'" (381 U.S. at 492–94 (Goldberg, J., concurring)) (citations omitted).

12. *See* United States v. Carolene Products Co., 304 U.S. 144, 152 (1938) ("[R]egulatory legislation affecting ordinary commercial transactions is not to be pronounced unconstitutional unless in the light of the facts made known or generally assumed it is of such a character as to preclude the assumption that it rests upon some rational basis within the knowledge and experience of the legislators.").

13. Constitutional limits on lengthy prison terms are further discussed in chapter 7.

14. United States v. Carolene Products Co., *supra*, 304 U.S. at 152.

15. *See* idem at 153 n.4. Criminal defendants, even prior to conviction, have not been deemed a vulnerable minority in need of special protection, even though they are precisely the kind of despised and powerless group that will not be adequately protected by normal political processes. *See* Richard S. Frase, *Excessive Prison Sentences, Punishment Goals, and the Eighth Amendment: "Proportionality" Relative to What?* 89 Minn. L. Rev. 571, 648–49 (2005), and *infra* part III.

16. United States v. Virginia, 518 U.S. 515 (1996).

17. Pike v. Bruce Church, Inc., 397 U.S. 137 (1970).

18. United States v. O'Brien, 391 U.S. 367 (1968).

19. *See* State Farm Mut. Auto. Ins. Co. v. Campbell, 538 U.S. 408 (2003); BMW of N. Am., Inc. v. Gore, 517 U.S. 559 (1996).

20. Dolan v. City of Tigard, 512 U.S. 374 (1994).

21. *See* Bajakajian v. United States, 524 U.S. 321 (1998).

22. *See, e.g.,* Solem v. Helm, 463 U.S. 277, 284–86 (1983) ("The Eighth Amendment…prohibits not only barbaric punishments, but also sentences that are disproportionate to the crime committed…. The principle that a punishment should be proportionate to the crime is deeply rooted and frequently repeated in common-law jurisprudence."); *see also* Roper v. Simmons, 543 U.S. 551 (2005) (holding that the Eighth and Fourteenth amendments prohibit as disproportionate the imposition of the death penalty on offenders who were under the age of eighteen when they committed the crime subject to that penalty). *But see* Ewing v. California, 538 U.S. 11, 31–32 (2003) (concurring opinions of Scalia and Thomas, JJ, concluding that the Eighth Amendment contains no proportionality guarantee). The Court's Eighth Amendment punishment decisions are further discussed in chapter 7.

23. City of Boerne v. Flores, 521 U.S. 507, 545 (1997).

24. The many examples of explicit and implicit proportionality principles in U.S., foreign, regional, and international law are discussed in several of the authors' published works. *See, e.g.,* E. Thomas Sullivan, *Antitrust Remedies in the U.S. and the E.U.: Advancing a Standard of Proportionality*, 48 ANTITRUST BULLETIN 377, 414–20 (2003); Frase, *supra* note 15 at 598–627.

25. Chapter 7 provides a more detailed discussion of these proportionality principles.

26. *See* HCJ 2056/04, Village Council v. Gov't of Israel, 58(5) P.D. 807, para. 44 (statement of applicable proportionality principles) and paras. 59–61 (application of the principles to alternative measures that are not equally effective). This decision is also available in (2004) 43 I.L.M. 1099.

27. The intensity of proportionality review depends in large part on how clearly the principle is defined; "[o]bviously, the more accurately the principle of proportionality is defined, the more intensive the judicial review effected thereby will be." Walter van Gerven, *The Effect of Proportionality on the Actions of Member States of the European Community: National Viewpoints from Continental Europe,*

in THE PRINCIPLE OF PROPORTIONALITY IN THE LAWS OF EUROPE 37, 61 (Evelyn Ellis ed., Hart 1999). It follows, then, that a legal system that incorporates the principle of proportionality may choose "how sophisticated the proportionality principle" should be (idem). Van Gerven has posited that the "constitutional nature of the legal system concerned, [] the nature of the acts to be assessed…, [] the importance of the interests involved and [] the variety of interests to be taken into account" should inform a system's decision about the appropriate intensity of proportionality review (idem).

28. *See generally* Jackson, *supra* note 1, at 835–42; Kathleen M. Sullivan, *The Justices of Rules and Standards*, 106 HARV. L. REV. 22 (1992).

29. NICHOLAS EMILIOU, THE PRINCIPLE OF PROPORTIONALITY IN EUROPEAN LAW: A COMPARATIVE STUDY 142 (Kluwer Law Int'l 1996).

30. Despite the reluctance of some members of the Supreme Court to allow American legal theory to borrow from the experience of other nations, information about foreign and international experience has been seeping into the high court's opinions to aid in the development of methods for treatment of issues already faced by foreign or international courts. See a recent debate between Justice Scalia and Justices Kennedy and O'Connor, on the place of international and foreign experience in the Court's Eighth Amendment jurisprudence, in Roper v. Simmons, 543 U.S. 551 (2005). *See also* Vicki C. Jackson, *Ambivalent and Comparative Constitutionalism: Opening Up the Conversation on "Proportionality," Rights and Federalism*, 1 U. PA. J. CONST. L. 583 (1999) (exploring the reasons for the "ambivalent resistance of U.S. constitutional law to explicit learning and borrowing from other nations' constitutional decisions and traditions").

PART I

1. HUGO GROTIUS, THE RIGHTS OF WAR AND PEACE INCLUDING THE LAW OF NATURE AND OF NATIONS (1625) (M. Walter Dunne 1901).

2. *See infra* notes 74–75 of chapter 1 and accompanying text.

3. *See infra* notes 92–104 of chapter 1 and accompanying text.

4. *See infra* ch. 3.

5. Idem.

6. *See infra* ch. 4.

CHAPTER 1

1. CICERO, ON OBLIGATIONS bk. 1, § 11, *available at* http://www.oup.co.uk/pdf/ 0-19-924018-3.pdf. *See also* ST. AUGUSTINE, CITY OF GOD, bk. 19, ch. 12, *available at* http://www.ccel.org/ccel/schaff/npnf102.iv.XIX.12.html; 2 PIERINO BELLI, A TREATISE ON MILITARY MATTERS AND WARFARE 59 (Herbert C. Nutting trans., Milford 1936) (writing that "in war there is no other objective than peace, and there is no peace apart from justice…").

2. Cicero, *supra* note 1, bk. 1, § 11.

3. *See* Rebecca Grant, *In Search of Lawful Targets*, 86 Air Force Magazine 38, 38 (2003), *available at* http://www.afa.org/magazine/feb2003/02targets03.pdf ("The first concepts of lawful conduct in war sought to make war an instrument of national policy rather than just an exercise in barbarity").

4. St. Augustine, *supra* note 1.

5. Idem, bk. 19, ch. 7.

6. Idem.

7. St. Thomas Aquinas, The Summa Theologica (Benziger Bros. ed. 1947).

8. Idem, Second Part of the Second Part, question 40, art. 1.

9. Idem.

10. Idem.

11. Idem.

12. Idem.

13. Idem.

14. Idem.

15. Idem (quoting Augustine).

16. Idem.

17. Hugo Grotius, De Jure Belli ac Pacis (On the Law of War and Peace) (1625) (Francis W. Kelsey trans., Clarendon 1925), *available at* http://www.lonang.com/exlibris/grotius/gro-102.htm.

18. "Throughout the Christian world I observed a lack of restraint in relation to war, such as even barbarous races should be ashamed of; I observed that men rush to arms for slight causes, or no cause at all, and that when arms have once been taken up there is no longer any respect for law, divine or human; it is as if, in accordance with a general decree, frenzy had openly been let loose for the committing of all crimes." Hugo Grotius, Prolegomena to the Law of War and peace 21 (Oskar Piest ed., Francis W. Kelsey trans., Liberal Arts Press 1957) (hereinafter Prolegomena).

19. Idem.

20. Idem at 18. Quite similarly, Sir Robert Phillimore, member of Her Majesty's Honorable Privy Council and Judge of the High Court of Admiralty, described war as an "exercise of the international right of action, to which, from the nature of the thing and the absence of any common superior tribunal, nations are compelled to have recourse, in order to assert and vindicate their rights." 3 Sir Robert Phillimore, Commentaries upon International Law 77 (2d ed. 1873).

21. Prolegomena, *supra* note 18, at 18.

22. Hugo Grotius, The Rights of War and Peace Including the Law of Nature and of Nations (1625) (M. Walter Dunne 1901), bk. 1, ch. 1, § 3, *available at* http://oll.libertyfund.org/index.php?option=com_staticxt&staticfile=show.php%3Ftitle=553&Itemid=27.

23. Idem.

24. Idem.

25. Idem, bk. 1, ch. 2, § 1.

26. Idem, § 3.

27. Idem, § 2.

28. Idem, § 5.

29. Idem, bk. 2, ch. 22, § 17 ("It is necessary to observe that a war may be just in its origin, and yet the intentions of its authors may become unjust in the course of its prosecution.... It is laudable, for instance, to maintain national honour; it is laudable to pursue a public or a private interest, and yet those objects may not form the justifiable grounds of the war in question").

30. Idem, bk. 1, ch. 3, §§ 4–5. *Accord* BELLI, *supra* note 1, at 6–11 (contending that, in general, sovereignty creates the right to declare war); PHILLIMORE, *supra* note 20, at 77.

31. GROTIUS, *supra* note 22, bk. 2, ch. 22, § 4.

32. Idem, bk. 2, ch. 24, § 4.

33. Phillimore established the requirements of a just war as follows: that a war be waged by proper authority to restore a violated right and order among the states and that the means "must be in strict conformity with this end." PHILLIMORE, *supra* note 20, at 77–78.

34. GROTIUS, *supra* note 22, bk. 2, ch. 1, § 2.

35. Idem, bk. 2, ch. 1, § 16.

36. HUGO GROTIUS, DE JURE BELLI AC PACIS (ON THE LAW OF WAR AND PEACE) (1625) bk. 1, ch. 2, § 8 (Francis W. Kelsey trans., Clarendon 1925), *available at* http://www.lonang.com/exlibris/grotius/gro-102.htm.

37. GROTIUS, *supra* note 22, bk. 2, ch. 1, § 16.

38. Idem, § 17.

39. Idem.

40. Idem, bk. 2, ch. 23, § 6.

41. Idem, §§ 7–10.

42. Idem, bk. 2, ch. 24, § 4.

43. Idem, § 5.

44. Grotius did not use the word "proportionality" in this regard. Yet, the essence of the principles he elucidated in his treatise is quite similar to the present-day requirement of proportionality.

45. GROTIUS, *supra* note 22, bk. 2, ch. 24, § 5.

46. Idem.

47. Idem.

48. Idem.

49. Idem, § 9.

50. Idem, bk. 3, ch. 1, § 2.

51. Judith Gail Gardam, *Proportionality and Force in International Law*, 87 AM. J. INT'L L. 391, 397 (1993).

52. In fact, the full name of the convention is the Convention for the Amelioration of the Condition of Soldiers Wounded in Armies in the Field. PHILLIMORE, *supra* note 20, at 157.

53. Geneva Convention of 1864, art. I, reprinted in PHILLIMORE, *supra* note 20, at 157–60.

54. Idem, art. V, reprinted in PHILLIMORE, *supra* note 20, at 158. Four years later, the international community addressed—in the St. Petersburg Declaration of 1868 Renouncing the Use, in Time of War, of Explosive Projectiles under 400 Grammes Weight, *available at* http://www.icrc.ch/IHL.nsf/FULL/130?OpenDocument (hereinafter Declaration)—the concept of military objective, whose importance lies in its being a benchmark against which to measure the proportionality of military means. *See infra* note 97 and accompanying text (showing the correlation between the principles of proportionality and military objective in the Geneva Convention of 1949). The document recognized weakening of the enemy's military forces as the only legitimate military objective. Military force could not be used uselessly to "aggravate the sufferings of disabled men, or render their death inevitable." Declaration, *supra.*

55. PHILLIMORE, *supra* note 20, at 83.

56. Idem at 155.

57. Idem at 156.

58. Hague Convention respecting the Laws and Customs of War on Land, pmbl., Oct. 18, 1907, 36 Stat. 2277, 1 Bevans 631, *available at* http://www.icrc.ch/IHL.nsf/FULL/195?OpenDocument (hereinafter the Hague Convention).

59. Idem. The fact that the conventions codify the customary rules of war probably means these rules also apply to nonsignatory parties.

60. This convention was adopted at both peace conferences at The Hague. As the 1907 version made very few insignificant alterations in the text of the convention adopted in 1899, we refer to the 1907 text of the convention.

61. The Hague Convention, *supra* note 58, art. 22.

62. In line with the Geneva Convention of 1864, the Hague Convention prohibited the killing of surrendering enemy combatants (idem, art. 23(c)). It also banned the use of poison and poisoned weapons (idem, art. 23(a)) and condemned bombardment or attack by any other means of undefended cities (idem, art. 25). Moreover, it obliged military commanders to warn the authorities, "except in cases of assault," of any impending bombardment (idem, art. 26).

63. The Hague Convention specifically prohibited any seizure or destruction of enemy property "unless such destruction or seizure be imperatively demanded by the necessities of war" (idem, art. 23(g)).

64. Brian D. Orend, *War*, in THE STANFORD ENCYCLOPEDIA OF PHILOSOPHY (Summer 2002 ed., Edward N. Zalta ed.), http://plato.stanford.edu/archives/sum2002/entries/war (hereinafter War).

65. Idem.

66. While this is true, Judith G. Gardam argues that "the emergence, during the nineteenth century, of the opinion that resort to war was a sovereign right of states did not relegate proportionality in its *jus ad bellum* sense entirely to disuse." Gardam, *supra* note 51, at 403. Gardam wrote that the doctrine of proportionality found its

jus ad bellum application in the customary rules of resorting to force that emerged, referring particularly to the *Caroline* incident (idem; see also *infra* notes 68–71 and accompanying text describing the *Caroline* incident).

67. *See* Gardam, *supra* note 51, at 403 (writing that the doctrine of proportionality worked with the customary rules providing justifications for uses of force).

68. Nicholas J. S. Davies, *The Crime of War: From Nuremberg to Fallujah*, Online Journal (2004), http://onlinejournal.com/artman/publish/article_82.shtml (last visited Mar. 20, 2008).

69. Idem.

70. Idem.

71. Idem (second omission in original).

72. None of the international documents adopted during the period between the two world wars added anything new to the application of the principle of proportionality in the law of armed conflict. However, other related measures were taken by the international community, including the prohibition of the use of asphyxiating, poisonous, or other gases and of bacteriological methods of warfare, as well as the adoption in 1929 of a new Convention for the Amelioration of the Condition of the Wounded and Sick in Armies in the Field and a new Convention relative to the Treatment of Prisoners of War. *See* International Committee of the Red Cross, International Humanitarian Law—Treaties & Documents, http://www.icrc.org/ihl.nsf/TOPICS?OpenView (last visited Mar. 20, 2008), for the full text of these and other treaties and international documents.

73. *See supra* note 2 and accompanying text.

74. UN Charter, art. 2, para. 4, *available at* http://www.un.org/aboutun/charter.

75. Idem, art. 51.

76. *See* War, *supra* note 64.

77. *See, e.g.*, Military and Paramilitary Activities in and Against Nicaragua (Nicar. v. U.S.), 1986 I.C.J. 14, 94 (June 27).

78. Idem.

79. Idem at 122–23.

80. Idem at 120–23.

81. Idem at 122–23.

82. Idem at 123.

83. Oil Platforms (Iran v. U.S.), 2003 I.C.J. 161, 198 (Nov. 6).

84. The incident occurred in the midst of the Iran-Iraq War.

85. *Oil Platforms*, 2003 I.C.J. at 175.

86. Idem at 175–76.

87. Idem at 196–97.

88. Idem at 198.

89. Idem.

90. Idem.

91. Idem at 198–99.

92. Legality of the Threat or Use of Nuclear Weapons, Advisory Opinion, 1996 I.C.J. 226, 259 (July 8) (hereinafter *Advisory Opinion*).

93. Gardam, *supra* note 51, at 411.

94. *Advisory Opinion*, 1996 I.C.J. at 266.

95. The International Criminal Tribunal for the Former Yugoslavia confirmed this view. Prosecutor v. Galic, Case No. IT-98-29-T, Judgment, ¶ 58 n.104 (2003) (hereinafter Prosecutor v. Galic). The provisions of Article 57(2)(a)(iii) and (b) of Additional Protocol I require that a party refrain or cancel an attack if it is anticipated to cause "loss of civilian life, injury to civilians, damage to civilian objects, or a combination thereof, which would be excessive to the concrete and direct military advantage anticipated."

96. The decision by a commander or other responsible person must be judged at the time it was made. This is in line with the language "an attack which may be expected to cause incidental loss" used in Articles 51(5)(b), 57(2)(a)(iii) and (b) of Additional Protocol I to the Geneva Convention of 1949.

97. Additional Protocol I to the Geneva Convention of 1949 art. 51(5)(b), *available at* http://www.icrc.ch/IHL.nsf/FULL/470?OpenDocument (hereinafter Protocol I); *see also* Prosecutor v. Galic, *supra* note 95, ¶ 58 ("The basic obligation to spare civilians and civilian objects as much as possible must guide the attacking party when considering the proportionality of an attack."); 11 TRIALS OF WAR CRIMINALS BEFORE THE NUREMBERG MILITARY TRIBUNALS 1253–54 (1950) ("There must be some reasonable connection between the destruction of property and the overcoming of enemy forces").

98. Protocol I, *supra* note 97, art. 51(5)(b).

99. Gardam, *supra* note 51, at 407. *But see* U.S. DEP'T OF DEFENSE, CONDUCT OF THE PERSIAN GULF WAR: FINAL REPORT TO CONGRESS 697 (1992), *available at* http://www.ndu.edu/library/epubs/cpgw.pdf (hereinafter DEFENSE REPORT) (recognizing that the principle of proportionality "prohibits military action in which the negative effects...*clearly* outweigh the military gain" and arguing that the balancing may be done "in overall terms against campaign objectives") (emphasis added).

100. Protocol I, *supra* note 97, art. 53. The article also prohibits the use of these objects in support of military effort. This prohibition applies to both the attacker and the defender.

101. Idem, art. 54.

102. Idem, art. 55. The Department of Defense explains that this provision is "not intended to prohibit battlefield damage caused by conventional operations." DEFENSE REPORT, *supra* note 99 at 714.

103. Protocol I, *supra* note 97, art. 56(1) ("Works or installations containing dangerous forces, namely dams, dykes and nuclear electrical generating stations, shall not be made the object of attack, even where these objects are military objectives, if such attack may cause the release of dangerous forces and consequent severe losses among the civilian population"). The protection ceases when these facilities are

employed in direct, regular, and significant support of military operations and no other feasible way exists to stop this support (idem, art. 56(2)).

104. Even when targeting legitimate military targets, any "excessive long-term damage to the economic infrastructure and natural environment with a consequential adverse effect on the civilian population" should be avoided. International Criminal Tribunal for the Former Yugoslavia (ICTY): Final Report to the Prosecutor by the Committee Established to Review the NATO Bombing Campaign Against the Federal Republic of Yugoslavia, 39 I.L.M. 1257, 1263 (2000) (hereinafter Final Report). The extent of allowable damage to the natural environment depends on the importance of the selected military target (idem). Any alternative, less-damaging means of warfare must also be considered, though to be required they would have to be equally effective in attaining the military objective (idem). The commander has a certain amount of operational discretion in selecting the military target and balancing the likely damage with the benefit from the completed military operation (idem).

105. Prosecutor v. Galic, *supra* note 95, ¶ 58.

106. Final Report, *supra* note 104, at 1271.

107. Idem.

108. According to Article 58 of Protocol I, *supra* note 97, parties to the conflict are required to remove civilians under their control from the vicinity of military objectives.

109. Prosecutor v. Galic, *supra* note 95, ¶ 61; Final Report, *supra* note 104, at 1271.

110. Final Report, *supra* note 104, at 1271–72.

111. Idem. *But see supra* note 99 and accompanying text.

112. Final Report, *supra* note 104, at 1282–83.

113. Idem at 1283. The specific incidents include the attack on a passenger train in Grdelica Gorge on Apr. 12, 1999 (10 civilians killed, 15 injured; idem at 1273); the attack on the Djakovica Convoy on Apr. 14, 1999 (approximately 70–74 civilians killed; idem at 1275); the bombing of the Serbian TV and radio station RTS (estimated 17 civilians killed; idem at 1277); and the attack on the Chinese embassy in Belgrade on May 7, 1999 (3 Chinese citizens killed; idem at 1280).

114. Gardam, *supra* note 51, at 409.

115. Idem.

116. Idem. *See also* Roger Normand & Chris af Jochnick, *The Legitimation of Violence: A Critical Analysis of the Gulf War*, 35 Harv. Int'l L.J. 387 (1994) (arguing that the U.S. military engaged in unnecessary destruction of Iraqi civilian infrastructure to "achieve economic or political objectives, rather than simply attacking military targets to defeat the Iraqi Army"). Realizing the importance of environmental protection against the effects of weapons used in armed conflict, the International Court of Justice held that "while the existing international law relating to the protection and safeguarding of the environment does not specifically prohibit the use of nuclear weapons, it indicates important environmental factors that are properly to be taken into account in the context of the implementation of the

principles and rules of the law applicable in armed conflict." *Advisory Opinion*, *supra* note 92, at 243. The United States Department of Defense attempted to justify the collateral civilian casualties and damage, arguing that they are inevitable when civilian and military objects are mingled together, a situation very often present in modern society. DEFENSE REPORT, *supra* note 99, at 702. The Defense Department named several reasons that, in its opinion, justified the collateral civilian casualties and damage in the Persian Gulf War (idem). First, it contended that many objects in modern society have mixed military and civilian use (idem). For example, it noted that destruction of facilities essential to civilian life, such as bridges, highways, electrical power grids, and communications facilities, was vital because they also had significant military functions (idem). A number of these facilities were located in urban areas, which increased the number of civilian casualties during the aerial attacks (idem). Second, it accused the Iraqi regime of using Iraqi and Kuwaiti civilian populations as shields of military objects and intentionally commingling civilian and military objects (idem at 699). The Defense Report stated that "[t]he presence of civilians will not render a target immune from attack" and that both the attacker and the defender are responsible to minimize civilian casualties: the attacker—by discriminating military targets and ensuring that minimal damage is done to civilian population and facilities; and the defender—by separating civilian population and objects from military objects (idem at 701). In its analysis, the Defense Department relied on customary international law because neither Iraq nor the United States was at the time a party to Protocol I, of which Article 49(1) impliedly imposes the obligation to minimize civilian casualties on both the attacker and the defender (idem at 691).

117. THE NATIONAL SECURITY STRATEGY OF THE UNITED STATES OF AMERICA 6 (September 2002) (hereinafter NAT'L SECURITY STRATEGY).

118. Idem.

119. At the same time, no previous president has ever foresworn the use of a preemptive strike, even the first use of tactical nuclear weapons in the European theater. *See* Todd E. Pettys, *Our Anticompetitive Patriotism*, 39 U.C. DAVIS L. REV. 1353, 1404 (2006) (quoting Senator John Kerry, presidential debate in Coral Gables, Florida, 40 WEEKLY COMP. PRES. DOC. 2175, 2188 (Sept. 30, 2004)). Forswearing the first use of such weapons, it is argued, would weaken the "deterrence" rationale. *See Strategic Deterrence and Nuclear War*, 76 AM. SOC. INT'L L. PROCEEDINGS 23, 26 (Apr. 22–24, 1982) (comments by Eugene V. Rostow, director, U.S. Arms Control and Disarmament Agency).

But clearly, not ruling out a preemptive strike is not the same as asserting it as an explicit, muscular foreign policy. Moreover, an overly aggressive explication of preemptive strike can have a counterintuitive effect on deterrence by causing other nations to take action to deter one—as in the case today of Iran and North Korea. In short, the intended deterrent effect can be undercut.

120. NAT'L SECURITY STRATEGY, *supra* note 117, at 15.

121. Idem. *Accord* GROTIUS, *supra* note 22, bk. 2, ch. 1, § 16; Neta C. Crawford, *Just War Theory and the U.S. Counterterror War*, 1/1 PERSPECTIVES ON POLITICS 5, 14 (March 2003).

122. NAT'L SECURITY STRATEGY, *supra* note 117, at 15.

123. Crawford, *supra* note 121, at 7.

124. NAT'L SECURITY STRATEGY, *supra* note 117, at 15. One question that remains is whether attacking sovereign states that show some association with and support of the terrorist groups comports with the principles of just war. *See* Crawford, *supra* note 121 (discussing the weaknesses of the preemptive war doctrine and recognizing that the concept of "just war" may significantly reduce the proportionality of self-defense because, when the declared mission is so broad as fighting evil, the "self-defense and preemption tend to expand and may lead to military excess as 'the search for a perfect or utopian (and perhaps one-sided) peace leads to the unnecessary prolongation and intensification of war'") (citation omitted).

125. Idem.

126. *See* GROTIUS, *supra* note 22, bk. 2, ch. 1, § 17.

127. *See* Jim Rutenberg, *Conceding Missteps, Bush Urges Patience on Iraq*, N.Y. TIMES, Oct. 26, 2006, A1.

128. *See* RON SUSKIND, THE ONE PERCENT DOCTRINE (Simon & Schuster 2006).

129. NAT'L SECURITY STRATEGY, *supra* note 117, at 15. *Cf.* Crawford, *supra* note 121, at 8–12 (noting that some believe that the concept of war has been transformed after Sept. 11 because war is no longer always fought against a visible adversary—a sovereign state—which has a well-defined territory, identifiable army, and the need for mobilization to launch an attack).

130. Colin L. Powell, *U.S. Forces: Challenges Ahead*, 71 FOREIGN AFFAIRS 32, 40 (1992) ("Wars kill people. That is what makes them different from all other forms of human enterprise.").

131. GROTIUS, *supra* note 22, bk. 2, ch. 23, §§ 7–10. *See also* idem, ch. 24, § 4.

132. Colin Powell served as a military advisor to Secretary Weinberger, who in 1984 articulated the six-part Weinberger Doctrine, which would be used to determine when and how to commit U.S. troops: "(1) vital national interests must be at stake; (2) overwhelming force must be employed to ensure victory; (3) political and military objectives must be clearly defined; (4) force structures and dispositions must be adjusted as events on the ground dictate; (5) there must be 'some reasonable assurance' of public and congressional support; (6) force must be the last resort." ROBERT C. DIPRIZIO, ARMED HUMANITARIANS: U.S. INTERVENTIONS FROM NORTHERN IRAQ TO KOSOVO 3 (Johns Hopkins Univ. Press 2002) (citing Casper W. Weinberger, "The Uses of Military Power," address to the National Press Club, Washington, D.C., Nov. 28, 1984).

133. Powell, *supra* note 130, at 38.

134. *See* DIPRIZIO, *supra* note 132, at 3.

135. Powell, *supra* note 130, at 40.

136. Idem.

137. *See supra* note 114 and accompanying text.

138. *See supra* notes 43–47 and accompanying text.

139. Powell, *supra* note 130, at 37–38.

140. Idem at 38.

141. Idem.

142. The principle of proportionality has also found its way into a field related to the law of war—international countermeasures. The International Court of Justice applied the principle of proportionality to countermeasures in *The Gabcikovo-Nagymaros Project* (Hung./Slovk.), 1997 I.C.J. 7 (Feb. 5). The court said that a countermeasure must be proportionate to the injury suffered, taking into account the importance of the violated right. *The Gabcikovo-Nagymaros Project, supra* at 56. The court particularly held that Czechoslovakia unilaterally violated the principle of proportionality controlling a shared resource by preventing Hungary from enjoying its equitable share of the use of the Danube River (idem). According to the court, countermeasures are to be measured in relation to the injury suffered, not the wrong committed. This prevents the harm inflicted by the countermeasures from outweighing that of the original wrong. Mary Ellen O'Connell, *Debating the Law of Sanctions,* 13 Eur. J. Int'l L. 63, 76 (2002). O'Connell notes the indeterminacy of the principle of proportionality in dealing with international countermeasures, which indeterminacy, however, she argues can be overcome (idem at 77). Countermeasures may be kept in place for an indefinite number of years (idem). "The potential effectiveness of the measures is not a fundamental criterion" (idem at 78). While most of the time countermeasures might not work, they tell the offending party that its deed will not go unpunished (idem).

143. *See* Nicholas Emiliou, The Principle of Proportionality in European Law: A Comparative Study 5 (Kluwer Law Int'l. 1996).

144. Part I of the Constitution Act, 1982, being Schedule B to the Canada Act 1982, ch. 11 (UK), *available at* http://laws.justice.gc.ca/en/const/index.html.

145. Idem.

146. *See* Yale Law Sch., Global Constitutionalism: Privacy, Proportionality, the Political Case IV-22–23 (Paul Gewirtz & Jacob Katz Cogan eds., Yale Law Sch. 2001) (hereinafter Global Constitutionalism) (quoting R. v. Oakes, [1986] 1 S.C.R. 103, 139–40).

147. Idem at IV-22.

148. Idem.

149. Global Constitutionalism, *supra* note 146, at IV-24 (quoting Robert J. Sharpe & Katherine E. Swinton, The Canadian Charter of Rights and Freedoms 42–58 (1998)).

150. Idem.

151. Idem (citing Quebec Ass'n of Protestant Sch. Bds. v. Quebec (A.G.), [1984] 2 S.C.R. 66).

152. Idem (citing Zylberberg v. Sudbury (Bd. of Educ.), [1988] 52 D.L.R. (4th) 577 (Ont. C.A.)).

153. [1998] 1 S.C.R. 493, *cited in* GLOBAL CONSTITUTIONALISM, *supra* note 146, at IV-25 (quoting SHARPE & SWINTON, *supra* note 149, at 42–58).

154. [1992] 2 S.C.R. 731, *cited in* GLOBAL CONSTITUTIONALISM, *supra* note 146, at IV-25 (quoting SHARPE & SWINTON, *supra* note 149, at 42–58).

155. R. v. Oakes, [1986] 1 S.C.R. 103, 139–40, *quoted in* GLOBAL CONSTITUTIONALISM, *supra* note 146, at IV-22.

156. *See Oakes*, [1986] 1 S.C.R. at 139–40 (citing R. v. Big M Drug Mart Ltd., [1985] 1 S.C.R. 295, 352), *quoted in* GLOBAL CONSTITUTIONALISM, *supra* note 146, at IV-22.

157. *Oakes*, 1 S.C.R. at 139–40, *quoted in* GLOBAL CONSTITUTIONALISM, *supra* note 146, at IV-22–23.

158. Idem.

159. GLOBAL CONSTITUTIONALISM, *supra* note 146, at IV-24 (quoting SHARPE & SWINTON, *supra* note 149, at 42–58).

160. For instance, context affects the type of justification and proof the court may require in a particular case. In *R. v. Butler*, the court held the Parliament's "reasoned apprehension of harm" that obscenity may cause to society was sufficient to rationally relate the prohibition of obscenity to prevention of "violence, cruelty, and dehumanization in sexual relations." [1992] 1 S.C.R. 452, *cited in* GLOBAL CONSTITUTIONALISM, *supra* note 146, at IV-28. Context has also been important in justifying the protection of vulnerable groups of people. Thomson Newspapers v. Canada (A.G.), [1998] 1 S.C.R. 877, *quoted in* GLOBAL CONSTITUTIONALISM, *supra* note 146, at IV-28–29 (citing precedent supporting the notion that a group's vulnerability, subjective fears of harm, and the "inability to measure scientifically a particular harm… are all factors of which the court must take account in assessing whether a limit has been demonstrably justified…").

161. GLOBAL CONSTITUTIONALISM, *supra* note 146, at IV-25 (quoting SHARPE & SWINTON, *supra* note 149, at 42–58).

162. *Oakes*, [1986] 1 S.C.R. at 139–40 (citing R. v. Big M Drug Mart Ltd., [1985] 1 S.C.R. 295, 352), *quoted in* GLOBAL CONSTITUTIONALISM, *supra* note 146, at IV-23.

163. GLOBAL CONSTITUTIONALISM, *supra* note 146, at IV-26 (quoting SHARPE & SWINTON, *supra* note 149, at 42–58).

164. Idem.

165. Ford v. Quebec (A.G.), [1988] 2. S.C.R. 712, *cited in* GLOBAL CONSTITUTIONALISM, *supra* note 146, at IV-26 (quoting SHARPE & SWINTON, *supra* note 149, at 42–58).

166. GLOBAL CONSTITUTIONALISM, *supra* note 146, at IV-26 (quoting SHARPE & SWINTON, *supra* note 149, at 42–58).

167. Peter W. Hogg, *Section 1 Revisited*, 1 NAT'L J. OF CONST. LAW 1, 19 (1991), *quoted in* GLOBAL CONSTITUTIONALISM, *supra* note 146, at IV-35.

168. Chief Justice Lamer wrote in Dagenais v. Canadian Broad. Corp., [1994] 3 S.C.R. 835, 887–90, *quoted in* GLOBAL CONSTITUTIONALISM, *supra* note 146, at IV-30–31, that legislative measures may achieve the desired objective or part of the desired objective. This is why, he said, the balancing "requires both that the underlying objective of a measure and the salutary effects that actually result from its

implementation be proportional to the deleterious effects the measure has on fundamental rights and freedoms" (idem). Chief Justice Lamer explained that, while the importance of the objective may outweigh the contemplated negative effects of its implementation on individual rights, the actual results achieved may be "[in]sufficient to justify these negative effects" (idem).

169. R. v. Oakes, [1986] 1 S.C.R. 103, 139–40, *quoted in* GLOBAL CONSTITUTIONALISM, *supra* note 146, at IV-23.

170. Idem.

171. GLOBAL CONSTITUTIONALISM, *supra* note 146, at IV-27 (quoting SHARPE & SWINTON, *supra* note 149, at 42–58).

172. Idem at IV-29.

173. *See, e.g.,* idem at IV-32–34 (quoting Thomson Newspapers v. Canada (A.G.), [1998] 1 S.C.R. 877).

174. EMILIOU, *supra* note 143, at 66. Because Germany is a welfare state, the principle of proportionality is employed to control government discretion in advancing its social and economic policies to protect individual rights and preserve the formal legality necessary for any known model of the rule of law. *See* BRIAN Z. TAMANAHA, ON THE RULE OF LAW: HISTORY, POLITICS, THEORY 120 (Cambridge Univ. Press 2004).

175. EMILIOU, *supra* note 143, at 66 (citations omitted).

176. *Cannabis Case,* BVerfGE 90, 145 (Constitutional Court of Germany 1994), *reprinted in* GLOBAL CONSTITUTIONALISM, *supra* note 146, at IV-3, 5 (hereinafter *Cannabis Case*). *See also* EMILIOU, *supra* note 143, at 65.

177. *Cannabis Case, supra* note 176, at IV-5.

178. EMILIOU, *supra* note 143, at 65–66.

179. Idem at 66.

180. BVerfGE 80, 137 (Constitutional Court of Germany 1989), *reprinted in* GLOBAL CONSTITUTIONALISM, *supra* note 146, at IV-14, 15 (hereinafter *Reiten im Walde Case*).

181. Article 2(1) of the German Constitution says: "Everyone has the right to the free development of his personality insofar as he does not violate the rights of others or offend against the constitutional order or the moral code." Grundgesetz für die Bundesrepublik Deutschland, art. 2(1) (federal constitution of Germany), *available at* http://www.psr.keele.ac.uk/docs/german.htm.

182. *Reiten im Walde Case, supra* note 180, at IV-15 (second and third alterations in original). In this case, the court considered the right to ride horses in parks as protected under Article 2(1) of the constitution (idem).

183. *Cannabis Case, supra* note 176, at IV-4.

184. *Cannabis Case, supra* note 176, at IV-5; *Reiten im Walde Case, supra* note 180, at IV-15.

185. *Reiten im Walde Case, supra* note 180, at IV-16.

186. *Cannabis Case, supra* note 176, at IV-5; *Reiten im Walde Case, supra* note 180, at IV-15.

187. The actual name of the Constitution of Germany in English is "Basic Law of the Federal Republic of Germany." See an English translation of the constitution at http://www.psr.keele.ac.uk/docs/german.htm (last visited Mar. 22, 2008).

188. *Reiten im Walde Case, supra* note 180, at IV-15 (alteration in original).

189. Idem.

190. *Lebach Case*, BVerfGE 35, 202 (Constitutional Court of Germany 1973), *reprinted in* Global Constitutionalism, *supra* note 146, at II-49, 50 (hereinafter *Lebach Case*).

191. *Reiten im Walde Case, supra* note 180, at IV-16–17.

192. *Cannabis Case, supra* note 176, at IV-3.

193. Idem at IV-6–9.

194. Idem at IV-6.

195. Idem at IV-8–9.

196. Idem at IV-10.

197. Idem.

198. Idem at IV-10–14.

199. Idem at IV-12–13.

200. Idem at IV-13–14.

201. Idem at IV-14.

202. *Lebach Case, supra* note 190, at II-49.

203. Idem at II-51.

204. Idem at II-50.

205. Idem at II-53.

206. Idem.

207. Idem at II-53–54.

208. Idem.

209. *Reiten im Walde Case, supra* note 180, at IV-14.

210. Idem.

211. Idem at IV-16.

212. Idem.

213. Idem at IV-16.

214. Idem at IV-16–17.

215. Idem at IV-17.

216. Idem.

217. Emiliou, *supra* note 143, at 96.

218. *See* idem at 97–111.

219. Idem at 97.

220. Idem.

221. *See* idem at 81–84.

222. Idem at 83.

223. Idem at 83, 97.

224. Idem at 83, 113–14.

225. Idem at 113.

226. Idem at 114.

227. Idem.

228. Konstytucja Rzeczypospolitej Polskiej, art. 6 (1952) (Constitution of the Republic of Poland), *quoted in* GLOBAL CONSTITUTIONALISM, *supra* note 146, at IV-37. The current version of this provision is contained in Konstytucja Rzeczypospolitej Polskiej, art. 22 (1997) (Constitution of the Republic of Poland), *available at* http://www.sejm.gov.pl/prawo/konst/angielski/kon1.htm (last visited Mar. 20, 2008).

229. Decision dated Apr. 26, 1995, No. K. 11/94 (Constitutional Court of Poland), *reprinted in* GLOBAL CONSTITUTIONALISM, *supra* note 146, at IV-37, 38.

230. Idem at IV-39.

231. Idem.

232. Idem at IV-40.

233. Idem.

234. Idem.

235. Idem at IV-40–41.

236. Idem at IV-41.

237. Idem.

238. Idem at IV-42.

239. *See* Criminal Code of Ukraine of 2001, art. 69 (unofficial translation), *available at* http://www.legislationline.org/upload/legislations/2e/4b/e7cc32551f671cc10183dac 480fe.htm (last visited Mar. 20, 2008).

240. *See* idem.

241. Case Concerning the Authority of Criminal Courts to Impose a Lesser Sentence than Prescribed by the Law, Decision of the Constitutional Court of Ukraine No. 15-rp/2004, Nov. 2, 2004, 45 Ofitsiyniy Visnyk Ukrainy 41, art. 2975 (Nov. 26, 2004), *available at* http://zakon.rada.gov.ua/cgi-bin/laws/main.cgi?nreg=v015p710%2D 04&p=1107713872139426 (last visited Mar. 20, 2008) (in Ukrainian) (hereinafter *Case Regarding Article 69*).

242. Idem.

243. Idem.

244. Idem.

245. *See* EMILIOU, *supra* note 143, at 134. The *Fédéchar* case, Case 8/55, Fédération Charbonnière de Belgique v. High Authority, 1954–1956 E.C.R. 292, 299, is the first case where the European Court of Justice held that an administrative action must be proportionate to the scale of the illegal action (idem). The *Fromançais* case, Case 66/82, Fromançais SA v. Fonds d'orientation et de regularisation des marches agricoles (FORMA), 1983 E.C.R. 395, 404 (per curiam), developed the doctrine of proportionality further by indicating that necessity and proportionality in the narrower sense were the two elements of the test of proportionality (idem). The three-element definition of the principle of proportionality used in Germany was adopted by the European Court of Justice in Case C-331/88, The Queen v. Minister of Agriculture, Fisheries and Food and Secretary of State for Health, ex parte

Fedesa and others, 1990 E.C.R. I-4023, 4063 (per curiam), and Cases C-133, 300 & 362/93, Crispoltoni v. Fattoria Autonoma Tabacchi, 1994 E.C.R. I-4863, 4905. Idem ("The principle of proportionality... requires that measures adopted by Community institutions do not exceed the limits of what is appropriate and necessary in order to attain the objectives legitimately pursued by the legislation in question; when there is a choice between several appropriate measures recourse must be had to the least onerous, and the disadvantages caused are not to be disproportionate to the aims pursued."); *see also* idem at 169 ("Indeed, German law has made perhaps the greatest contribution to the development of the general principles applied by the Court of Justice, including the principle of proportionality and the principle of protection of legitimate expectations").

246. Idem at 169.

247. Idem at 135.

248. Idem.

249. Idem at 135–36.

250. Case 11/70, Internationale Handelsgesellschaft mbH v. Einfuhr- und Vorratsstelle fur Getreide und Futtermittel, 1970 E.C.R. 1125, 1136 (per curiam).

251. *See* EMILIOU, *supra* note 143, at 136–37.

252. *See, e.g.*, Treaty Establishing the European Community, arts. 34, 40, 88, & 192, *available at* http://europa.eu.int/eur-lex/lex/en/treaties/dat/12002E/htm/C_2002325EN. 003301.html (last visited Mar. 20, 2008) (hereinafter EC treaty).

253. *See, e.g.*, idem, arts. 5, 11, 18, & 42.

254. *See, e.g.*, idem, art. 134.

255. *See* EMILIOU, *supra* note 143, at 138 (citing Case 19/61, Mannesmann v. High Auth., 1962 E.C.R. 357, 371 (per curiam) (stating that the principle of proportionality was a manifestation of the "principle of justice")).

256. Idem at 139–42. *See generally* Paolo G. Carozza, *Subsidiarity as a Structural Principle of International Human Rights Law*, 97 AM. J. INT'L L. 38 (2003) (arguing in favor of the principle of subsidiarity's utility in governing international human rights law).

257. EC treaty, *supra* note 252, art. 5.

258. EMILIOU, *supra* note 143, at 139 (citing COMMISSION OF THE EUROPEAN COMMUNITIES (now EUROPEAN COMMISSION), TASK FORCE REPORT ON THE ENVIRONMENT AND THE INTERNAL MARKET AT X (December 1989).

259. Idem at 140.

260. EC treaty, *supra* note 252, art. 5.

261. EMILIOU, *supra* note 143, at 140.

262. This is the European equivalent of the "congruence and proportionality" test for federal enforcement actions under Section 5 of the Fourteenth Amendment of the U.S. Constitution.

263. EMILIOU, *supra* note 143, at 134 (quoting Case C-331/88, *Fedesa*, 1990 E.C.R. I-4023, 4063 (per curiam); Case 362/93, *Crispoltoni*, 1994 E.C.R. I-4863, 4905 (per curiam)).

264. Idem at 189.

265. Idem at 191.

266. Idem.

267. Idem at 192 (citations omitted). The court reasoned that "[t]he legality of a Community act cannot depend on retrospective considerations of its efficacy." Where the future effect of a decision "cannot be accurately foreseen," the legislature's rule will be upheld unless "manifestly incorrect" given the information at its disposal when the rule was adopted.

268. Idem.

269. Idem (citing Case C-331/88, *Fedesa*, 1990 E.C.R. at 4063).

270. Idem.

271. Idem at 192–93.

272. Idem at 193.

273. Idem.

274. Idem.

275. Idem.

276. *See* Yutaka Arai-Takahashi, The Margin of Appreciation Doctrine and the Principle of Proportionality in the Jurisprudence of the ECHR (Intersentia 2002). Arai-Takahashi discusses the interplay of the doctrine of margin of appreciation and the principle of proportionality under the European Convention for Human Rights (ECHR).

CHAPTER 2

1. Nicholas Emiliou, The Principle of Proportionality in European Law: A Comparative Study 129 (Kluwer Law Int'l 1996) ("When an English judge, for instance, states that byelaws made by local authorities would probably be held void on the ground of unreasonableness if they involved such oppressive or gratuitous interference with the rights of those subject to them as could find no justification in the minds of reasonable men, he reaches the same result a German jurist would reach by applying the principle of proportionality") (citation and internal quotation marks omitted).

2. Idem at 39.

3. Idem.

4. Idem.

5. Idem.

6. (1854) 156 Eng. Rep. 145, 151 (Ex. Ct.); *see also* Restatement (Second) of Contracts § 351(1) (1981) ("Damages are not recoverable for loss that the party in breach did not have reason to foresee as a probable result of the breach when the contract was made").

7. Evra Corp. v. Swiss Bank Corp. v. Cont'l Ill. Nat'l Bank & Trust Co. of Chicago, 673 F. 2d 951, 957 (7th Cir. 1982).

8. Idem at 958 (citation omitted).

9. 673 F. 2d 951 (7th Cir. 1982).

10. Idem at 956.

11. RESTATEMENT (SECOND) OF CONTRACTS § 351(3) (1981).

12. Idem § 351 cmt. f.

13. Idem.

14. The Supreme Court has not considered this theory, having only twice cited the RESTATEMENT (SECOND) OF CONTRACTS § 351, and in neither case subsection 3. *See* Hercules, Inc. v. United States, 516 U.S. 417, 431, 434 (1996) (Breyer, J., dissenting); Exxon Co., U.S.A. v. Sofec, Inc., 517 U.S. 830, 840 (1996).

15. *See, e.g.,* Ak. Tae Woong Venture, Inc. v. Westward Seafoods, Inc., 963 P. 2d 1055 (Alaska 1998) (holding that a commercial fishing company was not entitled to an extended award of lost profits from a seafood processor who breached contract because it would be disproportionate to the defendant's breach); Lamkins v. Int'l Harvester Co., 182 S.W. 2d 203 (Ark. 1944) (holding that the seller of a tractor is not liable for loss resulting from inability to plant crops because it was not reasonable to believe that he "tacitly consented to be bound for more than ordinary damages in case of default on his part"); Kerr S.S. Co. v. Radio Corp. of Am., 157 N.E. 140 (N.Y. 1927) (holding that "where the terms of a telegram give no hint of the nature of the transaction" and defendant had no notice that failure to deliver would result in special damage to the plaintiff, "the liability is for nominal damages or for the cost of carriage if the tolls have been prepaid"); Newsome v. W. Union Tel. Co., 69 S.E. 10 (N.C. 1910) (awarding only nominal damages to buyer of whiskey who claimed negligence in telegram transmittal because "[d]amages which are uncertain and speculative, or which are not the natural and probable result of the breach, are too remote to be recoverable"). *But see* Perini Corp. v. Greate Bay Hotel & Casino, Inc., 129 N.J. 479 (N.J. 1992) (finding ample evidence that a casino construction contractor was aware of the high stakes involved at the time of contracting and therefore rejecting the contractor's argument that for a $600,000 contract it would not have accepted a risk of $14.5 million in liability).

16. Int'l Ore & Fertilizer Corp. v. SGS Control Serv., Inc. (*Int'l Ore II*), 38 F. 3d 1279 (2d Cir. 1994).

17. The district court relied on an earlier Second Circuit opinion in which the judge writing for the court explained, in dicta, that if SGS intended to assume the risk of such great liability ($547,688), it would have charged substantially more than $220 for its services. It would not have been rational for the company to enter into a contract where it knowingly risked so much for so little. Vitol Trading S.A., Inc. v. SGS Control Serv., 874 F. 2d 76, 81 (2d Cir. 1989). In *Int'l Ore II*, the appellate court explained that a majority of judges had not joined this part of the opinion. 38 F. 2d at 1284.

18. Int'l Ore & Fertilizer Corp. v. SGS Control Serv., Inc. (*Int'l Ore I*), 743 F. Supp. 250, 257 (S.D.N.Y. 1990).

19. RESTATEMENT (SECOND) OF CONTRACTS § 351 cmt. f (1981), *construed in Int'l Ore I*, 743 F. Supp. at 257.

20. *Int'l Ore II*, 38 F. 3d at 1281.

21. Idem at 1285.

22. Idem. The dissent in this case agreed with the district court that the contract damages were disproportionate because there was a great disparity between the contract price and the damages awarded and the plaintiff was in the better position to anticipate and avert the risk (idem at 1288–89; Mishler, J., dissenting).

23. Sundance Cruises Corp. v. Am. Bureau of Shipping, 7 F. 3d 1077 (2d Cir. 1993).

24. Idem at 1078–79.

25. Idem at 1084.

26. Idem.

27. Idem.

28. See R. Harper Heckman & Benjamin R. Edwards, *Time Is Money: Recovery of Liquidated Damages by the Owner*, 24 CONSTRUCTION LAWYER 28, 29 (Fall 2004), for a thorough discussion of the use and benefits of liquidated damages provisions, including the ease in allocating damages associated with construction disputes, the creation of firm expectations for all parties involved about what damages for delay will be, the avoidance of significant proof issues associated with establishing and quantifying a delay claim, and the potential savings of attorneys' fees, expert fees, and other costs incident to "proving up" an owner's delay damages.

29. RESTATEMENT (SECOND) OF CONTRACTS § 356 cmt. a (1981).

30. Priebe & Sons v. United States, 332 U.S. 407, 413 (1947).

31. *See* RESTATEMENT (FIRST) OF CONTRACTS § 339 cmt. b (1932).

32. RESTATEMENT (SECOND) OF CONTRACTS § 356 cmt. a (1981).

33. RESTATEMENT (FIRST) OF CONTRACTS § 339 cmt. b (1932).

34. *E.g.*, United Airlines, Inc. v. Austin Travel Corp., 867 F. 2d 737, 740 (2d Cir. 1989) (citing as the general rule that liquidated damages provisions are upheld "unless the liquidated amount is a penalty because it is plainly or grossly disproportionate to the probable loss anticipated when the contract was executed"); *In re* Plywood Co. of Pa., 425 F. 2d 151, 155 (3d Cir. 1970) ("[T]he liquidated damages stipulated must not be disproportionate to the probable loss judged as of the time of making the contract."); Sw. Eng'g Co. v. United States, 341 F. 2d 998, 1003 (8th Cir. 1965) (holding that "[w]here parties have by their contract agreed upon a liquidated damage provision as a reasonable forecast of just compensation for breach of contract, and damages are difficult to estimate accurately, such provision should be enforced" even "if in the course of subsequent developments, damages prove to be greater than those stipulated"). *See also* Ridgley v. Topa Thrift and Loan Ass'n, 953 P. 2d 484, 488 (Cal. 1998) (concluding that a state statute limits the validity of liquidated damages provisions to those that bear a "reasonable relationship to the range of actual damages that the parties could have anticipated would flow from a breach"); Hofer v. W.M. Scott Livestock Co., 201 N.W. 2d 410, 413 (N.D. 1972) ("A provision for payment of a stipulated sum as a liquidation of damages will ordinarily be sustained if it appears that at the time the contract was made the damages in the event of the breach will be incapable or very difficult of accurate

estimation, that there was a reasonable endeavor by the parties as stated to fix fair compensation, and that the amount stipulated bears a reasonable relation to probable damages and not disproportionate to any damages reasonably to be anticipated.") (quoting Anderson v. Cactus Heights Country Club, 125 N.W. 2d 491, 493 (S.D. 1963)); Rio Grande Valley Sugar Growers, Inc. v. Campesi, 592 S.W. 2d 340, 342 n.2 (Tex. 1979) ("In order to enforce a liquidated damage clause, the court must find: (1) that the harm caused by the breach is incapable or difficult of estimation, and (2) that the amount of liquidated damages called for is a reasonable forecast of just compensation."); Reliance Ins. Co. v. Utah Dept. of Transp., 858 P. 2d 1363, 1367 (Utah 1993) ("[I]f the parties were honestly trying to arrange in advance a fair basis for determining actual damages, it makes no difference whether this arrangement turns out to be too much or too little") (citations omitted).

35. *E.g.*, Lynch v. Andrew, 481 N.E. 2d 1383, 1386 (Mass. App. Ct. 1985) ("[C]ontract provisions which clearly and reasonably establish liquidated damages should be enforced, if not so disproportionate to the losses and expenses caused by the defendant's breach as to constitute a penalty") (citation and internal quotation marks omitted); Haromy v. Sawyer, 654 P. 2d 1022, 1023 (Nev. 1982) ("In order to prove a liquidated damage clause constitutes a penalty, the challenging party must persuade the court that the liquidated damages are disproportionate to the actual damages sustained by the injured party"); Wirth & Hamid Fair Booking v. Wirth, 192 N.E. 297, 301 (N.Y. 1934) ("[Liquidated damages] must bear reasonable proportion to the actual loss.") (citing Seidlitz v. Auerbach, 129 N.E. 461 (N.Y. 1920)); Ledbetter Bros., Inc. v. NCDOT, 314 S.E. 2d 761 (N.C. Ct. App. 1984) (enforcing liquidated damages provision where actual damages were at least 50 percent of liquidated damages assessed and liquidated damages amounted to only about 1.5 percent of the contract price).

36. *E.g.*, Farmers Export Co. v. M/V Georgis Prois, etc., 799 F. 2d 159, 162 (5th Cir. 1986) ("The amount fixed is reasonable if it approximates the actual loss that has resulted from a particular breach, even though it may not approximate the loss that might have been anticipated under other possible situations, *or if the breach* approximates the loss anticipated at the time of making the contract, even though it does not approximate the actual loss") (citing Restatement (Second) of Contracts § 356 cmt. b (1981)); Truck Rent-A-Center, Inc. v. Puritan Farms 2nd, Inc., 361 N.E. 2d 1015, 1018–19 (N.Y. 1977) (considering both that a "payment of a sum of money grossly disproportionate to the amount of actual damages provides for a penalty and is unenforceable" and that a liquidated damage provision must bear "a reasonable proportion to the probable loss" and concluding that the amount stipulated as liquidated damages was reasonably arrived at by the parties).

37. Restatement (Second) of Contracts § 356(1) (1981).

38. *See* idem § 351; *supra* part 1.4.1 (discussing foreseeable damages).

39. Restatement (Second) of Contracts § 356 cmt. b (1981).

40. Idem.

41. *See, e.g.*, 15 Corbin on Contracts §79.4 (rev. ed. 2003) (noting that the general freedom of contract encompasses the privilege of entering into a bargain and also having it enforced); Baltimore & Ohio Sw. Ry. Co. v. Voigt, 176 U.S. 498, 505 (1900) ("[T]he right of private contract is no small part of the liberty of the citizen, and…the usual and most important function of courts of justice is…to maintain and enforce contracts [rather] than to enable parties thereto to escape from their obligations on the pretext of public policy, unless it clearly appear [*sic*] that they contravene public right or the public welfare"). *See generally* Charles Fried, Contract as Promise: A Theory of Contractual Obligation (Harvard Univ. Press 1981) (defending the classical theory of contract and arguing that the law should protect the right of autonomous individuals to impose obligations on themselves by an exercise of free will that the state and its courts must respect); Richard A. Epstein, *Toward a Revitalization of the Contract Clause*, 51 U. Chi. L. Rev. 703 (1984) (arguing for a revitalization of the contract clause to protect economic liberties from judicial interference); G. Richard Shell, *Contracts in the Modern Supreme Court*, 81 Cal. L. Rev. 433 (1993) (comparing the modern Supreme Court's jurisprudence to that of previous eras and concluding that the modern Court, by favoring strict enforcement of agreements, has made a radical break with the Warren Court where public policy defenses to contract are concerned).

42. 205 U.S. 105 (1907); *see also* Sw. Eng'g Co. v. United States, 341 F. 2d 998, 1003 (8th Cir. 1965) (finding that the fact that the party seeking the liquidated damages suffered no actual damages did not preclude an award of liquidated damages); Heckman & Edwards, *supra* note 28, at 31 ("It is not unfair to hold the contractor performing the work to such agreement [liquidated damages clause] if by reason of later developments damages prove to be less or nonexistent. Each party by entering into such contractual provision took a calculated risk and is bound by reasonable contractual provisions pertaining to liquidated damages.").

43. *Bethlehem Steel*, 205 U.S. at 119. The Court explained that in the past courts tended to construe liquidated damages provisions as penalties and would award nothing but actual damages. Later, however, "the courts became more tolerant of such provisions, and have now become strongly inclined to allow parties to make their own contracts, and to carry out their intentions, even when it would result in the recovery of an amount stated as liquidated damages, upon proof of the violation of the contract, and without proof of the damages actually sustained" (idem). In addition, courts are also willing to uphold liquidated damages provisions that set the damages significantly lower than actual damages. Parties may disclaim consequential damages, subject only to unconscionability review. *See* Paul B. Marrow, *The Unconscionability of a Liquidated Damages Clause*, 22 Pace L. Rev. 27, 35 (2001).

44. Idem at 121.

45. Sun Printing & Publ'g Ass'n v. Moore, 183 U.S. 642, 668–71 (1902) (rejecting the idea that disproportion alone voids a liquidated damages provision and holding that "the stipulation for value…was binding upon the parties, the trial court

rightly refused to consider evidence tending to show that the admitted value was excessive, and the circuit court of appeals properly gave effect to the expressed intention of the parties"). The Court further stated that when the parties' intent was clear, a court of law could not invalidate a disproportionate liquidated damages provision even if a court of equity could properly do so (idem at 674, quoting Clement v. Cash, 21 N.Y. 253, 257 (N.Y. 1860)).

46. Idem at 673.

47. Wise v. United States, 249 U.S. 361, 366–67 (1919).

48. *Sun Printing*, 183 U.S. at 672–73.

49. Idem at 642.

50. Idem at 662.

51. Idem.

52. Idem at 672–73.

53. Idem at 664.

54. Idem at 672.

55. *Bethlehem Steel*, 205 U.S. 105, 121 (1907).

56. Kothe v. R.C. Taylor Trust, 280 U.S. 224 (1930).

57. Idem at 226.

58. Idem.

59. Idem.

60. 20 U.S. 13 (1822) (holding that a payment of $1,000 dollars in case of failure to finish building houses by a certain date was an unenforceable penalty).

61. Idem at 18.

62. Idem at 17.

63. 241 U.S. 184 (1916).

64. Idem at 190. *See also* Wise v. United States, 249 U.S. 361 (1919).

65. Robinson v. United States, 261 U.S. 486, 488 (1923). *But see* Priebe & Sons v. United States, 332 U.S. 407, 413 (1947) (reasoning that if the parties intended the liquidated damages provision to be "an added spur to performance" or to create security, the court will determine it a penalty).

66. *Tayloe*, 20 U.S. at 17. *Contra* Grenier v. Compratt Constr. Co., 454 A. 2d 1289 (Conn. 1983) (looking beyond the label applied in the contract documents to the reasonableness of the clause itself and enforcing a liquidated damages provision that was expressly labeled as a penalty).

67. *Tayloe*, 20 U.S. at 15.

68. Idem at 18. The Court further explained that any amount of money paid for nonperformance is a penalty and will not be considered liquidated damages unless the parties prove such (idem at 17).

69. 249 U.S. 361 (1919).

70. Idem at 364.

71. Idem at 367.

72. *See* United States v. Carroll Towing Co., 159 F. 2d 169, 173 (2d Cir. 1947).

73. Idem.

74. *See* Restatement (Third) of Torts: Liability for Physical Harm § 3 (2005).
75. *See, e.g.*, McIntyre v. Balentine, 833 S.W. 2d 52 (Tenn. 1992).
76. 421 U.S. 397 (1975). *See also* Donald J. Polden & E. Thomas Sullivan, *Contribution and Claim Reduction in Antitrust Litigation: A Legislative Analysis*, 20 Harv. J. Legis. 397 (1983).
77. *Reliable Transfer*, 421 U.S. at 405.
78. Idem at 407.
79. Idem at 407, 411. The Supreme Court has made clear that despite the adoption of proportionate damages, the proximate cause requirement and related superseding cause doctrine still apply. *See* Exxon Co., U.S.A. v. Sofec, Inc., 517 U.S. 830 (1996). The system "apportions damages based upon comparative fault only among tortfeasors whose actions were proximate causes of an injury" (idem at 837).
80. 511 U.S. 202 (1994). *See also supra* note 76.
81. Idem at 204.
82. Idem at 221 (citation omitted).
83. *Pro tanto* means "to that extent," "for so much," or "as far as it goes." Black's Law Dictionary 1259 (8th ed. 2004). A *pro tanto* approach to calculating the appropriate contribution of nonsettling defendants subtracts the actual dollar amount of any settlement with codefendants from the total judgment awarded.
84. The Court rejected the first approach, *pro tanto* setoff with a right of contribution, which "discourages settlement, because settlement can only disadvantage the settling defendant." *McDermott*, 511 U.S. at 211. In addition, it leads to unnecessary ancillary indemnification litigation (idem at 212).
85. The Court rejected the second approach, *pro tanto* setoff without contribution, because it was less in line with the *Reliable Transfer* rule and was likely to lead to inequitable apportionments of liability (idem at 212–13).
86. Idem at 212. The Court concluded that the *pro tanto* rule came at "too high a price in unfairness" and the proportionate share approach would also lead to a high settlement rate due to "[t]he parties' desire to avoid litigation costs, to reduce uncertainty, and to maintain ongoing commercial relationships" (idem).
87. Idem at 209. In the field of antitrust and competition law see D.J. Polden & E.T. Sullivan, *supra* note 76; E. Thomas Sullivan, *New Perspectives in Antitrust Litigation: Towards a Right of Comparative Contribution*, 1980 U. Ill. L. Rev. 389 (1980).
88. *See* Gerber v. MTC Elec. Tech. Co., 329 F. 3d 297 (2d Cir. 2003) (approving of the use of a "capped proportionate share" formula when determining a judgment credit in a securities class action settlement, under which formula credit would be the greater of the *pro tanto* rule or proportionate share rule, using defendant's proportion of fault as proven at trial); Denney v. Jenkens & Gilchrist, 230 F.R.D. 317, 325 n.32, 339–40 (S.D.N.Y. 2005) (recognizing proportionate share as a valid way of determining a judgment credit in a class action settlement in a RICO case); *In re* Worldcom, Inc. ERISA Litig., 339 F. Supp. 2d 561, 568–69 (S.D.N.Y. 2004) (holding that the proportionate share judgment reduction formula was appropriate in a class action settlement in an ERISA case).

89. 443 U.S. 256 (1979).

90. The Longshore and Harbor Workers' Compensation Act, 33 U.S.C. § 901 (2000).

91. *Edmonds*, 443 U.S. at 281 (Blackmun, J., dissenting).

92. Idem (majority opinion).

93. Antitrust damages are automatically trebled under 15 U.S.C. §15 (2000). Congress originally created treble damages in 1890 as a statutory deterrent; this is not a common law development.

94. 429 U.S. 477, 489 (1977) (quoting Zenith Radio Corp. v. Hazeltine Research, 395 U.S. 100, 125 (1969)) (alteration in original).

95. See *Los Angeles Memorial Coliseum Commission v. National Football League*, 791 F. 2d 1356, 1371–73 (9th Cir. 1986), for a good analysis of the required causal link between a remedy and the harm to be redressed (idem at 1372).

96. 431 U.S. 720, 746 (1977).

97. Idem.

98. Gregory Mktg. Corp. v. Wakefern Food Corp., 787 F. 2d 92, 98 (3d Cir. 1986).

99. Idem.

100. Idem (quoting Mid-West Paper Prods. Co. v. Continental Group, 596 F. 2d 573, 587 (3d Cir. 1979)). *Accord* Loeb Indus., Inc. v. Sumitomo Corp., 306 F. 3d 469, 483 (7th Cir. 2002) ("[T]he antitrust laws create a system that, to the extent possible, permits recovery in rough proportion to the actual harm a defendant's unlawful conduct causes in the market without complex damage apportionment. This scheme at times favors plaintiffs (*Hanover Shoe* [Inc. v. United Shoe Machinery Corp., 392 U.S. 491 (1968)]) and at times defendants *(Illinois Brick [supra])*, but it never operates entirely to preclude market recovery for an injury"); *In re* Indus. Gas Antitrust Litig., 681 F. 2d 514, 520 (7th Cir. 1982) ("Thus, the conflicting interests of deterrence through private antitrust enforcement and redress for injury must be balanced against the avoidance of excessive treble damages litigation. An appropriate balance is achieved by granting standing only to those who, as consumers or competitors, suffer immediate injuries with respect to their business or property, while excluding persons whose injuries were more indirectly caused by the antitrust conduct"); Montreal Trading Ltd. v. Amax Inc., 661 F. 2d 864, 867 (10th Cir. 1981) ("With a treble damages entitlement, the result [of allowing indirect purchasers to recover] could be multiple recoveries and total damage awards wholly out of proportion with 'the fruits of the illegality,' easily bankrupting the named defendants").

101. *See generally* E.T. Sullivan, *supra* note 87, at 403–15 (discussing proportionality in connection with antitrust injunctive/structural remedies).

102. FTC v. Nat'l Lead Co., 352 U.S. 419, 428–31 (1957) (holding that an FTC order may sweep so broadly as to prevent the violator of competition laws from using lawful means to violate the law and that the respondents "must remember that those caught violating the [antitrust laws] must expect some fencing in"); United States v. U.S. Gypsum Co., 340 U.S. 76, 88–89 (1950); United States v. Paramount Pictures, 334 U.S. 131, 148 (1948); Int'l Salt Co. v. United States, 332 U.S. 392, 400

(1947) ("When the purpose to restrain trade appears from a clear violation of law, it is not necessary that all of the untraveled roads to that end be left open and that only the worn one be closed. The usual ways to the prohibited goal may be blocked against the proven transgressor and the burden put upon him to bring any proper claims for relief to the court's attention"). *But see* Zenith Radio Corp. v. Hazeltine Research, Inc., 395 U.S. 100, 132–33 (1969) (stating that a remedial order may be issued to stop the illegal conduct and to prevent related unlawful acts from occurring in the future, thus allowing the judicial remedial power to extend outside the particular conduct found illegal in the case under consideration but limiting such extension only to "related *unlawful* acts") (citation omitted; emphasis added).

103. United States v. E.I. Du Pont de Nemours & Co., 366 U.S. 316, 326 (1961) ("The key to the whole question of an antitrust remedy is of course the discovery of measures effective to restore competition."); *Gypsum*, 340 U.S. at 88 ("A trial court upon a finding of a conspiracy in restraint of trade and a monopoly has the duty to compel action by the conspirators that will, so far as practicable, cure the ill effects of the illegal conduct, and assure the public freedom from its continuance."); Jacob Siegel Co. v. FTC, 327 U.S. 608, 612–13 (1946) (requiring that the selected remedy rationally relate to the unlawful practices); New York v. Microsoft Corp., 224 F. Supp. 2d 76, 110 (D.D.C. 2002) (noting that, despite the rule that an antitrust remedy could exceed the specific anticompetitive conduct, the restrictions that form part of the remedial order must be closely related to the anticompetitive conduct).

104. 253 F. 3d 34 (D.C. Cir. 2001).

105. Idem at 106 (alterations in original; citations and internal quotation marks omitted; emphasis added). *See also Microsoft*, 231 F. Supp. 2d at 220.

106. *See supra* part 2.2.1.

107. United States v. U.S. Gypsum Co., 340 U.S. 76, 89–90 (1950).

108. 340 U.S. 76.

109. Idem at 89–90.

PART II

1. Yale Law Sch., Global Constitutionalism: Privacy, Proportionality, the Political Case IV-60 (Paul Gewirtz & Jacob Katz Cogan eds., Yale Law Sch. 2001) (hereinafter Global Constitutionalism).

2. *See* Kathleen M. Sullivan, *The Justices of Rules and Standards*, 106 Harv. L. Rev. 22, 61 (1992) ("Balancing tests have infiltrated modern constitutional law to the extent that categorical two-tier review is incompletely realized or breaks down. The label 'intermediate scrutiny' situates these standards between the bipolar rule-like tiers of strict review and rationality review.").

3. *See* Erwin Chemerinsky, Constitutional Law 529–31 (Aspen Pub. 2001); Global Constitutionalism, *supra* note 1, at IV-61–63.

4. E. Thomas Sullivan, *Antitrust Remedies in the U.S. and the E.U.: Advancing a Standard of Proportionality*, 48 ANTITRUST BULLETIN 377, 418–20 (2003) (cataloging the uses of the principle of proportionality in American jurisprudence).

5. *See* State Farm Mut. Auto. Ins. Co. v. Campbell, 538 U.S. 408, 426 (2003) ("In sum, courts must ensure that the measure of punishment is both reasonable and proportionate to the amount of harm to the plaintiff and to the general damages recovered."); BMW of N. Am., Inc. v. Gore, 517 U.S. 559, 569 (1996).

6. Dolan v. City of Tigard, 512 U.S. 374, 391 (1994) (adopting a test of "rough proportionality" to determine whether the burden imposed by the city building permit conditions bore reasonable relationship to the projected impact of a proposed development).

7. City of Boerne v. Flores, 521 U.S. 507, 545 (1997) ("[W]hether Congress has exceeded its § 5 powers turns on whether there is a 'congruence and proportionality between the injury to be prevented or remedied and the means adopted to that end.'").

8. *See supra* note 22 of Introduction and accompanying text. *See generally* Richard S. Frase, *Excessive Prison Sentences, Punishment Goals, and the Eighth Amendment: "Proportionality" Relative to What?* 89 MINN. L. REV. 571, 598–627 (2005).

9. United States v. Bajakajian, 524 U.S. 321, 334 (1998) ("The touchstone of the constitutional inquiry under the Excessive Fines Clause is the principle of proportionality: The amount of the forfeiture must bear some relationship to the gravity of the offense that it is designed to punish.... We now hold that a punitive forfeiture violates the Excessive Fines Clause if it is grossly disproportional to the gravity of a defendant's offense.").

10. The Court added a third tier, intermediate scrutiny, to the system of standards in gender discrimination, dormant commerce clause, and content-neutral speech restriction cases. *See supra* Introduction. According to Kathleen Sullivan, intermediate scrutiny is the only true standard among the three tiers of review because, unlike the categorical rules of strict scrutiny and rational basis, intermediate scrutiny allows for judicial discretion in balancing competing values. K.M. Sullivan, *supra* note 2, at 61.

11. *See* idem at 60 ("One analogue in modern constitutional law to old-time categorization is the Court's post–New Deal effort to establish a fixed two-tier system of judicial review: strict scrutiny for fundamental liberties and suspect classes; deferential rationality review for garden-variety socioeconomic legislation. True, these tiers employ nominal balancing rhetoric, but the Court ties itself to the twin masts of strict scrutiny and rationality review in order to resist (or appear to resist) the siren song of the sliding scale. Bipolar two-tier review did penance for the appearance of naked value choices that had brought the Court into disrepute in the Lochner era. Thus, in true categorical fashion, two-tier review generally decides cases through characterization at the outset, without the need for messy explicit balancing. The classification at the threshold cuts off further serious debate: 'this is an x case and therefore the government (or rightholder) wins.' This is a rule-like regime.") (footnotes omitted).

12. *See* idem.

13. *See supra* notes 5 and 7.

14. *See, e.g.*, Harmelin v. Michigan, 501 U.S. 957 (1991) (upholding a sentence of life without parole for drug possession by a first offender). The Court's prison proportionality cases are further discussed in a later chapter.

15. *See supra* notes 8–9.

CHAPTER 3

1. *Global Constitutionalism: Privacy, Proportionality, the Political Case*, the compilation of materials on constitutional law published by Yale Law School, mentions the strong criticism of the Supreme Court's then two-tier model of equal protection review by Justice Thurgood Marshall. YALE LAW SCH., GLOBAL CONSTITUTIONALISM: PRIVACY, PROPORTIONALITY, THE POLITICAL CASE IV-62–63 (Paul Gewirtz & Jacob Katz Cogan eds., Yale Law Sch. 2001) (hereinafter GLOBAL CONSTITUTIONALISM). At first blush, it may seem that Justice Marshall's criticism would have been satisfied with the emergence of intermediate scrutiny in gender classification cases. Indeed, he argued that the rigid two-tier system of equal protection review no longer represented the state of the Supreme Court's jurisprudence and the needs of modern society: "However understandable the Court's hesitancy to invoke strict scrutiny, all remaining legislation should not drop into the bottom tier, and be measured by the mere rationality test." Bd. of Ret. v. Murgia, 427 U.S. 307, 319 (1976) (Marshall, J., dissenting), *quoted in* GLOBAL CONSTITUTIONALISM, *supra*, at IV-63. However, the Court has not been quick to extend the application of intermediate scrutiny into areas other than gender classifications.

2. In several cases where the Court announced the application of the rational basis test, the level of scrutiny was less deferential than expected under mere rationality. *See, e.g.*, Lawrence v. Texas, 539 U.S. 558 (2003) (striking down a law criminalizing consensual sodomy between individuals of the same sex in the privacy of their home); Romer v. Evans, 517 U.S. 620 (1996) (striking down an amendment to the Colorado Constitution, adopted by a voting initiative, that banned laws prohibiting discrimination based on sexual orientation); City of Cleburne v. Cleburne Living Ctr., 473 U.S. 432 (1985) (declaring unconstitutional a local zoning ordinance that prevented the operation of a home for people with a mental disability).

3. *See supra* notes 10–12 of Part II's introduction and accompanying text. Kathleen Sullivan argues that, because "[i]t defines bright-line boundaries and then classifies fact situations as falling on one side or the other," which at the outset predetermines the outcome of judicial review of cases implicating a range of interests, the two-tier system of judicial constitutional scrutiny is rulelike. Kathleen M. Sullivan, *The Justices of Rules and Standards*, 106 HARV. L. REV. 22, 59–60 (1992).

4. Idem. *See also* United States v. Virginia, 518 U.S. 515, 567 (1996) (Scalia, J., dissenting).

5. *See, e.g., Cleburne*, 473 U.S. 432 (rational basis with bite); Craig v. Boren, 429 U.S. 190 (1976) (intermediate scrutiny).

6. Vieth v. Jubelirer, 541 U.S. 267, 294 (2004); *see also* Erwin Chemerinsky, Constitutional Law 529 (Aspen Pub. 2001).

7. Griswold v. Connecticut, 381 U.S. 479, 503–504 (1965) (White, J., concurring).

8. Clark v. Jeter, 486 U.S. 456, 461 (1988) ("Classifications based on race or national origin and classifications affecting fundamental rights are given the most exacting scrutiny.") (citations omitted). *See also* Chemerinsky, *supra* note 6, at 528–29, 698–99.

9. *Griswold*, 381 U.S. at 504.

10. Idem.

11. 304 U.S. 144, 153 n.4 (1938).

12. *See Cannabis Case*, BVerfGE 90, 145 (Constitutional Court of Germany 1994), *reprinted in* Global Constitutionalism, *supra* note 1, at IV-3, 5 (hereinafter *Cannabis Case*).

13. 539 U.S. 306, 326 (2003) (citations omitted).

14. Idem at 326–27.

15. Idem at 326.

16. *Grutter*, 539 U.S. 306.

17. Idem at 328.

18. Idem. *But see* Gratz v. Bollinger, 539 U.S. 244 (2003) (holding that assigning more weight to race than to other personal factors in the admissions process to an undergraduate program violated the Equal Protection Clause).

19. *See, e.g., Grutter*, 539 U.S. at 350 (Thomas, J., dissenting). Justice Thomas, in particular, contended that strict scrutiny requires a rigorous analysis of each government objective proffered to justify the use of race in government decisions (idem at 351–54). In support of his statement, Justice Thomas referred to *Korematsu v. Unites States*, 323 U.S. 214 (1944), and *Richmond v. J.A. Croson Co.*, 488 U.S. 469 (1989), to describe the type of review required by strict scrutiny.

20. Idem at 333–41.

21. Idem at 341.

22. Idem.

23. Idem. The dissenters contended that using race as a plus in the admissions process was not a necessary means for achieving student diversity. *See, e.g.*, idem at 361–62 (Thomas, J., dissenting). They claimed that the majority overlooked lowering the admissions requirements as an equally effective race-neutral alternative (idem at 366–67).

24. *See, e.g.*, BVerfGE 80, 137 (Constitutional Court of Germany 1989), *reprinted in* Global Constitutionalism, *supra* note 1, at IV-14, 17 (hereinafter *Reiten im Walde Case*) (balancing the rights of horseback riders and hikers to use park trails).

25. 505 U.S. 833 (1992).

26. Idem at 878 (plurality decision).

27. Idem.

28. 410 U.S. 113 (1973).

29. Idem at 163.

30. Idem at 163–64.

31. Loving v. Virginia, 388 U.S. 1 (1967).

32. Skinner v. Oklahoma *ex rel.* Williamson, 316 U.S. 535 (1942).

33. Pierce v. Society of the Sisters of the Holy Names of Jesus & Mary, 268 U.S. 510 (1925); Meyer v. Nebraska, 262 U.S. 390 (1923).

34. Griswold v. Connecticut, 381 U.S. 479 (1965).

35. Eisenstadt v. Baird, 405 U.S. 438 (1972); *Griswold*, 381 U.S. 479.

36. Rochin v. California, 342 U.S. 165 (1952).

37. Cruzan v. Dir., Mo. Dep't of Health, 497 U.S. 261 (1990).

38. *See* Chemerinsky, *supra* note 6, at 695–799.

39. Planned Parenthood of Se. Pa. v. Casey, 505 U.S. 833, 878 (1992) (plurality decision).

40. *See supra* note 6 and accompanying text.

41. *See supra* note 10 of part II.

42. Chemerinsky, *supra* note 6, at 330.

43. Idem.

44. 397 U.S. 137 (1970).

45. Idem at 142.

46. *See, e.g., Lebach Case*, BVerfGE 35, 202 (Constitutional Court of Germany 1973), *reprinted in* Global Constitutionalism, *supra* note 1, at II-49, 49–50 (hereinafter *Lebach Case*) (measuring and comparing the importance of the competing constitutional interests of the right of individuals to maintain their personal dignity and the media's right to provide information).

47. *See, e.g.,* Bibb v. Navajo Freight Lines, Inc., 359 U.S. 520 (1959) (doubting the suitability of rear-wheel contoured mud flaps on trucks and trailers to achieve traffic safety on state roads based on the lower court's finding that the contoured mud flap "possesses no advantages over the conventional or straight mud flap previously required in Illinois").

48. *Pike*, 397 U.S. at 142.

49. Idem.

50. *See, e.g., Lebach Case, supra* note 46, at II-49–55 (balancing the right to free speech and the individual rights of a convicted felon to privacy).

51. *See* Global Constitutionalism, *supra* note 1, at IV-63–68 (briefly describing the evolution of Justice Breyer's proposal for the application of the principle of proportionality in American free speech jurisprudence).

52. 528 U.S. 377, 402 (2000).

53. United States v. O'Brien, 391 U.S. 367, 377 (1968) ("Whatever imprecision inheres in these terms, we think it clear that a government regulation is sufficiently justified if it is within the constitutional power of the Government; if it furthers an important or substantial governmental interest; if the governmental interest is

unrelated to the suppression of free expression; and if the incidental restriction on alleged First Amendment freedoms is no greater than is essential to the furtherance of that interest.").

54. Turner Broad. Sys., Inc. v. F.C.C., 512 U.S. 622, 642 (1994).

55. Idem at 641–42. Some exceptions exist to the application of strict scrutiny to content-based speech regulation (idem), but their discussion is outside the scope of this work.

56. 391 U.S. 367 (1968).

57. Idem at 377.

58. Nicholas Emiliou, The Principle of Proportionality in European Law: A Comparative Study 25, 134 (Kluwer Law Int'l 1996).

59. O'Brien, 391 U.S. at 377.

60. Emiliou, *supra* note 58, at 25, 134.

61. Turner Broad. Sys., Inc. v. F.C.C., 512 U.S. 622, 662 (1994) ("To satisfy this standard, a regulation need not be the least speech-restrictive means of advancing the Government's interests. 'Rather, the requirement of narrow tailoring is satisfied so long as the . . . regulation promotes a substantial government interest that would be achieved less effectively absent the regulation'") (quoting Ward v. Rock Against Racism, 491 U.S. 781, 799 (1989); alteration in original; internal quotation marks omitted).

62. O'Brien, 391 U.S. at 377.

63. Emiliou, *supra* note 58, at 25, 134. There is a tendency among the European courts to dilute the requirement of strict necessity when reviewing social and economic regulation. *See, e.g.*, idem at 32 (explaining that in Germany, "[i]n the area of regulation of the economy . . . the legislature has been granted a wide scope for intervention [of basic economic rights].").

64. *Turner Broad. Sys.*, 512 U.S. at 662.

65. *See* Emiliou, *supra* note 58, at 25, 134.

66. Broadrick v. Oklahoma, 413 U.S. 601, 615 (1973).

67. Idem at 613.

68. Virginia v. Hicks, 539 U.S. 113, 119 (2003).

69. 539 U.S. 113 (2003).

70. Idem at 124 (refusing to apply the overbreadth doctrine because the regulation under consideration did not affect any protected speech but instead was aimed at preventing unlawful conduct on the territory of a fenced residential community).

71. Idem at 122 n.3.

72. Idem at 119–20.

73. Idem at 122.

74. Idem at 124 (quoting Broadrick v. Oklahoma, 413 U.S. 601, 615 (1973)).

75. Idem.

76. Central Hudson Gas & Elec. Corp. v. Pub. Serv. Comm'n of N.Y., 447 U.S. 557, 565 (1980).

77. Idem at 566.

78. Idem.

79. Idem.
80. Idem (emphasis added).
81. *Compare* Greater New Orleans Broad. Ass'n, Inc., 527 U.S. 173, 188 (1999) ("The Government is not required to employ the least restrictive means conceivable, but it must demonstrate narrow tailoring of the challenged regulation to the asserted interest…") *and* Bd. of Trustees of the State Univ. of N.Y. v. Fox, 492 U.S. 469, 480 (1989) ("[W]e have not gone so far as to impose upon [would-be regulators] that…the manner of restriction is absolutely the least severe that will achieve the desired end. What our decisions require is a fit between the legislature's ends and the means chosen to accomplish those ends—a fit that is not necessarily perfect, but reasonable; that represents not necessarily the single best disposition but one whose scope is in proportion to the interest served; that employs not necessarily the least restrictive means, but…a means narrowly tailored to achieve the desired objective.") (citations and internal quotation marks omitted) *with* 44 Liquormart, Inc. v. Rhode Island, 517 U.S. 484, 507 (1996) (invalidating a law as violative of the First Amendment because "[i]t is perfectly obvious that alternative forms of regulation that would not involve any restriction on speech would be more likely to achieve the State's goal…") *and* Rubin v. Coors Brewing Co., 514 U.S. 476, 491 (1995) (holding that "the availability of…options, all of which could advance the Government's interest in a manner less intrusive to respondent's First Amendment rights, indicates that [the statute in question] is more extensive than necessary"). *See also Central Hudson, supra,* 447 U.S. at 564 ("the regulatory technique must be in proportion to [the state's] substantial interest"); CHEMERINSKY, *supra* note 6, at 1061–67.
82. Central Hudson Gas & Elec. Corp. v. Pub. Serv. Comm'n of N.Y., 447 U.S. 557 (1980).
83. Idem at 570–72.
84. Idem at 570.
85. Idem at 571 (explaining that the commission could have attempted to correct the language of the advertising to avoid negative effects on its goal of conserving the energy); *see also* Beneficial Corp. v. FTC, 542 F. 2d 611, 618–20 (1976) (holding that a "remedy for the perceived violation can go no further in imposing a prior restraint on protected commercial speech than is reasonably necessary to accomplish the remedial objective of preventing the violation" and that the commission could have chosen a less restrictive remedy). *See generally* E. Thomas Sullivan, *First Amendment Defenses in Antitrust Litigation,* 46 Mo. L. Rev. 517, 538–42 (1981).
86. *Central Hudson,* 447 U.S. at 566 n.8.
87. United States v. Virginia, 518 U.S. 515, 533 (1996).
88. Idem.
89. Idem (quoting Califano v. Webster, 430 U.S. 313, 320 (1977) (per curiam) (alteration in original).
90. Idem (quoting Cal. Fed. Sav. & Loan Ass'n v. Guerra, 479 U.S. 272, 289 (1987); alteration in original).
91. Idem.

92. Idem at 534.

93. United States v. Carolene Products Co., 304 U.S. 144, 152 (1938).

94. Idem.

95. Heller v. Doe by Doe, 509 U.S. 312, 320–21 (1993).

96. Romer v. Evans, 517 U.S. 620, 631 (1996); *Heller,* 509 U.S. at 320–21.

97. U.S. R.R. Ret. Bd. v. Fritz, 449 U.S. 166, 178 (1980) (discussing what legitimate objectives Congress could have proffered for the challenged legislation).

98. 508 U.S. 307, 315 (1993) (quoting Lehnhausen v. Lake Shore Auto Parts Co., 410 U.S. 356, 364 (1973)).

99. Ry. Express Agency, Inc. v. New York, 336 U.S. 106, 110 (1949).

100. N.Y. City Transit Auth. v. Beazer, 440 U.S. 568, 592–93 (1979).

101. Heller v. Doe by Doe, 509 U.S. 312, 321 (1993).

102. *See* United States v. Carolene Products Co., 304 U.S. 144, 152 (1938). *See also* idem at 152 n.4.

103. CHEMERINSKY, *supra* note 6, at 470 (describing the pressure for the Court to provide more deference to government socioeconomic regulations).

104. 198 U.S. 45 (1905).

105. Idem at 57–58.

106. Idem at 57.

107. Idem at 61–62.

108. Idem at 57.

109. Idem.

110. Adkins v. Children's Hosp. of D.C., 261 U.S. 525, 557 (1923) (invalidating the challenged minimum wage law because it was one sided and did not take into account the employer's ability or inability to sustain the burden of a minimum wage).

111. Coppage v. Kansas, 236 U.S. 1 (1915) (invalidating as contrary to the freedom of contract a state law that prohibited an employer from demanding that its employees not join a trade union).

112. Weaver v. Palmer Bros. Co., 270 U.S. 402 (1926) (invalidating a law that prohibited the use of shoddy in comfortables because there was no evidence that "any sickness or disease was ever caused by the use of shoddy").

113. 291 U.S. 502 (1934).

114. Idem at 523 (footnotes omitted).

115. United States v. Carolene Products Co., 304 U.S. 144, 152 (1938). Ordinarily, the Supreme Court has been criticized for undermining the principle of federalism by striking down state laws that intrude on individual autonomy. *Gonzales v. Raich,* 545 U.S. 1 (2005), presents a converse situation. Using a rational basis standard of review, the Court in *Raich* held that the federal law prohibiting the manufacture, distribution, or possession of marijuana did not violate the commerce clause when it was applied to intrastate growers and users of marijuana for medical purposes, whose use and cultivation of the drug was authorized by a recently enacted California law. Thus, instead of protecting individual autonomy, the Supreme Court used the commerce clause to curb state initiatives aimed at expanding it.

116. 413 U.S. 528 (1973).
117. Idem at 529.
118. Idem at 538.
119. Idem at 534.
120. Idem.
121. Idem at 536.
122. Idem at 538.
123. 473 U.S. 432 (1985).
124. Idem.
125. Idem at 444–47.
126. Idem at 444.
127. Idem at 445. The Court noted a number of other reasons why it refused to afford persons with a mental disability a quasi-suspect status. One reason was that such persons are not politically powerless, given the broad political support for actions in their protection (idem). Another is even more attenuated. The Court explained that, because "it would be difficult to find a principled way to distinguish" those with a mental disability from other groups of individuals who also suffer from certain immutable disabilities, relative political powerlessness, and minimal public prejudice, it was "reluctant to set out on that course" and "decline[d] to do so" (idem at 445–46).
128. Idem at 450.
129. 517 U.S. 620 (1996).
130. Idem at 632.
131. Idem at 631.
132. 539 U.S. 558 (2003).
133. Idem at 578–79.
134. Idem. The Court indicated that the defined liberty was not absolute and that it could, under certain circumstances—like those involving minors, public exposure, or harm to third parties—be overridden by a strong public interest (idem at 578). Importantly, the Court excluded morality alone from the list of possible countervailing interests (*see* idem). The Court in dictum suggested, however, that the decision in this case did not entitle homosexual persons to seek government recognition of any relationship they desired to establish (idem).
135. *See supra* note 24.
136. *See* EMILIOU, *supra* note 58, at 41–43.

CHAPTER 4

1. *See supra* notes 102–15 of chapter 3 and accompanying text; *see generally supra* ch. 3.
2. The word "punitive" means "relating to punishment; having the character of punishment or penalty; inflicting punishment or a penalty." BLACK'S LAW DICTIONARY 1234 (6th ed. 1990).

3. State Farm Mut. Auto. Ins. Co. v. Campbell, 538 U.S. 408, 416 (2003) (citing Cooper Indus., Inc. v. Leatherman Tool Group, Inc., 532 U.S. 424, 432 (2001) (citing RESTATEMENT (SECOND) OF TORTS § 903 (1979))).

4. *See* Thomas B. Colby, *Beyond the Multiple Punishment Problem: Punitive Damages as Punishment for Individual, Private Wrongs*, 87 MINN. L. REV. 583, 618 (2003) (relating that in the nineteenth century, after a significant broadening of the concept of actual damages, punitive damages lost their compensatory gloss and became strictly deterrent and retributive in nature).

5. Idem (citing *Cooper Indus.*, 532 U.S. at 438 n.11); *see also* BMW of N. Am., Inc. v. Gore, 517 U.S. 559, 568 (1996); Pac. Mut. Life Ins. Co. v. Haslip, 499 U.S. 1, 19 (1991).

6. *BMW*, 517 U.S. at 568.

7. St. Louis, I.M. & S. Ry. Co. v. Williams, 251 U.S. 63, 66 (1919).

8. *Haslip*, 499 U.S. at 17.

9. *Williams*, 251 U.S. at 66–67.

10. *BMW*, 517 U.S. 559. The Court had invalidated a punitive damages award on one prior occasion. It held in *Southwestern Telegraph & Telephone Co. v. Danaher* that, because there was "no intentional wrongdoing, no departure from any prescribed or known standard of action, and no reckless conduct," the $6,300 penalty inflicted on the company was "so plainly arbitrary and oppressive as to be nothing short of a taking of its property without due process of law" (238 U.S. 482, 490–91 (1915)). We do not place this decision on the same level with *Gore* because we believe the Court's reasoning in *Danaher* hinged on the impropriety of any punitive damages award in that case rather than on the excessiveness of the amount of punitive damages.

11. 492 U.S. 257 (1989).

12. Idem at 260.

13. Idem at 275.

14. Justices Brennan and Marshall joined the opinion only with the understanding that the door was not closed for due process challenges of punitive damages (idem at 280).

15. Idem at 278–80.

16. 499 U.S. 1 (1991).

17. Idem at 23–24.

18. Idem at 17.

19. 509 U.S. 443 (1993).

20. Idem at 457–58.

21. Idem at 457.

22. Idem at 458.

23. Idem at 462. Using potential harm as the measure of the plaintiff's injury compared to the amount of punitive damages makes the guidepost of the constitutionally allowable ratio less reliable due to the fact that potential harm, unlike direct harm, is in great measure based on speculation about future events.

24. 517 U.S. 559 (1996) (striking down as excessive an award of $2 million in punitive damages to a customer for the harm resulting from the dealer's failure to notify the customer that he was purchasing at full price a BMW automobile that had been repainted).

25. 538 U.S. 408 (2003) (striking down as excessive an award of $145 million, where the compensatory damages amounted to only $1 million for bad-faith failure to settle within policy limits, fraud, and intentional infliction of emotional distress).

26. *See, e.g., BMW*, 517 U.S. at 568.

27. Idem.

28. Idem. In addition to substantive due process requirements, the Supreme Court established several procedural safeguards against arbitrary punitive damages awards. *See* Cooper Indus., Inc. v. Leatherman Tool Group, Inc., 532 U.S. 424 (2001) (requiring *de novo* appellate review of punitive damages awards); Honda Motor Co. v. Oberg, 512 U.S. 415 (1994) (holding that the due process clause of the Fourteenth Amendment requires judicial review of jury punitive damages awards); Pac. Mut. Life Ins. Co. v. Haslip, 499 U.S. 1 (1991) (requiring postverdict review of punitive damages awards by jury).

29. *BMW* at 572–73.

30. *State Farm*, 538 U.S. at 421. Pamela Karlan has argued that this aspect of proportionality "is about federalism" (Pamela S. Karlan, *"Pricking the Lines": The Due Process Clause, Punitive Damages, and Criminal Punishment*, 88 MINN. L. REV. 880, 913 (2004)). Karlan argued that while "[t]here is relatively little constitutional limitation on the sort of behavior a state can criminalize or for which it can impose civil liability...there is some constitutional limit on the degree of permissible deviation from national norms" (idem). Thus, the principle of proportionality protects states in their sovereign ability to "adopt different positions on how to impose punishment and on how much punishment to impose" but limits the states' ability to overreach their bounds and inappropriately affect behavior in other states (idem).

31. Idem.

32. Idem at 421–22.

33. Idem at 422; *BMW*, 517 U.S. at 574 n.21.

34. *BMW*, 517 U.S. at 574.

35. Idem at 575.

36. Idem at 575, 580; State Farm Mut. Auto Ins. Co. v. Campbell, 538 U.S. 408, 419–23 (2003).

37. *State Farm*, 538 U.S. at 419; *see also BMW*, 517 U.S. at 576–80. There has been some criticism of the first guidepost on the grounds that its application leads to inconsistent results in lower courts' decisions. *See* Steven L. Chanenson & John Y. Gotanda, *The Foggy Road for Evaluating Punitive Damages: Lifting the Haze from the* BMW/State Farm *Guideposts*, 37 U. MICH. J.L. REFORM 441 (2004) (cataloguing lower court cases with inconsistent results).

38. *State Farm*, 538 U.S. at 419.

39. Idem at 422–23.

40. Idem at 422.

41. Idem at 423. To support this proposition, the Court quotes from Justice Breyer's concurrence in *BMW*: "Larger damages might also 'double count' by including in the punitive damages award some of the compensatory, or punitive, damages that subsequent plaintiffs would also recover" (idem; quoting *BMW*, 517 U.S. at 593 (Breyer, J., concurring)).

42. Idem.

43. Idem.

44. *See* idem at 423–24.

45. *See* idem.

46. For substantive criticism of the "total harm" system of punitive damages, see Colby, *supra* note 4.

47. Catherine M. Sharkey, *Punitive Damages as Societal Damages*, 113 Yale L.J. 347 (2003).

48. Idem at 402–14.

49. *See In re Simon II Litigation*, 211 F.R.D. 86, 185–86 (E.D.N.Y. 2002), for a brief discussion of the problem of uncorrelatability of a portion of punitive damages to a class of plaintiffs. The court in that case observed that the punitive function of punitive damages for nonmembers of the class could be utilized through research and treatment grants (idem at 186).

50. Sharkey, *supra* note 47, at 393–99.

51. Idem at 400–402; see also *TVT Records v. Island Def Jam Music Group*, 279 F. Supp. 2d 413, 419–20 & n.11 (S.D.N.Y. 2003), in which the court discussed the nature of punitive damages based on the disproportionalities created by the defendant in society; there are certain societal harms caused by the defendant, but the particularized victims are not always readily identifiable.

52. *See, e.g.*, State Rubbish Collectors Ass'n v. Siliznoff, 240 P. 2d 282 (Cal. 1952).

53. See Note, *An Economic Analysis of the Plaintiff's Windfall from Punitive Damages Litigation*, 105 Harv. L. Rev. 1900 (1992), for a good analysis of plaintiff windfall and associated problems.

54. To successfully perform this function without undermining punitive damages' goals of deterrence and retribution, a split-recovery statute must arguably meet the following requirements: (1) There is a cap on the maximum amount that may be allocated to the state; (2) a judge has discretion to determine the actual size of the state's share within the limits of a statutory cap; (3) the plaintiff's attorney's fees must be determined based on the entire punitive damages award and paid by the state and the plaintiff proportionally to the actual shares of punitive damages received; and (4) the state's share of a punitive damages award must be directed by the judge to a special fund whose activity is specifically tailored to mitigate the negative effects of the defendant's wrongful conduct on society.

55. See Victor E. Schwartz et al., *I'll Take That: Legal and Public Policy Problems Raised by Statutes That Require Punitive Damages Awards to Be Shared with the State*, 68 Mo. L. Rev. 25 (2003), for criticism of split-recovery statutes.

56. *State Farm*, 538 U.S. at 424–28; *BMW*, 517 U.S. at 580. In *BMW*, in order to show the long history supporting the principle that punitive damages should bear a reasonable relation to compensatory damages, the Court catalogued cases advancing that principle, including *Saunders v. Mullen*, 24 N.W. 529 (1885) ("When the actual damages are so small, the amount allowed as exemplary damages should not be so large."); and *Grant v. McDonogh*, 7 La. Ann. 447, 448 (1852) ("[E]xemplary damages allowed should bear some proportion to the real damage sustained…").

57. *State Farm*, 538 U.S. 424–25 (citing language from *TXO Production Corp. v. Alliance Resources Corp.*, 509 U.S. 443 (1993), about the possible use of potential harm for determining the ratio of punitive damages to the plaintiff's harm); *BMW*, 517 U.S. at 581.

58. *TXO*, 509 U.S. at 460–62. *Accord* Asa-Brandt, Inc. v. ADM Investor Servs., Inc., 344 F. 3d 738, 747 (8th Cir. 2003) ("The jury was presented with evidence that, if Wesley's scheme had worked, the Farmers would have been required to pay Wesley sums totaling more than $3.9 million. The record supports the view, therefore, that a punitive damage award of nearly $1.25 million is a fraction of the harm likely to result from Wesley's conduct.") (citation and internal quotation marks omitted).

59. *TXO*, 509 U.S. at 461–62.

60. *State Farm*, 538 U.S. at 414; *BMW*, 517 U.S. at 582.

61. *State Farm*, 538 U.S. at 425; *BMW*, 517 U.S. at 582; Pac. Mut. Life Ins. Co. v. Haslip, 499 U.S. 1, 18 (1991) ("We need not, and indeed we cannot, draw a mathematical bright line between the constitutionally acceptable and the constitutionally unacceptable [punitive damages] that would fit every case.").

62. *State Farm*, 538 U.S. at 425. The Court held that the punitive award in *BMW*, 517 U.S. at 582–83, a ratio of 500:1, and the punitive award in *State Farm*, 538 U.S. at 427–29, a ratio of 145:1, were excessive particularly based on this guidepost of reasonableness.

63. *See, e.g., State Farm*, 538 U.S. at 425.

64. Idem at 425; *see also BMW*, 517 U.S. at 582. The Fifth Circuit applied this reasoning in *Lincoln v. Case*, 340 F. 3d 283 (5th Cir. 2003), holding, after remitting the award of punitive damages to the amount of the maximum civil penalty allowed under the Fair Housing Act for a first-time offender, that a higher ratio was appropriate in an action for discrimination under the Fair Housing Act where particularly egregious conduct resulted in a small compensatory damages award.

65. *State Farm*, 538 U.S. at 427 ("Here the argument that State Farm will be punished in only the rare case, coupled with references to its assets…had little to do with the actual harm sustained by the Campbells."). The earlier *BMW* decision appeared to be of the opposite opinion, stating that higher ratios could be reasonable to punish wrongful conduct that causes harm that is difficult to assess. *BMW*, 517 U.S. at 582. To compute the amount of a punitive damages award required for effective deterrence, a multiplier formula multiplies the amount of actual harm by the factor of probability that the defendant's conduct will go undetected. *See*

A. Mitchell Polinsky & Steven Shavell, *Punitive Damages: An Economic Analysis*, 111 HARV. L. REV. 869, 887–96 (1998).

66. *State Farm*, 538 U.S. at 427–28. The Court relied on Justice Breyer's language in *BMW*, 517 U.S. at 591 (Breyer, J., concurring): "[Wealth] provides an open-ended basis for inflating awards when the defendant is wealthy.... That does not make its use unlawful or inappropriate; it simply means that this factor cannot make up for the failure of other factors, such as 'reprehensibility,' to constrain significantly an award that purports to punish a defendant's conduct."

67. Idem at 426. On remand, the Supreme Court of Utah disagreed, holding that the record supporting compensatory damages was sufficiently thorough to exclude punitive elements. Campbell v. State Farm Mut. Auto. Ins. Co., 98 P. 3d 409, 417–18 (Utah 2004).

68. *BMW*, 517 U.S. at 583. Scholars argue that, instead of the reprehensibility of the defendant's conduct, courts should rely on sanctions for comparable misconduct as a benchmark for determining the constitutional validity of punitive damages. *See* Chanenson & Gotanda, *supra* note 37. According to the authors, reliance on the judicially determined degree of reprehensibility transforms what should be an objective test of the constitutionality of punitive damages into a predominantly subjective type of analysis (idem at 443). They further argue that greater weight in the constitutional review of punitive damages must be given to the third guidepost, which is an objective measure of the social disutility of the defendant's conduct (idem at 444). The authors propose a presumptive test based on the third *BMW* guidepost (idem). According to this test, failure to clear an award under the third guidepost (i.e., when a punitive damages award exceeds the highest comparable authorized monetary statutory penalty) will be a strong indication of unconstitutionality (idem). Failing the second and third guideposts would render a punitive damages award unconstitutional (idem). Failing the third guidepost but satisfying the second would require an analysis of reprehensibility (idem). The authors note that only a finding of particularly egregious conduct will save a punitive damages award that exceeds the highest comparable monetary penalty (idem). Passing the third guidepost will still require that a punitive damages award be cleared under the first two guideposts (idem).

69. *BMW*, 517 U.S. at 583–85; *see also State Farm*, 538 U.S. at 428.

70. *BMW*, 517 U.S. at 584.

71. Idem at 584–85. *See generally* Zhang v. American Gem Seafoods, Inc., 339 F. 3d 1020 (9th Cir. 2003).

The First Circuit rejected the defendants' suggestion in *Zimmerman v. Direct Federal Credit Union*, 262 F. 3d 70, 83 (1st Cir. 2001), to compare the punitive damages award with punitive damages awards in similar cases, noting that reliance on statutory penalties was more appropriate because, according to *BMW*, the emphasis in comparing punitive damages with other civil or criminal penalties was on the legislature's assessment of reprehensibility. On remand from *State Farm*, the Supreme Court of Utah criticized the vagueness of the U.S. Supreme

Court's comparability assessment and argued that since the U.S. Supreme Court was ready to accept an award of punitive damages in the amount of $1 million, which was one hundred times more than the highest civil penalty of $10,000, $9 million in punitive damages in this case would be similarly acceptable. *State Farm*, 98 P. 3d 409, 418–19. The Supreme Court of Utah obviously confused the different goals of compensatory and punitive damages. Compensatory damages reflect the amount of actual harm suffered by the plaintiff and are not subject to the same dangers of arbitrariness as punitive damages.

72. *State Farm*, 538 U.S. at 428.

73. Idem.

74. Idem. *Cf. BMW*, 517 U.S. at 583.

75. *State Farm*, 538 U.S. at 428 (emphasis added).

76. Nonnormative, or ad hoc, government interference with individual property rights by way of jury awards of punitive damages has already caused the Court to employ the requirement of proportionality to ensure constitutional validity of punitive damages. *See* BMW v. Gore, 517 U.S. 559 (1996). The Court appears to view as particularly troubling the proneness to arbitrary encroachment on individual autonomy of ad hoc government decisions, like punitive damages awards or land-use permit conditions. *See* State Farm Mut. Auto. Ins. Co. v. Campbell, 538 U.S. 408, 417–18 (2003); Dolan v. City of Tigard, 512 U.S. 374, 385 (1994). Clearly visible is the divide in the Court's constitutional treatment between legislatively imposed imprisonment, fines, or land-use conditions and ad hoc punitive damages awards, forfeitures (the size of forfeitures ordinarily depends on the circumstances of each case), and individual land-use permit conditions. For example, *BMW* and *State Farm* apply the doctrine of proportionality exclusively to discretionary punitive damages awards. *See State Farm*, 538 U.S. 408; *BMW*, 517 U.S. 559. In contrast, the *Dolan* Court adopted a more rigorous standard of review for individualized one-time land-use permit conditions but spared legislatively imposed zoning requirements from this heightened scrutiny. 511 U.S. at 385 (distinguishing the conditions imposed on the owner of the property to receive a land development permit from the "legislative determinations classifying entire areas of the city," which were approved in *Agins v. City of Tiburon*, 447 U.S. 255 (1980)).

77. 512 U.S. 374 (1994).

78. 483 U.S. 825 (1987). *See also* DANIEL R. MANDELKER, JULES B. GERARD & E. THOMAS SULLIVAN, FEDERAL LAND USE LAW § 2.04(3) (16th ed. 2002).

79. *Dolan*, 512 U.S. at 386.

80. NICHOLAS EMILIOU, THE PRINCIPLE OF PROPORTIONALITY IN EUROPEAN LAW: A COMPARATIVE STUDY 65 (Kluwer Law Int'l 1996).

81. Possessory exactions are "dedications to public use as a condition of approval" of a land-use permit. John J. Delaney, *Applicability of Nollan-Dolan Rough Proportionality Requirements to Non-possessory Exactions and Exactions Imposed by Legislative Enactment*, SF08 ALI-ABA 639, 643 (2000).

82. Idem at 648–49.

83. Lingle v. Chevron U.S.A., Inc., 544 U.S. 528 (2005) (holding that an inquiry into the nature of due process examining the fit between the public purpose and the exaction on the property of a person was not applicable to takings).

84. City of Monterey v. Del Monte Dunes at Monterey, Ltd., 526 U.S. 687, 702–703 (1999).

85. Nollan v. Cal. Coastal Comm'n, 483 U.S. 825 (1987).

86. Idem at 828.

87. Idem at 828–29 (alteration in original).

88. Idem at 829.

89. Idem at 836.

90. Idem.

91. Idem.

92. Idem.

93. Idem at 836–37.

94. Idem at 837.

95. Idem at 838–41.

96. 512 U.S. 374 (1994).

97. Idem at 380.

98. Idem at 387.

99. 447 U.S. 255, 260 (1980).

100. *Dolan*, 512 U.S. at 385 (2d and 3d alterations in original).

101. In *Agins*, the plaintiffs challenged as facially unconstitutional the zoning restrictions placed on their five-acre parcel of land as part of the city's general land-use and open-space development plan (447 U.S. at 257).

102. *Dolan*, 512 U.S. at 385. This important distinction indicates the Court's concern over discretionary adjudicative municipal decisions that condition land-use permits on dedication of land. The Court believes that without some limitation on the discretion of local authorities, land-use permit conditions may be utilized to disguise takings of property without the constitutionally mandated compensation (Nollan v. Cal. Coastal Comm'n, 483 U.S. 825, 837 (1987)). The Court appears to be less concerned with legislatively imposed zoning requirements (*see Dolan*, 512 U.S. at 385) most likely because the political process involved in legislative formulation of zoning requirements provides a sufficient check on local authorities.

103. *Dolan*, 512 U.S. at 385.

104. Idem.

105. Idem at 387.

106. Idem at 387–88.

107. Idem at 388. Justice Stevens severely criticized the majority's decision to impose the burden of establishing rough proportionality on the city, claiming that the essential nexus test is sufficient to satisfy the requirements of the takings clause (idem at 403; Stevens, J., dissenting). He said that the inquiry must venture beyond the issue of essential nexus only "if the developer establishes that a concededly

germane condition is so grossly disproportionate to the proposed development's adverse effects that it manifests motives other than land use regulation on the part of the city" (idem). Thus, Justice Stevens proposed to significantly limit the application of the doctrine of proportionality in the constitutional evaluation of permit conditions to cases of gross disproportionality. He argued that the Court's analysis resurrected "a species of substantive due process analysis that it firmly rejected decades ago [implying *Lochner*]" (idem at 405). This view fails to realize that the majority specifically adapted the rough proportionality inquiry to the type of transactions at issue here by adopting a sufficiently relaxed intermediate level of proportionality analysis tailored to allow effective local land-use regulation. In particular, the majority rejected the test of strict proportionality, recognizing that the interest involved did not require this level of scrutiny (idem at 390; majority opinion). It implicitly argued, however, that the proneness of land-use permit conditions to undermine individual property rights under the guise of land-use regulation elevates the competing individual property rights to a level of importance that requires substitution of meaningful constitutional balancing for the traditional deference to the government (idem at 385, 391–96). Justice Souter dissented, arguing that if there is a lack of reasonable relationship between the government exaction and the projected impact of the proposed development, it is not because the exaction is disproportional but because there exists no essential nexus between the imposed condition and the proposed development (idem at 412; Souter, J., dissenting). He claimed that the requirement of rough proportionality is not needed because what the Court engaged in here was merely *Nollan*'s essential nexus analysis, which was sufficient for these purposes (idem). Justice Souter disagreed with the majority on its application of *Nollan* in this case, especially because it placed the burden of producing the evidence of reasonable relationship on the city (idem at 413).

108. Idem at 389–91 (majority opinion). Justice Stevens argued that none of the cases surveyed by the majority established a requirement similar to the "rough proportionality" requirement the majority instituted in this case (idem at 398; Stevens, J., dissenting). More important, said Justice Stevens, none of the statutes imposed a burden on the city to make an individualized showing that the proposed conditions satisfied the requirement of proportionality (idem). He argued that what most of the states incorporated in their takings statutes was merely the requirement of essential nexus developed by the Court in *Nollan* (idem). Justice Stevens also criticized the fact that the majority's analysis failed to take into account any benefits that might arise for the owner in this case in connection with the imposed conditions and the city's subsequent improvement of the drainage system (idem at 399–400).

109. Idem at 389 (majority opinion) (rejecting the rational basis standard because it is "too lax to adequately protect petitioner's right to just compensation if her property is taken for a public purpose").

110. Idem at 389–90.

111. Idem at 391.

112. Idem.
113. Idem at 393.
114. Idem.
115. The Court noted, in particular, that " [i]f petitioner's proposed development had somehow encroached on existing greenway space in the city, it would have been reasonable to require petitioner to provide some alternative greenway space for the public either on her property or elsewhere" (idem at 394).
116. Idem at 395. In his dissent, Justice Stevens argued that the majority went against the well-established eminent domain principle that the impact on the owner's property rights must be measured in relation to the entire parcel, not just the destruction of one strand in the bundle of rights (idem at 400–401; Stevens, J., dissenting) (citing Penn Central Transp. Co. v. New York City, 438 U.S. 104 (1978)). The majority responded that the exaction contemplated here was sufficiently important to constitute a taking because the permit conditions at issue in this case would "eviscerate" one of the most important sticks in Mrs. Dolan's bundle of rights—her right to exclude others from her property (idem at 393–94; majority opinion).
117. Idem at 395–96. See also Mandelker, Gerard & E.T. Sullivan, *supra* note 78, for an overview of related federal land-use law.
118. *See* Emiliou, *supra* note 80, at 192–93 (explaining that the level of proportionality required by the European Court of Justice vis-à-vis the exercise of discretionary regulatory powers depends on the position of the violated interest in the established legal order and specifically pointing out the Court's deference to the exercise of discretionary regulatory powers in the field of economic policy).
119. *See supra* note 110 and accompanying text.
120. This realization is implicit in the Court's attempt to stress the severity of land-use permit conditions, which frequently require that the owner "deed portions of the property to the city" (*Dolan*, 512 U.S. at 385).
121. Nollan v. Cal. Coastal Comm'n, 483 U.S. 825, 836 (1987).
122. Idem at 835–37.
123. *See supra* notes 109–12 and accompanying text.
124. *Nollan*, 483 U.S. at 837.
125. Idem.
126. *Dolan*, 512 U.S. at 393–96.
127. Idem at 393–95.
128. Idem.
129. Idem at 393.
130. Idem at 395–96.
131. *See* idem at 412 (Souter, J., dissenting).
132. There is limited suggestion in the opinion that the Court intended to institute the requirement of rough proportionality exclusively for individualized discretionary permit conditions when it distinguished them from legislative zoning (*Dolan*, 512 U.S. at 385).

133. The Court's analysis focused predominantly on the dangers of possessory exactions to the exercise of individual private property rights (idem at 388–89); *see also* Nollan v. Cal. Coastal Comm'n, 483 U.S. 825, 837 (1987).

134. 526 U.S. 687 (1999).

135. Idem at 702.

136. Idem (citing Armstrong v. United States, 364 U.S. 40, 49 (1960)).

137. Idem.

138. Idem at 703.

139. Idem at 702.

140. *See* idem (holding that the rough proportionality test does not extend beyond the "land-use decisions conditioning approval of development on the *dedication of property to public use*") (emphasis added).

141. Ehrlich v. City of Culver City, 512 U.S. 1231 (1994).

142. Ehrlich v. City of Culver City, 911 P. 2d 429, 438–39 (Cal. 1996). The court very aptly explained the rationale for heightened scrutiny in exactions cases, maintaining that the concern of the U.S. Supreme Court was over the discretionary context in which local authorities could circumvent the requirement of due compensation for a taking by utilizing possessory or nonpossessory exactions as conditions on the issuance of development permits (idem at 439). Justice Arabian provided the following helpful explanation of the rationale behind the heightened scrutiny applied in the *Nollan-Dolan* test: "As Justice Scalia's opinion in *Nollan* makes clear, such a discretionary context presents an inherent and heightened risk that local government will manipulate the police power to impose conditions *unrelated* to legitimate land use regulatory ends, thereby avoiding what would otherwise be an obligation to pay just compensation. In such a context, the heightened *Nollan-Dolan* standard of scrutiny works to dispel such concerns by assuring a constitutionally sufficient link between ends and means." (idem; citation omitted).

143. Ehrlich v. City of Culver City, 519 U.S. 929 (1996) (denying petition for writ of certiorari).

144. 544 U.S. 528 (2005).

145. 447 U.S. 255, 260 (1980).

146. *Chevron*, 544 U.S. at 532.

147. Idem at 536 (quoting First English Evangelical Lutheran Church of Glendale v. County of Los Angeles, 482 U.S. 304, 314 (1987)).

148. Idem at 542–44.

149. Idem at 543.

150. Idem at 547–48. The rights of private property owners were further curtailed by the recent Supreme Court decision in *Kelo v. City of New London*, 125 S. Ct. 2655 (2005). The Court held that the "public use" requirement for takings contained in the Fifth Amendment has transformed its meaning to "public purpose" (idem at 2662). Absent any indication of an illegitimate purpose for taking property from one individual to benefit another, a taking of private property made in accordance with a carefully devised development plan

to upgrade property would qualify as a taking for public purpose, in compliance with the Fifth Amendment's "public use" requirement (idem at 2664–65). The Court distinguished a taking of property from one private party and a grant of that property to another performed outside of an integrated local development plan from the taking under consideration, which was carried out in accordance with a comprehensive integrated development plan of the city (idem at 2666–67). The Court's decision left private property owners with the unenviable protection of the general requirement of rationality with its broad deference to the government precluding any meaningful judicial review. *But see* idem at 2669 (Kennedy, J., concurring) (stating that courts should use a rational basis standard of review in determining whether a taking was for public use and ensuring—based on the Court's decisions in *Cleburne v. Cleburne Living Center, Inc.*, 473 U.S. 432, 446–47, 450 (1985), and *Department of Agriculture v. Moreno*, 413 U.S. 528, 533–36 (1973), in which the Court used rational basis review to establish that the government classifications under consideration intended to injure a specific class of people—that the rational basis standard is capable of detecting particular instances in which a taking has been effected for private purpose).

151. *Chevron*, 544 U.S. at 543.

152. Idem.

153. Idem at 545.

154. *See* Parking Ass'n of Ga., Inc. v. City of Atlanta, 515 U.S. 1116 (1995) (Thomas, J., dissenting). Notwithstanding his position in *Parking Association of Georgia*, Justice Thomas joined the majority opinion in *Chevron*. 544 U.S. 528.

155. (b) Attorney's fees

> In any action or proceeding to enforce a provision of [various civil rights statutes], the court, in its discretion, may allow the prevailing party, other than the United States, a reasonable attorney's fee as part of the costs, except that in any action brought against a judicial officer for an act or omission taken in such officer's judicial capacity such officer shall not be held liable for any costs, including attorney's fees, unless such action was clearly in excess of such officer's jurisdiction.

42 U.S.C. § 1988 (2000).

156. Like punitive damages, which are awarded to serve the goal of deterring intentional tortious conduct (State Farm Mut. Auto. Ins. Co. v. Campbell, 538 U.S. 408, 416 (2003)), attorney's fees are awarded to successful plaintiffs to promote the role of a plaintiff as a private prosecutor in § 1988 cases. *See* City of Riverside v. Rivera, 477 U.S. 561 (1986).

157. BMW of N. Am., Inc. v. Gore, 517 U.S. 559, 568 (1996). *See supra* part A.

158. *Rivera*, 477 U.S. at 573–74.

159. Farrar v. Hobby, 506 U.S. 103, 114–16 (1992).

160. 461 U.S. 424, 440 (1983).

161. The level of the plaintiffs' success will determine the billable hours that will be included in the calculation of attorney's fees, Rivera, 477 U.S. at 584 (Powell, J., concurring). Other factors may also be considered. *See infra* note 165.

162. *Hensley*, 461 U.S. at 434 ("Hours that are not properly billed to one's *client* also are not properly billed to one's *adversary* pursuant to this statutory authority.") (citation omitted).

163. Idem at 434–35.

164. Idem at 440.

165. Idem. The Court referenced a twelve-factor test as the relevant measure for determining the reasonableness of attorney's fees. The factors to be considered for this purpose are as follows:

> (1) the time and labor required; (2) the novelty and difficulty of the questions; (3) the skill requisite to perform the legal service properly; (4) the preclusion of employment by the attorney due to acceptance of the case; (5) the customary fee; (6) whether the fee is fixed or contingent; (7) time limitations imposed by the client or the circumstances; (8) *the amount involved and the results obtained*; (9) the experience, reputation, and ability of the attorneys; (10) *the "undesirability" of the case*; (11) the nature and length of the professional relationship with the client; and (12) awards in similar cases.

Idem at 430 (quoting Johnson v. Ga. Highway Express, Inc., 488 F. 2d 714, 717–19 (5th Cir. 1974)) (emphasis added). Factors 8 and 10 contain an element of balancing, typical to most proportionality inquiries, of the desirability of the action (i.e., the deterrence value of the action) and the degree of success achieved with the amount of an award of attorney's fees.

166. Idem at 428–29. Respondents focused on determining the reasonable amount of fees based on the plaintiffs' success on the causes of action the plaintiffs' attorneys advanced rather than suggesting a proportionality analysis.

167. *See supra* note 161 and accompanying text.

168. *See* BMW of N. Am., Inc. v. Gore, 517 U.S. 559, 580 (1996).

169. 477 U.S. 561, 574 (1986) (plurality opinion).

170. The Court here is referring to the *Hensley* factors, *supra* note 165.

171. *Rivera*, 477 U.S. at 574 (plurality opinion).

172. Idem.

173. Idem.

174. Idem at 575.

175. Idem at 574. The plurality said that "Congress did not intend for fees in civil rights cases, *unlike most private law cases*, to depend on obtaining substantial monetary relief" (idem at 575; emphasis added). State and federal courts have indeed applied the principle of proportionality of attorney's fee awards in private cases. For example, in *Marassi v. Lau*, 859 P. 2d 605, 608 (Wash. Ct. App. 1993), the court explained that where there are multiple claims on a contract that provides for the

payment of attorney's fees and each party prevails on some claims, the described proportionality approach is preferable because in such cases the inquiry into who may be viewed as a prevailing party becomes excessively subjective (idem).

In civil class actions, courts have viewed the proportionality of the attorney's fees to the relief recovered by a class instructive in determining the reasonableness of attorney's fees. *See* Int'l Precious Metals Corp. v. Waters, 530 U.S. 1223, 1224–25 (2000) (O'Connor, J., concurring) (stating that approval of attorney's fees must be accompanied by an inquiry into whether there is "at least . . . some rational connection between the fee award and the amount of the actual distribution to the class" and recognizing the split among circuits relative to whether district courts abuse discretion when basing attorney's fee awards on actual distribution to the class); *In re* Activision Sec. Litig., 723 F. Supp. 1373, 1378 (N.D. Cal. 1989) (expressing preference for proportionality in determining attorney's fees over the lodestar method in common fund cases); Dotson v. Bell Atlantic-Md., Inc., 2003 WL 23508428, *11 (Md. Cir. Ct. 2003) (observing that proportionality of attorney's fees is not only important in determining the reasonableness of attorney's fees but also useful for future class plaintiffs in structuring their attorney's fees mechanisms).

176. *See, e.g.*, Marassi v. Lau, 859 P. 2d 605, 607–608 (Wash. Ct. App. 1993) (holding that, where an agreement provided for recovery of attorney's fees by a party who substantially prevailed and both the defendant and the plaintiff prevailed on distinct and severable claims advanced in the same proceeding, a proportionality approach should be used to award each party attorney's fees in proportion to the claims upon which each prevailed).

177. *Rivera*, 477 U.S. at 585 (Powell, J., concurring).

178. Idem.

179. Justice Powell was of the opinion that there are objective indicators, like requesting an injunction, to distinguish between the primary purpose being recovery of private damages or advancement of a public interest. *See* idem at 583–86.

180. Idem at 585.

181. Idem at 585–86. Justice Powell said, in particular, that "[a]lthough the finding of a Fourth Amendment violation hardly can be considered a new constitutional ruling," the violations at issue in this case were particularly troubling because the police expressed "general hostility to the Chicano community in the area" (idem at 586) (citation omitted).

Justice Rehnquist, on the other hand, disagreed with the plurality on a narrow definition of proportionality. He proposed to focus on the expectation of recovery as a measure of reasonable attorney's fees. In other words, the time spent litigating a case, based on which the attorney's fees are computed, must be related to what is reasonably expected to be recovered if the court finds for the plaintiff (idem at 592–93; Rehnquist, J., dissenting). Consequently, to the extent that rejecting the requirement of proportionality to recovered damages in this case may be interpreted to diminish the weight of such "billing judgment," Justice Rehnquist disagreed with the plurality's holding (idem at 595). He concluded that the facts in this case supported the view that the "billing judgment" was not exercised properly, given the attorney's knowledge of the history of low compensatory awards in this field of civil rights litigation (idem).

182. 506 U.S. 103, 114–16 (1992).

183. Idem at 115.

184. Idem.

185. Idem.

186. Idem.

187. *See* Cole v. Wodziak, 169 F. 3d 486, 487–88 (7th Cir. 1999) (casting doubt on *Rivera* because it was a plurality decision and holding that, according to *Farrar*, "[w]hen recovery is low *enough* in relation to the demand, however, the judge may jettison the lodestar apparatus and choose an appropriate fee using other means"); Migis v. Pearle Vision, Inc., 135 F. 3d 1041, 1048 (5th Cir. 1998) (holding that an attorney's fee award of six and a half times the amount of damages was excessive, given that the amount of damages recovered was twenty-six times less than what the plaintiff requested and that the district court abused its discretion when it did not take into account the difference between the requested amount of damages and the amount actually recovered, as well as the relation of the amount recovered to the attorney's fee award); Gudenkauf v. Stauffer Commc'ns, Inc., 158 F. 3d 1074, 1084–85 (10th Cir. 1998) (holding that in mixed-motive employment discrimination cases where damages are not awarded, the inquiry into the proportionality of attorney's fees must focus primarily on the plaintiff's success in proving that "an employer's discrimination, and not the employee's own misconduct, drove the employment decision") (citation omitted); Sheppard v. Riverview Nursing Ctr., Inc., 88 F. 3d 1332 (4th Cir. 1996) (stating that "[f]actoring proportionality concerns into the analysis helps guard against [excessive awards of attorney's fees not reasonably related to the benefit to the plaintiff or society]" and that "[i]n appropriate cases...courts should consider the reasons why injunctive relief was or was not granted, or the extent and nature of any declaratory relief" and arguing that *Farrar* adopted a more general notion of proportionality by inquiring whether "the public purposes served by resolving the dispute justifies [*sic*] the recovery of fees" (citing *Farrar*, 506 U.S. at 121–22 (O'Connor, J., concurring)).

188. *See supra* ch. 3(B) (discussing the dormant commerce clause in the context of intermediate scrutiny).

189. "The Congress shall have power to enforce, by appropriate legislation, the provisions [of the Fourteenth Amendment]." U.S. Const. amend. XIV, § 5.

190. *See, e.g.,* City of Boerne v. Flores, 521 U.S. 507 (1997).

191. 521 U.S. 507 (1997).

192. "The judicial power of the United States shall not be construed to extend to any suit in law or equity, commenced or prosecuted against one of the United States by Citizens of another State, or by Citizens or Subjects of any Foreign State." U.S. Const. amend. XI.

193. *City of Boerne*, 521 U.S. 507.

194. Idem at 509.

195. *See* Kimberly E. Dean, Note, *In Light of the Evil Presented*, 43 B.C. L. Rev. 697, 701 (2002).

196. Seminole Tribe of Fla. v. Florida, 517 U.S. 44 (1996). Congress is not permitted to use its enforcement power to expand the substantive rights recognized by the judiciary in its Fourteenth Amendment jurisprudence. *City of Boerne*, 521 U.S. at 508.

197. Vicki Jackson has argued that this deferential review of congressional action is appropriate given the status of state "rights" in U.S. constitutional law. "In order to avoid a quagmire of constitutional uncertainty in the U.S. constitutional setting, given both the lack of discrete areas reserved to the states as matters of regulatory jurisdiction and the constitutionally protected participation of states in consti-tuting the federal government, a judicial policy of highly deferential review of exercises of federal power (not claimed to violate individual rights) makes sense." Vicki C. Jackson, *Ambivalent and Comparative Constitutionalism: Opening Up the Conversation on "Proportionality," Rights and Federalism*, 1 U. Pa. J. Const. L. 583, 631–32 (1999) (footnote omitted). Jackson indicated that a more rigorous level of judicial review of federalism-based challenges to congressional actions would be appropriate if a well-defined "baseline measure of a 'right' to regulate [by the states], or a rule constraining the level of detail of federal enactments" were present in the U.S. constitutional system (idem at 627). Absent such a baseline measure, however, a deferential standard is needed "in order to minimize risks of judicial invalidation based on disagreement over 'policy' issues concerning the scope of federal regulation" (idem at 627–28).

198. *See* Tennessee v. Lane, 541 U.S. 509, 529 (2004); Nev. Dep't of Human Res. v. Hibbs, 538 U.S. 721, 728–40 (2003); Bd. of Trustees of Univ. of Ala. v. Garrett, 531 U.S. 356, 367–68 (2001); Kimel v. Fla. Bd. of Regents, 528 U.S. 62 (2000). A good illustration of these tendencies appears in circuit court opinions that review the validity of the Equal Pay Act (EPA), 29 U.S.C. § 206(d) (2000), and the Americans with Disabili-ties Act (ADA), 42 U.S.C. § 12101, et seq. (2000). The Sixth and the Seventh circuits upheld the validity of the EPA under Section 5 of the Fourteenth Amendment in *Kovacevich v. Kent State University*, 224 F. 3d 806 (6th Cir. 2000), and *Varner v. Illinois State University*, 226 F. 3d 927 (7th Cir. 2000), respectively, because the act sought to remove wage discrimination due to gender, to which the Supreme Court jurisprudence afforded a heightened degree of protection. The Sixth Circuit held that the EPA was congruent and proportional to those violations Congress sought to remedy, given the fact that the standard for liability under the EPA approxi-mated the constitutional equal protection analysis of gender discrimination and provided defenses for "other-than-sex" explanations (*Kovacevich*, 224 F. 3d at 819–20). The Seventh Circuit noted that, despite the fact that the EPA prohibited some constitutional conduct, the act contained exemptions for neutral expla-nations of wage disparity, which rendered it congruent and proportional to the

constitutional violation of gender discrimination that Congress was seeking to remedy (*Varner*, 226 F. 3d at 932–36).

By contrast, circuit courts proved less deferential to Congress's effort to prohibit state discrimination based on disabilities because the Supreme Court had already determined that disability discrimination was subject to rational basis review. *See* City of Cleburne v. Cleburne Living Ctr., Inc., 473 U.S. 432 (1985). The Third and Seventh circuits held as an unconstitutional abrogation of state sovereign immunity Title I of the ADA (prohibiting employment discrimination against people with disabilities) (Lavia v. Pa. Dep't of Corr., 224 F. 3d 190 (3d Cir. 2000); Erickson v. Bd. of Governors, 207 F. 3d 945 (7th Cir. 2000)). The Sixth Circuit likewise found that Title II of the ADA (prohibiting discrimination against people with disabilities in services, programs, or activities of a public entity) impermissibly abrogated state immunity (Popovich v. Cuyahoga County Ct. of Common Pleas, 227 F. 3d 627 (6th Cir. 2000)). All of these decisions relied heavily on the absence of legislative findings that states had a history of discrimination against persons with disabilities to justify the prophylactic measure that abrogated state immunity. *See, e.g., Lavia*, 224 F. 3d at 205; *Popovich*, 227 F. 3d at 640.

Congress is bound to this judicial standard because any attempt to alter the Court's determination of the standard of review will be considered an invalid substantive change, as opposed to a remedial action. *See supra* note 196.

199. *See, e.g.*, Nev. Dep't of Human Res. v. Hibbs, 538 U.S. 721, 735 (2003) ("[T]he States' record of unconstitutional participation in, and fostering of, gender-based discrimination in the administration of leave benefits is weighty enough to justify the enactment of prophylactic § 5 legislation.").

200. *See* idem at 737–40. Noting the narrowness of Congress's goal—to eliminate "the fault line between work and family" (idem at 738)—and the limitations placed on the scope of the act, the Court determined that the Family and Medical Leave Act (FMLA) "is congruent and proportional to its remedial object, and can be understood as responsive to, or designed to prevent, unconstitutional behavior" (idem at 740) (internal quotation marks omitted). Moreover, the Court recognized that past attempts to remedy the violations had failed, a fact that justified additional prophylactic measures (idem at 737). *See also* E. Thomas Sullivan, *Judicial Sovereignty: The Legacy of the Rehnquist Court*, 20 CONST. COMMENT. 171 (2003).

201. *See* E. Thomas Sullivan, *Judicial Sovereignty: The Legacy of the Rehnquist Court*, 20 CONST. COMMENT. 171, 178–84 (2003) (discussing the Court's "congruence and proportionality" test and noting that the legislation must be proportional to the means employed).

202. 527 U.S. 627, 630 (1999).

203. 528 U.S. 62, 81 (2000).

204. Idem at 88.

205. 529 U.S. 598, 626 (2000).

206. 531 U.S. 356, 372–74 (2001).

207. Idem at 369 ("[T]he Eleventh Amendment does not extend its immunity to units of local government…. It would make no sense to consider constitutional violations on their part, as well as by the States themselves, when only the States are the beneficiaries of the Eleventh Amendment.") (citation omitted). The Fifth Circuit considered the *Kimel/Garrett* approach as "a more vigorous application of the congruence and proportionality test" (Reickenbacker v. Foster, 274 F. 3d 974, 982 (5th Cir. 2001)).

208. *See supra* notes 262–67 of chapter 1 and accompanying text (discussing the notion of subsidiarity in European Community law).

209. 391 U.S. 430 (1968).

210. 349 U.S. 294, 301 (1955).

211. *Green*, 391 U.S. at 435 (quoting *Brown II*, 349 U.S. at 301).

212. Idem at 438 (quoting Griffin v. County Sch. Bd. of Prince Edward County, 377 U.S. 218 (1964)).

213. Idem at 439.

214. Idem.

215. *See* Freeman v. Pitts, 503 U.S. 467 (1992). Other categories such as resource allocation, quality of education, transportation, physical facilities, and extracurricular activities were also mentioned as relevant to the school districts' compliance with the constitutional equal protection principles (idem).

216. *See, e.g., Green*, 391 U.S. at 441–42 (rejecting as inadequate the district's freedom-of-choice plan because it failed to create school demographics that more closely approximated the racial makeup of the district's general population, despite an overall increase in the number of African American students attending formerly all-white schools).

217. 402 U.S. 1, 23–25 (1971). Other tools recommended by the Court to achieve integration and remedy previous segregation were mandatory busing and pairing and grouping of noncontiguous school zones (idem at 27–31).

218. Idem at 24.

219. Idem at 25.

220. Idem at 24.

221. *See infra* notes 228–32 and accompanying text. Institutions do have the discretion, however, to choose to consider race as one factor among others in assessing an individual's qualification for admittance (Gratz v. Bollinger, 539 U.S. 244 (2003); Grutter v. Bollinger, 539 U.S. 306 (2003)).

222. *Swann*, 402 U.S. at 26.

223. Idem.

224. Freeman v. Pitts, 503 U.S. 467, 494 (1992). Similar considerations of proportionality advanced the Court's position that a school district's unitary status is not achieved with respect to quality of education if "teachers in schools with disproportionately higher percentages of white students tended to be better educated and have more experience than their counterparts in schools with disproportionately high percentages of black students …" (idem at 483).

225. *See* idem at 496, 503–56 (Scalia, J., concurring).
226. 427 U.S. 424 (1976) (ruling that federal courts exceed their authority when they try to remedy changes in racial makeup caused by demographic changes). Justices Souter and Blackmun held an opposing view in their *Freeman* concurrences. They argued that past segregation can affect the current demographic trends and that findings need to be made as to whether a causal connection between the past dual system and current trends exists (*Freeman*, 503 U.S. at 507–508 (Souter, J., concurring), 515 (Blackmun, J., concurring)).
227. *Freeman*, 503 U.S. at 496–98.
228. United States v. Fordice, 505 U.S. 717 (1992).
229. *See* idem at 754 (Scalia, J., concurring in part and dissenting in part).
230. Idem at 743.
231. Idem.
232. Idem. Proportionality is also mentioned as a tool in determining compliance of higher educational institutions that receive federal funding with Title IX's (20 U.S.C. § 1681 (2000)) antidiscrimination provision. The regulation that implements Title IX stipulates: "A recipient which operates or sponsors interscholastic, intercollegiate, club or intramural athletics shall provide equal athletic opportunity for members of both sexes" (34 C.F.R. 106.41(c) (2006)). Key among the ten factors to be considered when "determining whether opportunities are available" is "[w]hether the selection of sports and levels of competition effectively accommodate the interests and abilities of members of both sexes" (idem). *See also* Roberts v. Colo. State Bd. of Agric., 998 F. 2d 824 (10th Cir. 1993).

Empowered to administer Title IX's antidiscrimination provision, the Office of Civil Rights assesses compliance with the accommodation provision in three basic policy areas: the determination of athletic interests and students' abilities; the selection of sports offered; and the levels of competition available during the opportunity for team competition (44 Fed. Reg. 71,413 at 41,417 (1979)).

The third policy area requires that "intercollegiate level participation opportunities for male and female students [be] provided in numbers substantially proportionate to their respective enrollments" (idem at 71,418). The substantial proportionality factor provides a sort of safe harbor for schools under Title IX, allowing schools to meet the antidiscrimination requirements by maintaining student participation in athletic activities in rough proportion to the gender makeup of the student body. There is no specified ratio to which schools must adhere; the relationship, however, must be fairly close. *See Roberts*, 998 F. 2d at 830 (holding that 10.5 percent disparity in female athletic participation and enrollment constituted the level of participation not substantially proportionate to enrollment). To achieve substantial proportionality under the accommodation test, a school may downgrade or reduce the opportunities of the overrepresented sex (idem).

As mentioned, the substantial proportionality between athletic participation of a specific gender and its respective enrollment is not an absolute requirement. It merely provides a safe harbor for schools by allowing them to establish a *prima facie* case of nondiscrimination. A school may rebut a presumption of gender discrimination that becomes operative in the absence of substantial proportionality by showing "that it has expanded and is continuing to expand opportunities for athletic participation by the underrepresented gender, or else [the school must] fully and effectively accommodate the interests and abilities among members of the underrepresented gender" (*Roberts*, 998 F. 2d at 829); *see also* Kelley v. Bd. of Trustees, 35 F. 3d 265 (7th Cir. 1994) (providing additional discussion of the substantial proportionality test).

233. Wesberry v. Sanders, 376 U.S. 1, 7–8 (1964).

234. Idem.

235. Reynolds v. Sims, 377 U.S. 533 (1964).

236. Idem at 583–84 ("In substance, we do not regard the Equal Protection Clause as requiring daily, monthly, annual or biennial reapportionment, so long as a State has a reasonably conceived plan for periodic readjustment of legislative representation. While we do not intend to indicate that decennial reapportionment is a constitutional requisite, compliance with such an approach would clearly meet the minimal requirements for maintaining a reasonably current scheme of legislative representation. And we do not mean to intimate that more frequent reapportionment would not be constitutionally permissible or practicably desirable. But if reapportionment were accomplished with less frequency, it would assuredly be constitutionally suspect.").

237. Lucas v. Forty-fourth General Assembly of State of Colo., 377 U.S. 713, 734 (1964).

238. Karcher v. Daggett, 462 U.S. 725, 740–42 (1983).

239. Idem at 730–31.

240. Idem at 731.

241. Idem.

242. *Karcher*, 462 U.S. at 740. A looser standard is established for state election districting. *See* Mahan v. Howell, 410 U.S. 315 (1973) (upholding a 16.4 percent variation in population among districts as nonexcessive and resulting from a rational objective of maintaining political lines).

243. *See* 42 U.S.C. § 1973 (2000) ("[N]othing in this section establishes a right to have members of a protected class elected in numbers equal to their proportion in the population.").

244. 478 U.S. 30 (1986).

245. 42 U.S.C. § 1973.

246. Voting Rights Act § 2(a), codified at 42 U.S.C. § 1973(a).

247. Idem § 2(b).

248. 478 U.S. at 50.

249. Idem at 46.

250. Johnson v. DeGrandy, 512 U.S. 997 (1994).

251. Voting Rights Act § 2(b), codified at 42 U.S.C. § 1973(b); *Johnson*, 512 U.S. at 1013–14.

252. *Johnson*, 512 U.S. at 1017–18.

253. Idem at 1018–19 & n.81.

254. *See* Samuel Issacharoff, *Supreme Court Destabilization of Single-member Districts*, 1995 U. Chi. Legal F. 205, 222 (1995); comments by panelist Pamela S. Karlan, *Conference: The Supreme Court, Racial Politics, and the Right to Vote*: Shaw v. Reno *and the Future of the Voting Rights Act*, 44 Am. U. L. Rev. 1, 9 (1994).

255. Shaw v. Reno, 509 U.S. 630 (1993).

256. Thornburg v. Gingles, 478 U.S. 30, 84 (1986) (O'Connor, J., concurring). The issue of whether proportionality is relevant to political gerrymandering arose in *Vieth v. Jubelirer*, 541 U.S. 267 (2004). The plurality in *Vieth* determined that political gerrymandering cases were nonjusticiable (idem at 286–90; plurality opinion). This decision effectively rejected the plaintiff's theory that partisanship in political gerrymandering was unacceptable. The plurality listed several reasons for its decision. First, determining when partisanship renders political gerrymandering unconstitutional would be an unmanageable constitutional obligation for the court (idem at 286). Second, the effects standard previously established in *Davis v. Bendemer*, 478 U.S. 109 (1986)—whether a political party has been "denied of its chance to effectively influence the process," *Vieth*, 541 U.S. at 286 (citing *Davis*, 478 U.S. at 132–33)—was rejected because the Court found that political affiliation was not so easily discernable and sufficiently permanent as race to serve as a basis for a constitutional standard and a remedy (idem at 286–90). Finally, the plurality rejected the plaintiffs' proposed standard because it rested on the principle, unsupported by the Constitution, that groups have a right to proportional representation (idem at 288).

CHAPTER 5

1. The Court's balancing approach is extensively discussed in Richard S. Frase, *What Were They Thinking? Fourth Amendment Unreasonableness in* Atwater v. City of Lago Vista, 71 Fordham L. Rev. 329, 348–89 (2002) (hereinafter Frase, "Atwater"). For more recent cases using balancing, see Sampson v. California, 126 S.Ct. 2193 (2006) (upholding an officer's suspicionless body search of a parolee), and Illinois v. Lidster, 540 U.S. 419 (2004) (upholding a roadblock designed to find witnesses to a fatal hit-and-run accident that had occurred at that spot one week earlier).

2. *See generally* 1 Joshua Dressler & Alan C. Michaels, Understanding Criminal Procedure §§ 8.06, 17.01–18.05 (4th ed. 2006), and Frase, "Atwater," *supra* note 1, at 348–89.

3. In Florida v. Royer, 460 U.S. 491, 500 (1983), and United States v. Place, 462 U.S. 696, 709 (1983), the Court invalidated temporary seizures in part because the police failed to use a less intrusive alternative. But later cases, while still requiring that the police pursue their investigation "diligently," rejected any formal "least intrusive means" standard. *See, e.g.*, United States v. Sokolow, 490 U.S. 1, 10–11 (1989) (use of drug courier profile); Skinner v. Railway Labor Executives' Assn., 489 U.S. 602, 629 n.9 (1989) (employee drug testing); Colorado v. Bertine, 479 U.S. 367, 374,

375 (1987) (car inventory); Illinois v. Lafayette, 462 U.S. 640, 647, 648 (1983) (jail inventory); United States v. Sharpe, 470 U.S. 675, 686–87 (1985) (duration of *Terry* stop); Belton v. New York, 453 U.S. 454, 458–460 (1981) (search incident to arrest); and United States v. Martínez-Fuerte, 428 U.S. 543, 557 n.12 (1976) (immigration checkpoint).

4. *See, e.g.,* Akhil Reed Amar, *Terry and Fourth Amendment First Principles,* 72 ST. JOHN'S L. REV. 1097, 1098, 1120–23 (1998); Sherry F. Colb, *The Qualitative Dimensions of Fourth Amendment "Reasonableness,"* 98 COLUM. L. REV. 1642, 1724–25 (1998); Frase, "Atwater," *supra* note 1, at 389–94; Christopher Slobogin, *Let's Not Bury* Terry: *A Call for Rejuvenation of the Proportionality Principle,* 72 ST. JOHN'S L. REV. 1053 (1998). Other Fourth Amendment articles that implicitly apply proportionality principles include Anthony G. Amsterdam, *Perspectives on the Fourth Amendment,* 58 MINN. L. REV. 349, 436–37 (1974); Timothy P. O'Neill, *Beyond Privacy, Beyond Probable Cause, Beyond the Fourth Amendment: New Strategies for Fighting Pretext Arrests,* 69 COLO. L. REV. 693, 719–24 (1998); and William J. Stuntz, *O.J. Simpson, Bill Clinton, and the Transubstantive Fourth Amendment,* 114 HARV. L. REV. 842, 869–76 (2001).

5. 335 U.S. 451, 459 (1948) (Jackson, J., concurring).

6. Atwater v. City of Lago Vista, 532 U.S. 318, 364, 371–72 (2001). Ms. Atwater was a long-time resident of the town, her identity was well known to the arresting officer, and there was no reason to fear imminent danger or continued violations if, as would be the normal procedure, she were released on citation. *See generally* Frase, "Atwater," *supra* note 1 (critiquing Court's ruling in *Atwater* and proposing workable subconstitutional limits on arrests in minor traffic cases).

7. Frase, "Atwater," *supra* note 1, at 373–74.

8. 466 U.S. 740, 753–54 (1984).

9. Idem at 751, 753 (citing Dorman v. United States, 435 F. 2d 385, 392 (1970)).

10. *McDonald,* 335 U.S. at 459 (Jackson, J., concurring).

11. *Welsh,* 466 U.S. at 754. The Court doubted that the defendant was a danger to the public since he had voluntarily returned home and gone to bed (idem at 753).

12. *See* DRESSLER & MICHAELS, *supra* note 2, § 9.02. *See also* Thomas Y. Davies, *The Fictional Character of Law-and-Order Originalism: A Case Study of the Distortions and Evasions of Framing-Era Arrest Doctrine in* Atwater v. Lago Vista, 37 WAKE FOREST L. REV. 239, 322–26 (2002) (discussing other common law distinctions between felony and misdemeanor arrest powers). The Court has never decided whether any aspect of the in-presence rule is enforceable under the Fourth Amendment (Frase, "Atwater," *supra* note 1, at 391).

13. 471 U.S. 1, 11–12 (1985). The Court implicitly adopted the deadly force limits of the Model Penal Code, Section 3.07(2)(b)(iv), and the lower court explicitly did so (idem at 6 n.7). The linkage of Fourth Amendment standards with Model Penal Code justification rules shows that constitutional and subconstitutional proportionality principles regulating use of force draw from similar underlying values. For further discussion of subconstitutional principles see chapter 6, part B.

14. Idem at 11.
15. 490 U.S. 386, 396 (1989).
16. 469 U.S. 221, 229 (1985).
17. *See, e.g.*, State v. Amburgy 701 N.E. 2d 728, 731 (Ohio App. 1997); State v. Holmes, 569 N.W. 2d 181, 185 (Minn. 1997).
18. *See e.g.*, Wilson v. Shelby County et al., 95 F. Supp. 2d 1258, 1262–63 (N.D. Ala. 2000) (eight federal circuits have condemned blanket strip search policies applied to minor-offense detainees); Welsh v. Wisconsin, 466 U.S. 740, 751 (1984) (lower courts have long considered offense seriousness an important factor in assessing whether exigent circumstances permit warrantless entry of a home). *See generally* Eugene Volokh, *Crime Severity and Constitutional Line-drawing*, 90 VA. L. REV. 1957 (2004); William A. Schroeder, *Factoring the Seriousness of the Offense into Fourth Amendment Equations: Warrantless Entries into Premises: The Legacy of Welsh v. Wisconsin*, 38 U. KAN. L. REV. 439, 444 n.26 (1990).
19. 342 U.S. 1 (1951).
20. Idem at 5. *But see* United States v. Salerno, 481 U.S. 739, 754–55 (1987) (the Eighth Amendment does not require setting bail at all, and the state's legitimate interests include prevention of further crime and/or threats to witnesses, as well as prevention of flight).
21. 18 U.S.C. §§ 3142(b) and (c). *See also* idem at § 3142(e), (f), and (g) (providing that the court may also deny release and issue a detention order upon finding that no combination of release conditions will reasonably ensure appearance and safety).
22. German proportionality limits on arrest and pretrial detention are discussed in Richard S. Frase & Thomas Weigend, *German Criminal Justice as a Guide to American Law Reform: Similar Problems, Better Solutions?* 18 B.C. INT'L & COMPAR. L. REV. 317, 326–29 (1995). *See also* French Code of Criminal Procedure, Preliminary Article, sec. III, which incorporates both means- and ends-proportionality concepts (all "restrictive measures" imposed on suspects and defendants must be "strictly limited to the necessities of the procedure [and] proportional to the seriousness of the alleged offense"); idem art. 144, para. 1 (the court may not order pretrial detention unless this is "the only way" to achieve one or more of defined purposes of detention).
23. *See, e.g.*, OHIO CONST. art. I., § 9 (no bail required for nonjailable offenses); MINN. STAT. § 629.471 (maximum bail in misdemeanor cases is normally double the highest authorized fine, though for some offenses the maxima are four or six times higher); Ex parte Thomas, 815 So. 2d 592, 595 (Ala. Crim. App. 2001) (as a rule of thumb, bail should equal $1,000 times the maximum sentence (in years) the accused could face on the charges); *In re* Periandri, 756 N.E. 2d 682, 684–85 (Ohio Ct. App. 2001) (Cuyahoga County Court of Common Pleas guidelines set higher maxima for more serious offenses); 1987 R.I. Lexis 408 (similar bail guidelines).
24. *See, e.g.*, Ex parte Durst, 148 S.W. 3d 496 (Tex. Ct. App. 2004) (lowering bail from $3 billion to $450,000; despite flight and evidence-tampering risks and defendant's great wealth, the amount set by the lower court was too high for bail-jumping and

evidence-tampering charges; in most cases, the court ruled, offense severity and expected sentence are the "controlling factors," though the "triple risk" in this case makes them only "important" factors; the court also found that lower bail combined with other release conditions would adequately ensure appearance).

25. For another example of the use of proportionality as an evidentiary tool see part E.

26. *See, e.g.*, Ex parte Lonardo, 89 N.E. 2d 502 (Ohio Ct. App. 1949) (bail of $75,000 was too high for the minor crime of "being a suspicious person"; defendants had numerous prior convictions, and the prosecutor argued they were dangerous organized crime figures); People ex rel. Sammons v. Snow, 173 N.E. 8 (Ill. 1930) (bail of $50,000 was too high for the crime of vagrancy; defendant had a record of numerous violent crimes and a prison escape).

27. 390 U.S. 570, 583 (1968). *Cf.* Corbitt v. New Jersey, 439 U.S. 212, 218, 221 n.9 (1978) and Brady v. United States, 397 U.S. 742, 746 (1970) (distinguishing *Jackson* and emphasizing the unnecessary-burden rationale of that case).

28. 483 U.S. 44, 55–56 (1987). In *Holmes v. South Carolina,* 547 U.S. 319 (2006) the Court cited *Rock* and unanimously held that exclusion of the defendant's proffered alternative-perpetrator evidence denied him a fair trial.

29. 380 U.S. 609, 613–15 (1965).

30. 529 U.S. 61, 65–66 (2000).

31. 406 U.S. 605, 610 (1972).

32. Idem at 611.

33. 544 U.S. 622, 624, 626 (2005) (quoting Holbrook v. Flynn, 475 U.S. 560, 568–69 (1986), and tracing the antishackling rule back to Blackstone's Commentaries).

34. Idem at 634–35.

35. 539 U.S. 166 (2003). *See also* Riggins v. Nevada, 504 U.S. 127 (1992) (trial competency) and Washington v. Harper, 494 U.S. 210 (1990) (dangerous prison inmate).

36. *Sell,* 539 U.S. at 179–180. *See also* idem at 180–82, 186.

37. 494 U.S. 210, 223–25 (1990).

38. *Cf.* Riggins v. Nevada, 504 U.S. 127, 140–41 (1992) (Kennedy, J., concurring) (trial-competency cases are different from and cause more concern than dangerous-inmate cases). For further discussion of cases that involve treatment of prisoners see chapter 7, part C.

39. *See, e.g.*, Susan Klein, *Redrawing the Criminal-Civil Boundary*, 2 Buffalo Crim. L. Rev. 679 (1999). However, civil forfeitures straddle this divide: They are subject to the Eighth Amendment excessive fines clause but are generally not subject to criminal procedure safeguards. For further discussion of forfeitures see chapter 7, part D.

40. *See* Kansas v. Hendricks, 521 U.S. 346, 356 (1997) (civil commitment); U.S. v. Salerno, 481 U.S. 739, 746–48 (1987) (detention without bail); U.S. v. Ward, 448 U.S. 242, 248 (1980) (civil penalty of $5,000); Bell v. Wolfish, 441 U.S. 520, 535 (1979) (conditions of pretrial detention). See further discussion of prison and jail cases in chapter 7, part C.

41. *See, e.g.*, Kennedy v. Mendoza-Martínez, 372 U.S. 144 (1963) (revocation of draft evader's citizenship).

42. *See, e.g.*, Hudson v. United States, 522 U.S. 93 (1997) (double jeopardy); Smith v. Doe, 538 U.S. 84 (2003) (ex post facto).

43. *See* JOHN H. ELY, DEMOCRACY AND DISTRUST: A THEORY OF JUDICIAL REVIEW 146 (Harvard Univ. Press 1980). For further discussion of strict scrutiny see chapter 3.

44. *See, e.g.*, United States v. Halper, 490 U.S. 435 (1989) (civil penalty for false claims bore no rational relation to compensation of government for its losses and enforcement costs. The Court repeatedly labeled the penalty as "disproportionate" (idem at 446 n.6, 449, 450, 452).

45. *Hudson*, 522 U.S. at 101 (disapproving *Halper* because that case seemed to treat the excessiveness factor as dispositive).

46. *Smith*, 538 U.S. at 103.

47. *Cf.* Roy G. Spece Jr., *Justifying Invigorated Scrutiny and the Least Restrictive Alternative as a Superior Form of Intermediate Review: Civil Commitment and the Right to Treatment as a Case Study*, 21 ARIZ. L. REV. 1049, 1054–56 (1979).

48. *See, e.g.*, State ex rel. K. W. v. Werner, 242 S.E. 2d 907, 913 (W.Va. 1978) (requiring that juveniles receive the least restrictive alternative treatment consistent with the purpose of their custody, citing state and federal cases); State v. Krol, 344 A. 2d 289, 300–301 (N.J. 1975) (indefinite commitment order must achieve public safety "in a fashion that reasonably minimizes infringements upon defendant's liberty and autonomy").

49. *See* U.S. v. Leon, 468 U.S. 897, 907 (1984) (admissibility is determined by "weighing the costs and benefits of preventing the use in the prosecution's case in chief of inherently trustworthy tangible evidence").

50. Rakas v. Illinois, 439 U.S. 128, 136–37 (1978).

51. *See, e.g.*, Pennsylvania v. Scott, 524 U.S. 357, 364 (1998) (parole revocation hearing); U.S. v. Havens, 446 U.S. 620, 627–28 (1980) (impeachment).

52. *See, e.g.*, Calandra v. U.S., 414 U.S. 338, 351–52 (1974) (costs of extending exclusionary rule to grand jury proceedings not justified by limited probable added deterrence of police misconduct). *See also* Teague v. Lane, 489 U.S. 288, 310 (1989) (costs imposed on states by retroactive application in habeas cases of new constitutional rules far outweigh benefits).

53. 422 U.S. 590, 603–604 (1975).

54. *See also* MODEL CODE OF PRE-ARRAIGNMENT PROCEDURE § 290.2(2) (unless constitutionally required, motions to suppress evidence "shall be granted only if the court finds that the violation was substantial," considering the degree and willfulness of violation, extent of privacy invasion, and extent that exclusion would help prevent violations).

55. Bentham's utilitarian proportionality principles are discussed further in chapter 7.

56. *See, e.g.*, State v. Fakler, 503 N.W. 2d 783, 787–88 (Minn. 1993); City of Kettering v. Hollen, 416 N.E. 2d 598, 600 (Ohio 1980).

57. 401 U.S. 222 (1971).

58. Idem at 225 (emphasis added).

59. 124 S. Ct. 2620, 2622, 2628, 2630 (2004). *See also* idem at 2627 ("[A]ny further extension of these [Miranda] rules must be justified by its necessity.").

60. 538 U.S. 760, 779 (2003) (Souter, J., concurring).

61. *See, e.g.,* Dickerson v. United States, 530 U.S. 428, 440 (2000) (*Miranda* procedures are constitutionally required in the absence of alternative safeguards that are "at least as effective in apprising accused persons" of their right of silence and in assuring a continuous opportunity to exercise it"); Mapp v. Ohio, 367 U.S. 643, 652 (1961) (the exclusionary rule is constitutionally required because some effective remedy is needed, and other remedies such as administrative discipline and damage suits have proved "worthless and futile"). *But see* Hudson v. Michigan, 126 S. Ct. 2159, 2167 (2006) (alternative remedies have improved since *Mapp*).

62. *See* Stephen A. Saltzburg & Daniel J. Capra, American Criminal Procedure: Cases and Commentary, 586–88 (8th ed. 2007).

63. 424 U.S. 319, 347–48 (1976) (holding that the cost and administrative burdens of requested welfare termination procedures would outweigh the likely benefits of these added safeguards).

64. Blanton v. City of North Las Vegas, 489 U.S. 538, 543 (1989). *See also* Baldwin v. New York, 399 U.S. 66, 69–70 (1970); Duncan v. Louisiana, 391 U.S. 145, 159 (1968).

65. 372 U.S. 335 (1963).

66. Scott v. Illinois, 440 U.S. 367 (1979) (jail sentence); Alabama v. Shelton, 535 U.S. 654 (2002) (suspended jail sentence). In contrast, the pretrial right to counsel during custodial interrogation, recognized in *Miranda v. Arizona*, applies regardless of the sentence authorized or imposed (Berkemer v. McCarty, 468 U.S. 420, 434 (1984)). However, all *Miranda* rights are inapplicable when police questioning is "reasonably prompted by a concern for public safety" (e.g., "Where's the gun?") (New York v. Quarles, 467 U.S. 649, 655–56 (1984)). The *Quarles* exception reflects ends-benefits proportionality and is analogous to the power police have to use deadly force when dealing with a dangerous suspect. *See supra* part A.

67. *Duncan*, 391 U.S. at 160. There was no similar historical basis for limiting counsel rights in minor cases (Argersinger v. Hamlin, 407 U.S. 25, 30 (1972)).

68. *Duncan*, 391 U.S. at 160.

69. 440 U.S. at 373.

70. *See, e.g.,* Minn. Const. art. I, § 6 (jury size); Minn. R. Crim. P. 5.02 (appointed counsel); idem at 9 (pretrial discovery); idem at 11, 12 (mandatory pretrial omnibus hearing for felonies and gross misdemeanors, optional pretrial conference and hearing for misdemeanors); idem at 26.01, subd. 1 (jury trial rights); idem at 28.02, subd. 4(3) (appeal time limits).

CHAPTER 6

1. Other constitutional limitations on criminal liability (as well as on noncriminal measures) are designed to protect First Amendment, equal protection,

and other fundamental rights. These limits are examined in the discussions of judicial review levels (e.g., strict and intermediate scrutiny, rational basis) in chapter 3.

2. Bouie v. City of Columbia, 378 U.S. 347, 353–54 (1964). *But see* Rogers v. Tennessee, 532 U.S. 451 (2001) (judicial abolition of common law requirement that the murder victim die within a year and a day from the defendant's acts was neither unexpected nor indefensible and thus did not violate due process).

3. City of Chicago v. Morales, 527 U.S. 41, 56 (1999). Such laws are also invalid because they "authorize and even encourage arbitrary and discriminatory enforcement" (idem).

4. 379 U.S. 559 (1965).

5. 355 U.S. 225, 228–30 (1957).

6. Joshua Dressler, Understanding Criminal Law 42 (4th ed. 2006); Herbert L. Packer, The Limits of the Criminal Sanction 79–99 (Stanford Univ. Press 1968).

7. *Lambert*, 355 U.S. at 229.

8. 370 U.S. 660 (1962).

9. Dressler, *supra* note 6, at 105; Packer, *supra* note 6, at 73–79.

10. *Robinson*, 370 U.S. at 667.

11. Idem at 666–67.

12. See William Stuntz, *The Uneasy Relationship Between Criminal Procedure and Criminal Justice*, 107 Yale L.J. 1, 68 n.234 (1997) (citing several 1962 articles).

13. 392 U.S. 514 (1968).

14. Dressler, *supra* note 6, at 107 (noting that dissenters and Justice White would not allow the conviction of an addict for using drugs). Justice White also stated that he would not vote to convict a homeless alcoholic for being drunk in public (*Powell*, 392 U.S. at 551).

15. Jones v. City of Los Angeles, 444 F. 3d 1118 (9th Cir. 2006); Tobe v. City of Santa Ana, 27 Cal. Rptr. 2d 386 (Cal. App. 1994); Pottinger v. City of Miami, 810 F. Supp. 1551 (S.D. Fla. 1992). *See generally* Benno Weisberg, *When Punishing Innocent Conduct Violates the Eighth Amendment: Applying the* Robinson *Doctrine to Homelessness and Other Contextual "Crimes,"* 96 J. Crim. L. & Criminol. 329 (2005) (Eighth Amendment should ban conviction for conduct that is criminal only under circumstances the defendant cannot avoid).

16. *Tobe*, 27 Cal. Rptr. 2d at 393–95; *Pottinger*, 810 F. Supp. at 1580–83.

17. See, e.g., State v. Guminga, 395 N.W. 2d 344, 346–47 (Minn. 1986); Davis v. City of Peachtree City, 304 S.E. 2d 701 (Ga. 1983); Commonwealth v. Koczwara, 155 A. 2d 825 (Pa. 1959) (barring custody sentence but not conviction). *Cf.* U.S. v. Park, 421 U.S. 658, 665 n.9 (1975) (upholding the conviction of the president of a national retail food chain for allowing rodent contamination in one of the company's warehouses, based solely on his CEO status).

18. See, e.g., *Guminga*, 395 N.W. 2d at 347 ("such an intrusion on personal liberty is not justified by the public interest protected, especially when there are

alternative means by which to achieve the same end, such as civil fines or license suspension").

19. *Cf.* PACKER, *supra* note 6, at 137–39 (retributive rationale for the reasonable doubt rule). In parallel fashion, the limiting retributive severity principle gives greater emphasis to avoiding penalties that are too severe than it does to avoiding those that are too lenient (see further discussion in chapter 7, part F).

20. *In re* Winship, 397 U.S. 358, 364 (1970).

21. H.L.A. HART, PUNISHMENT AND RESPONSIBILITY: ESSAYS IN THE PHILOSOPHY OF LAW 8, at 27, 236–37 (Oxford Univ. Press 1968).

22. PACKER, *supra* note 6, at 16, 62, 66.

23. PACKER, *supra* note 6, at 95. However, in *United States v. Lanier*, 520 U.S. 259, 266 (1997), the Court seemed to suggest that under at least some circumstances the rule of lenity is constitutionally required by the due process clauses. *See also* WAYNE R. LaFAVE, CRIMINAL LAW 88 n.28 (4th ed. 2003) (the "fair warning" principle underlies constitutional and subconstitutional doctrines of lenity, vagueness, ex post facto, and abolition of common law crimes).

24. LaFAVE, *supra* note 23, at 89; U.S. v. Bass, 404 U.S. 336, 348 (1971).

25. LaFAVE, *supra* note 23, at 77–78.

26. Amer. Law Inst., Model Penal Code and Commentaries, parts I & II (1985), § 2.05, cmt. 1.

27. MODEL PENAL CODE § 2.02(1). "Material" elements exclude technical matters such as the statute of limitations, jurisdiction, and venue (idem § 1.13(10)).

28. See DRESSLER, *supra* note 6, at 128–29 (*mens rea* is more of a retributive than a utilitarian requirement).

29. PACKER, *supra* note 6, at 69, 261.

30. *See* LaFAVE, *supra* note 23, at 278–79 (citing Alaska and Louisiana cases).

31. N.Y. PENAL LAW § 15.15(2), applied in People v. Ryan, 626 N.E. 2d 51 (N.Y., 1993).

32. *In re* Welfare of C.R.M., 611 N.W. 2d 802 (Minn. 2000) (requiring clear legislative intent to dispense with proof of *mens rea*, particularly for felony-level crimes, and holding that the crime of possessing a knife on school property requires knowingly being in possession).

33. 342 U.S. 246 (1952).

34. 438 U.S. 422, 438, 443–46 (1978).

35. 471 U.S. 419, 426 (1985).

36. Idem at 426. The Court also based its decision on the rule of lenity (discussed earlier).

37. *See* Cheek v. U.S., 498 U.S. 192 (1991) (tax evasion and failure to file); Ratzlaff v. U.S., 510 U.S. 135 (1994) (structuring of currency transactions). *See also* James v. U.S., 366 U.S. 213 (1961) (willful tax evasion could not be shown in light of the gloss that a prior case (overruled in *James*) had placed on the statute at issue).

38. 511 U.S. 600 (1994).

39. 513 U.S. 64 (1994).

40. *See generally* John S. Wiley, *Not Guilty by Reason of Blamelessness: Culpability in Federal Criminal Interpretation*, 85 Va. L. Rev. 1021, 1023 (1999).

41. Model Penal Code § 2.01(1) (criminal liability requires proof of "a voluntary act or the omission to perform an act of which [defendant] is physically capable").

42. Dressler, *supra* note 6, at 99.

43. 138 N.E. 2d 799 (N.Y. 1956) (affirming convictions for negligent homicide).

44. Dressler, *supra* note 6, at 53, 237–38. Exceptions to these rules can be found in many states, however, and laws that cut back retreat, necessity, or proportional-force requirements have been enacted with increasing frequency in recent years. *See generally* Renee Lettow Lerner, *The Worldwide Popular Revolt Against Proportionality in Self-defense Law*, 2 J. L. Econ. & Policy 331 (2006). *See also* Stuart P. Green, *Castles and Carjackers: Proportionality and the Use of Deadly Force in Defense of Dwellings and Vehicles*, 1999 U. Ill. L. Rev. 1.

45. *See, e.g.*, Dressler, *supra* note 6, at 238.

46. Model Penal Code § 3.02. See also chapter 5, part A, which discusses Fourth Amendment limits on police use of deadly force that resemble restrictions on the justified use of deadly force in law enforcement under Model Penal Code § 3.07.

47. *See, e.g.*, Dressler, *supra* note 6, at 224–25.

48. Some writers and criminal codes also include, under excuse rather than justification, cases of reasonable mistake as to justifying conditions. *See, e.g.*, Paul Robinson, Criminal Law 451–61 (1997).

49. Dressler, *supra* note 6, at 219, 226; Sanford H. Kadish, *Excusing Crime*, 75 Calif. L. Rev. 257, 263–66.

50. Dressler, *supra* note 6, at 54–58; Packer, *supra* note 6, at 143.

51. Packer, *supra* note 6, at 117–18 discusses a similar mountain-road example and agrees that reasons of fairness, not utility, argue for permitting a defense of excuse in such cases.

CHAPTER 7

1. *Compare* Pamela S. Karlan, *"Pricking the Lines": The Due Process Clause, Punitive Damages, and Criminal Punishment*, 88 Minn. L. Rev. 880, 903–14 (2004) (arguing that punitive damages awards justify stricter constitutional scrutiny than prison sentences because the former cannot be reviewed by lower federal courts; they are imposed by untrained local juries, not judges and legislators, and they can be objectively compared to the compensatory damages award in the same case), *with* Richard S. Frase, *Excessive Prison Sentences, Punishment Goals, and the Eighth Amendment: "Proportionality" Relative to What?* 89 Minn. L. Rev. 571, 609 (2005) (hereinafter *Proportionality*) (pointing out that damages do not involve physical liberty; that the typical, well-financed civil defendants can better defend themselves than most criminal defendants; and that trial judges can set aside excessive damages awards, whereas criminal defendants often have no subconstitutional remedies against excessive prison terms; also noting that in at least three

respects—de novo review, more frequent use of comparative analysis, and more lenient treatment of recidivists (only violations of a similar nature, committed in the same state, may be used to justify a punitive damages award)—the Court seems to be much more protective of civil defendants' bank accounts than it has been of criminal defendants' liberty).

2. *See, e.g.*, Wilkerson v. Utah, 99 U.S. 130 (1878) (upholding execution by firing squad).

3. 217 U.S. 349 (1910).

4. Idem at 367. *But see* Badders v. United States, 240 U.S. 391 (1916); Graham v. West Virginia, 224 U.S. 616 (1912) (upholding prison terms; no mention of *Weems*).

5. 356 U.S. 86, 100–101 (1958).

6. 370 U.S. 660 (1962) (crime of narcotics addiction violates Eighth Amendment).

7. 392 U.S. 514 (1968) (crime of public drunkenness is constitutional).

8. 433 U.S. 584, 592 n.4 (1977) (holding that the death penalty is grossly disproportionate to the crime of raping an adult woman, even if that penalty might measurably serve some punishment goals).

9. *See, e.g.*, Roper v. Simmons, 543 U.S. 551, 571 (2005).

10. *See, e.g.*, idem at 570–71 (2005) (offenders under eighteen at the time of the offense); Atkins v. Virginia, 536 U.S. 304, 319 (2002) (offenders with mental retardation); Tison v. Arizona, 481 U.S. 137, 158 (1987) (accomplice's major participation in a felony resulting in death, combined with reckless indifference to human life); Enmund v. Florida, 458 U.S. 782, 800–801 (1982) (felony murder accomplice's limited intent and role in the offense); *Coker*, 433 U.S. at 598 ("in terms of moral depravity and of the injury to the person and to the public, [rape of an adult woman] does not compare with murder"). Scholars have also emphasized retributive principles; *see, e.g.*, Margaret J. Radin, *The Jurisprudence of Death: Evolving Standards for the Cruel and Unusual Punishments Clause*, 126 U. Pa. L. Rev. 989, 1056 (1978) ("a punishment is excessive and unconstitutional…if it inflicts more pain than the individual deserves").

11. Bruce W. Gilchrist, *Disproportionality in Sentences of Imprisonment*, 79 Colum. L. Rev. 1119, 1147 (1979).

12. See further discussion of European standards in chapter 1. Actions that fail the rational basis test are excessive and therefore arguably disproportionate in the sense that they impose totally useless costs or burdens.

13. Several justices and scholars have taken this view of the death penalty generally. *See* Furman v. Georgia, 408 U.S. 238, 300–302 (Brennan, J., concurring); idem, 408 U.S. at 331–32, 342–59 (Marshall, J., concurring); Margaret R. Gibbs, *Eighth Amendment: Narrow Proportionality Requirement Preserves Deference to Legislative Judgment*, 82 J. Crim. L. & Criminology 955, 976 (1992) ("If there is a significantly less severe punishment adequate to achieve the purposes for which the punishment is inflicted, then this would also contribute to a conclusion of disproportionality."); Michael Herz, *Nearest to Legitimacy: Justice White and Strict Rational Basis Scrutiny*, 74 U. Colo. L. Rev. 1329, 1352 (2003) ("[W]hat matters in

determining whether capital punishment for a particular offense is 'needless' is the *incremental* deterrent effect of capital punishment as opposed to lengthy, or life-long, imprisonment.").

14. *See* Gregg v. Georgia, 428 U.S. 153, 173 (1976) (plurality opinion) ("punishment must not involve the unnecessary and wanton infliction of pain"). The *Gregg* opinion also stated "we cannot invalidate a category of penalties because we deem less severe penalties adequate to serve the ends of penology" (idem at 182–83). However, the later cases we cite (*Enmund, Atkins,* and *Roper*) imply a "less-would-do-just-as-well" approach, at least for certain offenders.

15. *Enmund,* 458 U.S. at 798–800 (accomplices); *Atkins,* 536 U.S. at 319–20 (offenders with mental retardation); *Roper,* 543 U.S. at 572 (offenders under eighteen).

16. *Roper,* 543 U.S. at 572.

17. *See, e.g.,* Morales v. Tilton, 465 F. Supp. 2d 972 (N.D. Cal. 2006), and cases cited therein. *See generally, Note, A New Test for Evaluating Eighth Amendment Challenges to Lethal Injections,* 120 HARV. L. REV. 1301 (2007).

18. *See, e.g., Morales,* 465 F. Supp. 2d at 974, 981.

19. *See* Wilkerson v. Utah, 99 U.S. 130, 135–36 (1878), stating that the Eighth Amendment prohibits "punishments of torture...and all others in the same line of unnecessary cruelty," and State of La. ex rel. Francis v. Resweber, 329 U.S. 459, 463 (1947), opining that the amendment bans "unnecessary pain" during execution.

20. 128 S. Ct. 1520 (2008).

21. Idem at 1532. At several points Justice Roberts also suggested that the risk of pain must be found to be "objectively intolerable." Idem at 1531, 1532, 1535, 1537. Justices Scalia and Thomas concurred in the judgment, but appeared to reject any consideration of unnecessary risk of pain; these two justices maintained that the Eighth Amendment only bans methods of execution that are "deliberately designed to inflict pain." Idem at 1556 (Thomas, J., concurring).

22. 463 U.S. 277, 290–92 (1983).

23. 445 U.S. 263 (1980).

24. Idem at 280, 293; Solem v. Helm, 463 U.S. 277, 301–302 (1983) (stating *Rummel* facts).

25. *Rummel,* 445 U.S. at 272 (citing Coker v. Georgia, 433 U.S. 584, 592 (1977)).

26. Idem at 275.

27. Idem at 275–76.

28. Idem at 302.

29. 454 U.S. 370 (1982) (per curiam).

30. Idem at 377–79 (Powell, J., concurring). Davis's severe sentence may also have been due in part to the fact that he was an African American man who, in a rural Virginia community, had dared to date white women and marry one. *See* Steven Grossman, *Proportionality in Non-capital Sentencing: The Supreme Court's Tortured Approach to Cruel and Unusual Punishment,* 84 KY. L. J. 107, 120 n.80 (1996).

31. 483 F. 2d 136, 140–43 (4th Cir. 1973).

32. 463 U.S. 277 (1983).

33. Idem at 289.

34. Idem at 289–90 (citing Rummel v. Estelle, 445 U.S. at 272 (1980)).

35. Idem at 290–91.

36. Idem at 290–93. Although not cited by Justice Powell, lower courts had previously recognized similar factors. In addition to Hart v. Coiner, 483 F. 2d 136 (4th Cir. 1973), see State v. Fain, 617 P. 2d 720, 725–26 (Wash. 1980) (adopting the four *Hart* factors); Martin v. Leverette, 244 S.E. 2d 39, 43 (W. Va. 1978) (same); *In re* Foss, 519 P. 2d 1073, 1078–79 (Cal. 1974) (factors similar to *Hart* 1 through 4); *In re* Lynch, 503 P. 2d 921 (Cal. 1972) (factors similar to *Hart* 1, 3, and 4); People v. Lorentzen, 194 N.W. 2d 827, 831–33 (Mich. 1972) (factors similar to *Hart* 3 and 4).

37. *Solem*, 463 U.S. at 290–91.

38. Powell argued that Helm's severe sentence was "unlikely to advance the goals of our criminal justice system in any substantial way" and in particular was unlikely to provide treatment for his alcoholism or other rehabilitation measures (idem at 297 n.22). He also noted that certain less punished South Dakota offenders were more "deserving" of punishment (idem at 299).

39. Idem at 296 n.21.

40. 501 U.S. 957 (1990).

41. This penalty was later invalidated under the Michigan constitution in People v. Bullock, 485 N.W. 2d 866 (Mich. 1992). State constitutional provisions are discussed in part E of this chapter.

42. 501 U.S. at 994–95.

43. Idem at 994.

44. Idem at 996–1009.

45. Idem at 1005.

46. Idem at 1002.

47. Idem at 1003. In 1998 the Michigan legislature concluded the opposite and repealed life-without-parole sentences applicable to first-time drug offenders, including those charged with drug sales. *See Recent Legislation: Criminal Procedure*, 76 U. Det. Mercy L. Rev. 679 (1999).

48. 501 U.S. at 1028–29 (Stevens, J., dissenting). Justice Stevens also argued that Harmelin's severe sentence was as capricious (i.e., random) and therefore as cruel and unusual as being struck by lightning (idem; Stevens, J., dissenting).

49. Idem at 989.

50. Idem at 999.

51. 538 U.S. 11 (2003).

52. Idem at 25–28. For a critique of O'Connor's evidence, *see Proportionality, supra* note 1, at 642 and sources cited therein.

53. 538 U.S. at 29–30.

54. Idem at 32 (Scalia, J., concurring).

55. Idem at 35 (Stevens, J., dissenting).

56. Idem at 41 (Breyer, J., dissenting) (citing *Solem* and Witte v. United States, 515 U.S. 389, 402–403 (1995) (a repeat offender is punished only for his conviction offense, deemed aggravated by prior convictions)).

57. In weighing the severity of Ewing's twenty-five-year minimum sentence, Breyer noted that the defendant was thirty-eight years old, was seriously ill, and "will likely die in prison." Idem at 39 (Breyer, J., dissenting).

58. Idem at 47, 52.

59. Idem at 52.

60. 538 U.S. 63 (2003).

61. 28 U.S.C. § 2254(d)(1).

62. *Lockyer*, 538 U.S. at 82.

63. See the earlier discussion of *Rummel* (Powell, J., dissenting), *Harmelin* (Stevens, J., dissenting), *Ewing* (Breyer, J., dissenting), *Andrade* (Souter, J., dissenting), *Hart v. Coiner* (four-factor test including whether a significantly less severe penalty would serve the legislative purpose) and lower court cases adopting the *Hart* standards.

64. *See Proportionality, supra* note 1, at 628–29.

65. *See* Richard S. Frase, *Comparative Perspectives on Sentencing Policy and Research, in* Sentencing and Sanctions in Western Countries 279–81 (Michael Tonry & Richard S. Frase eds., Oxford Univ. Press 2001) (hereinafter *Comparative Perspectives*); Norval Morris & Colin Howard, Studies in Criminal Law 147–96 (Clarendon 1964); Dirk van Zyl Smit & Andrew Ashworth, *Disproportionate Sentences as Human Rights Violations*, 67 Mod. L. Rev. 541, 542–44 (2004) (hereinafter *Disproportionate Sentences*).

66. For further discussion see *Proportionality, supra* note 1, at 627–45.

67. Deterrence effects are doubtful in general. *See* Andrew von Hirsch et al., Criminal Deterrence and Sentence Severity: An Analysis of Recent Research 41–43 (Hart 1999); *see also Proportionality, supra* note 1, at 642 (critiquing the *Ewing* Court's analysis of the deterrent and incapacitative effects of the California three-strikes law).

68. *See Proportionality, supra* note 1; *see also* part F, discussing assessments of costs and benefits under ends-proportionality analysis.

69. Desert overbreadth arguments led the Canadian Supreme Court to invalidate a seven-year mandatory minimum penalty for importing narcotics. *See Smith v. the Queen*, discussed in part F. Desert overbreadth arguments are also implicit in a number of U.S. cases invalidating mandatory penalties. Some of these cases are discussed in part E.

70. *See* Harmelin v. Michigan, 501 U.S. 957, 1028–29 (Stevens, J., dissenting); *See also* Franklin E. Zimring et al., Punishment and Democracy: Three Strikes and You're Out in California 194–200 (Oxford Univ. Press 2001) (three features of mandatory minimum statutes guarantee that these laws will result in excessive punishment of many offenders: the overaggregation and "worst-case" orientation inherent in picking a single penalty; the legislature's disregard of the

important difference between symbolic and actual sanctions; and its inability to consider all offender- and case-specific mitigating factors).

71. Prisoners awaiting trial are not directly covered by the Eighth Amendment, but courts have used the due process clauses to grant many of the same protections and also to protect these inmates from harsh treatment intended as punishment before conviction. *See* Bell v. Wolfish, 441 U.S. 520, 535–36, 538 (1979); Fuentes v. Wagner, 206 F. 3d 335, 344 (3rd Cir. 2000). For discussion of the standards used to identify impermissible pretrial punishment as opposed to a permissible nonpunitive, regulatory measure see chapter 5, part E).

72. Some state constitutions have provisions that protect persons in custody from "unnecessary rigor" or from being "abused." These provisions are discussed in part E.

73. Inmate suits challenging the denial of specific constitutional rights are not governed by the Eighth Amendment but sometimes incorporate implicit means-proportionality principles. *See, e.g.,* Turner v. Safley, 482 U.S. 78, 94–99 (1987) (near-total ban on inmate marriages was an excessive response to valid security and rehabilitative concerns and thus impermissibly burdened inmates' constitutional right to marry in light of available more narrowly tailored alternative measures).

74. 429 U.S. 97, 102–104 (1976).

75. 428 U.S. 153, 173, 183 (1976). The "evolving standards" language is from Trop v. Dulles, 356 U.S. 86, 101 (1958). See also Baze v. Rees, 128 S.Ct. 1520, 1531 (2008) (plurality opinion by Roberts, J.), using Eighth Amendment standards developed in prisoners' rights cases to evaluate risks associated with lethal injection procedures. *Baze* is further discussed in part A.

76. *See, e.g.,* Spain v. Procunier, 600 F. 2d 189 (9th Cir. 1979) (use of tear gas and neck chains); Stewart v. Rhodes, 473 F. Supp. 1185, 1193 (D. Ohio 1979) (lengthy chaining of inmates to beds).

77. *See, e.g.,* Wright v. McMann, 460 F. 2d 126 (2d Cir. 1972); Adams v. Carlson, 368 F. Supp. 1050 (E.D. Ill. 1973).

78. Wilson v. Seiter, 501 U.S. 294, 298–99 (1991).

79. Farmer v. Brennan, 511 U.S. 825, 839, 847 (1994).

80. 452 U.S. 337, 347 (1981) (upholding double-celling of prison inmates).

81. *Wilson,* 501 U.S. at 304, 308.

82. Whitley v. Albers, 475 U.S. 312, 320 (1986).

83. Idem at 320–21 (1986) (inmate shot in the leg during a prison riot and hostage taking); Hudson v. McMillian, 503 U.S. 1, 6–7 (1992) (prisoner punched and kicked while cuffed and shackled and being led to the lockdown area).

84. *Hudson,* 503 U.S. at 9–10.

85. Nonproportionality standards are more defensible when applied to certain claims (e.g., inadequate medical care, failure to protect, or harsh prison conditions) that involve measures that are banned as inhumane and a violation of human dignity.

86. 536 U.S. 730, 737–45 (2002).

87. 256 F. 3d 679, 683–84 (7th Cir. 2001).

88. 466 F. Supp. 2d 51 (D.D.C. 2006).

89. Trammel v. Keane, 338 F. 3d 155, 163, 166 (2d Cir. 2003).

90. *Hudson*, 503 U.S. at 7. *See also* Williams v. Benjamin, 77 F. 3d 756, 765 (4th Cir. 1996) (unnecessary infliction of pain for a prolonged time period supported inference that the guards were acting to punish the inmates rather than to quell the disturbance).

91. Whitley v. Albers, 475 U.S. 312, 319 (1986) (the test is not whether "it may appear in retrospect that the degree of force authorized or applied for security purposes was unreasonable, and hence unnecessary in the strict sense").

92. 18 U.S.C. § 3626.

93. Magna Carta §§ 20–21 (fines should be graded according to offense seriousness and should also not deprive the offender of his livelihood).

94. Browning-Ferris Industries v. Kelco Disposal, 492 U.S. 257, 264 (1989) (at least eight states that ratified the Constitution had some equivalent of the excessive fines clause in their state constitutions or declarations of rights).

95. Idem at 262. The Court's decisions limiting punitive damages awards under the due process clauses are discussed in chapter 4.

96. 509 U.S. 544, 558–59 (1993).

97. 509 U.S. 602, 609–10, 621–23 (1993).

98. 524 U.S. 321, 334–40 (1998).

99. Barry L. Johnson, Purging the Cruel and Unusual: The Autonomous Excessive Fines Clause and Desert-based Constitutional Limits on Forfeitures After United States v. Bajakajian, 2000 U. ILL. L. REV. 461, 492–98; Karlan, supra note 1, at 901; Rachel Van Cleave, *"Death is Different," Is Money Different? Criminal Punishments, Forfeitures, and Punitive Damages: Shifting Constitutional Paradigms for Assessing Proportionality*, 12 S. CAL. INTERDISC. L. J. 217, 251–22 (2003). See further discussion of retributive principles in part F.

100. Susan R. Klein, *The Discriminatory Application of Substantive Due Process: A Tale of Two Vehicles*, 1997 U. ILL. L. REV. 453, 482.

101. *See, e.g.*, U.S. v. Heldeman, 402 F. 3d 220, 223 (1st Cir. 2005) (forfeiture of defendant's $900,000 equity in his apartment following fraud and drug convictions held not excessive); *see also* U.S. v. Betancourt, 422 F. 3d 240, 250 (5th Cir. 2005) (forfeiture of $5.4 million lottery winnings from a ticket purchased with drug proceeds; excessive fines clause does not apply to contraband, fruits, or proceeds of illegal activity). *But see* U.S. v. 3814 N.W. Thurman St., 164 F. 3d 1191 (9th Cir. 1999) (seeming to adopt a narrow definition of crime fruits that are excluded from excessive fines protection).

102. *See, e.g.*, U.S. v. 3814 N.W. Thurman St., 164 F. 3d 1191 (9th Cir. 1999) (invalidating forfeiture of $200,686 increase in property owner's equity when fraudulently obtained loan was partly used to reduce liens on the property); One Car, 1996 Dodge X-Cab Truck v. State, 122 S.W. 3d 422 (Tex. Ct. App. 2003) (invalidating forfeiture of truck worth $11,000, containing trace amounts of methamphetamine).

103. *See, e.g.*, Wilson v. Commissioner of Revenue, 656 N.W. 2d 547 (Minn. 2003) (applying excessive fines clauses to punitive assessment levied personally against corporate officer of company employing a delinquent taxpayer after the company failed to honor a wage levy and holding that the $45,363 assessment was grossly disproportional both to the company's failure to levy and to other authorized wage levy sanctions in the state and other jurisdictions).

104. *See, e.g.*, State v. Rewitzer, 617 N.W. 2d 407 (Minn. 2000), using the *Solem* analysis to hold that $273,600 in fines and surcharges, imposed for the sale of twenty-four grams of marijuana and twenty-one grams of hallucinogenic mushrooms, violated both federal and state excessive fines clauses.

105. 923 P. 2d 163, 166 (Colo. Ct. App. 1995). *See also* People v. Pourat, 100 P. 3d 503 (Colo. Ct. App. 2004) (*Malone* ability-to-pay factor valid after *Bajakajian*, which did not rule on that issue).

106. 525 N.W. 2d 513 (Mich. Ct. App. 1994).

107. Idem at 515.

108. 699 A. 2d 767, 769 (Pa. Super. Ct. 1997).

109. *See, e.g.*, U.S. v. Heldeman, 402 F. 3d 220, 223 (1st Cir. 2005) ($900,000 forfeiture upheld principally by comparison to $6 million maximum fine, assuming consecutive $1 million fines on each of the six counts, noting that the forfeited amount was only 15 percent of the maximum possible fine).

110. State v. Venman, 564 A. 2d 574, 581–82 (Vt. 1989).

111. *See* State v. Fain, 617 P. 2d 720, 725 (Wash. 1980) (noting that one purpose stated in the state penal code is "[t]o differentiate on reasonable grounds between serious and minor offenses, and to prescribe proportionate penalties for each") (citing Rev. Code Wash. Sec. 9A.04.020(1)(d)).

112. *See, e.g.*, Sterling v. Cupp, 625 P. 2d 123 (Or. 1981) (search by opposite-sex guard).

113. *See, e.g.*, Abraham v. State, 585 P. 2d 526 (Alaska 1978) (remanded for hearings to effectuate defendant's constitutional right to rehabilitative treatment of his alcoholism; defendant spoke only Yupik (Eskimo) and alleged there were no prison programs for such people).

114. *See, e.g.*, Ascher v. Comm'r of Pub. Safety, 519 N.W. 2d 183, 187 (Minn. 1994) (rejecting the Fourth Amendment rule that permits suspicionless sobriety checkpoint stops of drivers despite identical wording of Minnesota and U.S. constitutional search-and-seizure provisions). *See generally* CHARLES H. WHITEBREAD & CHRISTOPHER SLOBOGIN, CRIMINAL PROCEDURE: AN ANALYSIS OF CASES AND CONCEPTS 1027–43 (4th ed. 2000) (reviewing state law expansions of constitutional rights related to search and seizure, interrogation, and other procedural issues).

115. *See generally, Length of Sentence as Violation of Constitutional Provisions Prohibiting Cruel and Unusual Punishment*, Howard J. Alperin, 33 A.L.R. 3d 335 (1970, updated through Feb. 12, 2008).

Some state cases have struck down sentences under the Eighth Amendment, or under both the federal and state constitutions, without separate discussion of the state constitutional provision. *See, e.g.*, Wilson v. State, 830 So.

2d 765 (Ala. Crim. App. 2001); Crosby v. State, 824 A. 2d 894 (Del. Super. Ct. 2003); People v. Gaskins, 923 P. 2d 292 (Colo. Ct. App. 1996); Humphrey v. Wilson, 652 S.E. 2d 501 (Ga. 2007). *See also* State v. Davis, 79 P. 3d 64 (Ariz. 2003) (invalidating mandatory consecutive sentences totaling fifty-two years without possibility of release for statutory rape); *but see* State v. Berger, 134 P. 3d 378 (Ariz. 2006), *cert. denied*, Berger v. Arizona, 127 S.Ct. 1370 (U.S. 2007) (distinguishing *Davis* and upholding mandatory consecutive terms totaling two hundred years without release for first-offense possession (downloading) of child pornography).

116. 537 P. 2d 384, 394 (1975) (invalidating a life sentence given to a child molester after the defendant had served twenty-two years in prison without release).

117. 626 N.E. 2d 803, 806 (Ind. 1993). Defendant was charged under a law, Ind. Code § 35-48-4-4.6, which provided a sentence of up to eight years for the sale of any simulated controlled substance, regardless of the drug being simulated.

118. 429 S.W. 2d 374, 378 (Ky. 1968) (aim of life-without-parole sentence is to incapacitate incorrigible offenders; no court could reasonably find that a fourteen-year-old offender will remain incorrigible for the rest of his life).

119. 739 So. 2d 301 (La. Ct. App. 1999).

120. Idem at 303, 304.

121. Idem at 303. However, a sentence of thirty years' hard labor without parole, imposed on remand, was upheld on appeal. State v. Hayes, 845 So. 2d 542 (La. Ct. App. 2003).

122. 485 N.W. 2d 866, 872, 876 (Mich. 1992). *But see* People v. Fluker, 498 N.W. 2d 431 (Mich. 1993) (*Bullock* applies to possession, not drug delivery). *See also* People v. Lorentzen, 194 N.W. 2d 827, 831–34 (Mich. 1972) (invalidating mandatory twenty-year minimum sentence).

123. People v. Sharpe, 839 N.E. 2d 492, 500 (Ill. 2005).

124. People v. Miller, 781 N.E. 2d 300, 307–309 (Ill. 2002).

125. People v. Lewis, 677 N.E. 2d 830, 831–33 (Ill. 1996) (invalidating the penalty for armed violence that was greater than that for identical offense of armed robbery).

126. *See, e.g., Miller*, 781 N.E. 2d at 307 (invalidating the life-without-parole sentence given to a fifteen-year-old who became a murder accomplice just before the shooting, noting that "this case presents the least culpable offender imaginable"). The other two clauses of the first test appear to prohibit severe punishments based on "original meaning" and desuetude.

127. *See, e.g.,* People v. Davis, 687 N.E. 2d 24, 28–29 (Ill. 1997) (invalidating the penalty for failure to have a firearm owner's card that was greater than the penalty for unlawful use of a weapon by a felon).

128. 839 N.E. 2d 492 (Ill. 2005). *Sharpe* also rejected a defense argument that the penalty enhancements at issue violated another part of Article I, Section 11 (following the proportionate-penalties clause), which required that penalties also be determined "with the objective of restoring the offender to useful citizenship"; the court cited

an earlier case that held that the possibility of rehabilitation is not to be given more weight than the seriousness of the offense (idem at 519).

129. 660 N.E. 2d 832, 847 (Ill. 1995).

130. *Sharpe*, 839 N.E. 2d at 517–18 (discussing People v. Bradley, 403 N.E. 2d 1029 (1980)).

131. 446 N.E. 2d 512 (Ill. 1983). The *Sharpe* opinion repeatedly objected to *Wisslead*'s "*cf.*" citation of prior due process cases, but those cases were clearly relevant since they involved comparisons to other crimes and were based on similar proportionality concerns.

132. In a line of cases beginning in the 1950s, Oregon appellate courts have found a violation of that state's proportionate-penalties clause where a lesser included offense receives more severe punishment than the greater offense. *See, e.g.*, Cannon v. Gladden, 281 P. 2d 233 (Or. 1955) (assault with intent to rape punishable with life; maximum for rape was twenty years).

133. *See, e.g.*, Ewing v. California, 538 U.S. 11, 31–32 (2003) (concurring opinions of Justices Scalia and Thomas); Allyn G. Heald, United States v. Gonzalez: *In Search of a Meaningful Proportionality Principle*, 58 Brook. L. Rev. 455 n.2 (1992); Nancy J. King, *Portioning Punishment: Constitutional Limits on Successive and Excessive Penalties*, 144 U. Pa. L. Rev. 101, 192 (1995); Stephen T. Parr, *Symmetric Proportionality: A New Perspective on the Cruel and Unusual Punishment Clause*, 68 Tenn. L. Rev. 41, 62 (2000).

134. *See, e.g.*, Gibbs, *supra* note 13, at 976 (principle akin to means proportionality); Gilchrist, *supra* note 11, at 1121–24, 1145–46 (same); Grossman, *supra* note 30, at 168–69 n.386 (same); Radin, *supra* note 10, at 1047–53 (utilitarian, "net social gain" principles); Richard G. Singer, *Sending Men to Prison: Constitutional Aspects of the Burden of Proof and the Doctrine of the Least Drastic Alternative as Applied to Sentencing Determinations*, 58 Cornell L. Rev. 51, 55, 72–89 (1972); Malcolm E. Wheeler, *Toward a Theory of Limited Punishment: An Examination of the Eighth Amendment*, 24 Stan. L. Rev. 838, 847–73 (1972) (noting Bentham's utilitarian proportionality principles, discussed in this chapter); Zimring et al., *supra* note 70, at 190 (principles akin to means and ends proportionality).

135. *See, e.g.*, Joshua Dressler, Understanding Criminal Law 16 (4th ed. 2006); Joel Feinberg, Doing & Deserving: Essays in the Theory of Responsibility (Princeton Univ. Press 1970); Michael S. Moore, Placing Blame: A General Theory of the Criminal Law (Oxford Univ. Press 1997); Paul H. Robinson & John M. Darley, Justice, Liability and Blame: Community Views and the Criminal Law (Westview 1995); Andrew von Hirsch, Censure and Sanctions (Oxford Univ. Press 1993).

136. *Compare* Andrew von Hirsch, Past or Future Crimes: Deservedness and Dangerousness in the Sentencing of Criminals 88–91 (Rutgers Univ. Press 1985) (arguing that repeat offenders deserve somewhat greater punishment), *with* George P. Fletcher, Rethinking Criminal Law 460–66 (Little, Brown 1978) (questioning whether prior record increases an offender's culpability to any

degree). *See generally* Julian V. Roberts, *The Role of Criminal Record in the Sentencing Process,* 22 CRIME AND JUSTICE: A REVIEW OF RESEARCH 303, 317–19 (Michael Tonry ed., Univ. Chicago Press 1997).

Some sentencing reforms, while supposedly based on a retributive model, provide substantially increased recommended sentences for offenders with extensive prior records. *See* Richard S. Frase, *State Sentencing Guidelines: Diversity, Consensus, and Unresolved Policy Issues,* 105 COLUM. L. REV. 1190, 1201 n.55 (2005) (hereinafter *Sentencing Guidelines*) (Minnesota and Kansas sentencing guidelines both adopt a just deserts model, yet recommended sentence durations are two to three times longer for offenders with the highest criminal history scores than for first offenders).

137. NORVAL MORRIS, MADNESS AND THE CRIMINAL LAW 182–87 (1982).

138. *See generally* ANDREW VON HIRSCH, CENSURE AND SANCTIONS (1993).

139. The retributive limits on criminal liability ("who may be punished"), recognized in U.S. constitutional and subconstitutional law, are discussed in chapter 6.

140. Morris's theory is described and evaluated in Richard S. Frase, *Limiting Retributivism, in* THE FUTURE OF IMPRISONMENT (Michael Tonry ed., Oxford Univ. Press 2004) (hereinafter *Limiting Retributivism*). *See also* Grossman, *supra* note 30, at 168–72 (arguing that Eighth Amendment proportionality should be construed in accordance with Morris's theory); Youngjae Lee, *The Constitutional Right Against Excessive Punishment,* 91 VA. L. REV. 677 (2005) (proposing Eighth Amendment retributive limits). Morris's limiting retributive theory has been adopted as the theoretical framework for the revised Model Penal Code sentencing provisions. *See* MODEL PENAL CODE § 1.02(2)(a) cmt. b (tentative draft 2007).

141. K.G. Armstrong, *The Retributivist Hits Back, in* THE PHILOSOPHY OF PUNISHMENT 138, 155 (H.B. Acton ed., Macmillan 1969); *see also* H.L.A. HART, PUNISHMENT AND RESPONSIBILITY: ESSAYS IN THE PHILOSOPHY OF LAW 237 (Oxford Univ. Press 1968) ("many self-styled retributivists treat appropriateness to the crime as setting a *maximum* within which penalties [are chosen on crime-control grounds]" (emphasis in original)). *See generally, Limiting Retributivism, supra* note 140, at 92–94 (numerous authors and model codes emphasize strict desert limits on maximum severity, with looser requirements of minimum severity).

142. *See generally* DRESSLER, *supra* note 135, at 14–16; Richard S. Frase, *Punishment Purposes,* 58 STAN. L. REV. 67, 67–83 (2005).

143. Kent Greenawalt, *Punishment, in* 3 ENCYCLOPEDIA OF CRIME AND JUSTICE, 1282, 1286–88 (2d ed., Joshua Dressler ed., 2001). *See generally,* Paul H. Robinson & John M. Darley, *The Utility of Desert,* 91 NW. U. L. REV. 453 (1997) (hereinafter *Desert*).

144. CESARE BECCARIA, AN ESSAY ON CRIMES AND PUNISHMENTS, chs. 23, 24 (1793).

145. JEREMY BENTHAM, BENTHAM'S THEORY OF LEGISLATION, ch. II (Oxford Univ. Press, 1914).

146. Idem, ch. I. *See also* H.L.A. HART, *supra* note 141, at 173 n.20.

147. BENTHAM, *supra* note 145, ch. II. *See also* BECCARIA, *supra* note 144, ch. 23 ("If an equal punishment be ordained for two crimes that do not equally injure society,

men will not be any more deterred from committing the greater crime, if they find a greater advantage associated with it."); VON HIRSCH ET AL., *supra* note 67, at 41–43 (discussing the marginal deterrent benefits of penalties proportioned to harms associated with different crimes).

148. Wheeler, *supra* note 134, at 851–52.

149. Radin, *supra* note 10, at 1055–56.

150. H.L.A. HART, *supra* note 141, at 25. *See generally, Desert, supra* note 143, at 453; MODEL PENAL CODE, Reporter's Note, at 43.

151. NORVAL MORRIS, THE FUTURE OF IMPRISONMENT 59–60, 75, 78 (Univ. Chicago Press 1974) (hereinafter *Morris, Future*).

152. BECCARIA, *supra* note 144, ch. 42.

153. BENTHAM, *supra* note 145, ch. I. Similar means-proportionality principles were endorsed in the French Declaration of the Rights of Man (1789). Article 8 of the declaration limited punishments to those that are "strictly and evidently necessary." Article 9 specified that, to protect the presumption of innocence, "if it should be considered necessary to arrest [a suspect], any undue harshness that is not required to secure his person must be severely curbed by Law."

154. *See, e.g., Morris, Future, supra* note 151; Radin, *supra* note 10, at 1043–56; Singer, *supra* note 134, at 55, 72–89; Michael Tonry, *Interchangeability, Desert Limits, and Equivalence of Function, in* PRINCIPLED SENTENCING: READINGS ON THEORY & POLICY (2d ed., Andrew von Hirsch & Andrew Ashworth eds., 1998); ZIMRING ET AL., *supra* note 70, at 190. The Model Penal Code and all three editions of the American Bar Association's sentencing standards explicitly or implicitly recognize the principle of parsimony. *Limiting Retributivism, supra* note 140, at 94–95. The principle is also endorsed in the proposed revisions of the Model Penal Code's sentencing provisions. MODEL PENAL CODE § 1.02(2)(a)(iii) cmt. f.

155. *Cf.* Roy G. Spece Jr., *Justifying Invigorated Scrutiny and the Least Restrictive Alternative as a Superior Form of Intermediate Review: Civil Commitment and the Right to Treatment as a Case Study*, 21 ARIZ. L. REV. 1049, 1054–56 (1979) (noting the difference between requiring choice of the "*least*" versus a "significantly less" burdensome alternative).

156. Kevin R. Reitz, *The Disassembly and Reassembly of U.S. Sentencing Practices, in* SENTENCING AND SANCTIONS IN WESTERN COUNTRIES 222–58 (Michael Tonry & Richard S. Frase eds., Oxford Univ. Press 2001) (hereinafter *Reitz, Disassembly*).

157. *See generally, Sentencing Guidelines, supra* note 136; *Reitz, Disassembly, supra* note 156.

158. *Sentencing Guidelines, supra* note 136, at 1211; Paul J. Hofer & Mark H. Allenbaugh, *The Reason Behind the Rules: Finding and Using the Philosophy of the Federal Sentencing Guidelines*, 40 AM. CRIM. L. REV. 19, 24 (2003). *See also* MODEL PENAL CODE, Reporter's Note, at 27–30, 187–88 (citing examples of state laws that incorporate explicit proportionality limits); idem at 35–36 (examples of implicit parsimony principles in state sentencing laws).

159. Richard S. Frase, *Sentencing Principles in Theory and Practice*, in 22 CRIME AND
     JUSTICE: A REVIEW OF RESEARCH, *supra* note 136, at 363–433 (hereinafter *Sentenc-
     ing Principles*).

160. *See, e.g.*, Roper v. Simmons, 543 U.S. 551, 575–78 (2005) (juvenile death penalty);
     Lawrence v. Texas, 123 S.Ct. 2472, 2481 (2003) (private consensual homosexual
     conduct); Atkins v. Virginia, 536 U.S. 304, 316 n.21 (2002) (death penalty imposed
     on an offender with mental retardation); Thompson v. Oklahoma, 487 U.S. 815,
     830–31 (1988) (juvenile death penalty).

161. *Comparative Perspectives, supra* note 65, at 277–79. Proportionality and parsimony
     principles are given particularly great weight in Australia and Minnesota. *See* Arie
     Freiberg, *Three Strikes and You're Out: It's Not Cricket: Colonisation and Resistance
     in Australian Sentencing, in* SENTENCING AND SANCTIONS IN WESTERN COUN-
     TRIES, *supra* note 156, at 38–39; *Sentencing Principles, supra* note 159.

162. Rome Statute of the International Criminal Court, U.N. Doc. A/CONF. 183/9
     arts. 78(1), 81(2)(a) (July 17, 1998). National courts and the European Court of
     Human Rights have barred extradition of offenders when the punishment they
     would receive in the demanding state would be disproportionate. *See* NORA
     V. DEMLEITNER ET AL., SENTENCING LAW AND POLICY: CASES, STATUTES, AND
     GUIDELINES, SECOND EDITION 577–78 (2007).

163. Smith v. the Queen, [1987] 40 D.L.R. (4th) 435.

164. Idem at 477, 481.

165. Idem at 482–83. The court also stated in dicta that "there must be a proportional-
     ity between the *effects* of the measures which are responsible for limiting the *Char-
     ter* right or freedom, and the objective which has been identified as of 'sufficient
     importance' [to overcome the charter right or freedom]" (idem at 483).

166. Idem at 483.

167. *See Disproportionate Sentences, supra* note 65, at 550–52. This means-proportion-
     ality requirement also provides a strong argument against any sentence of life
     without possibility of parole.

CONCLUSION

1. Kathleen M. Sullivan, *The Justices of Rules and Standards*, 106 HARV. L. REV. 22,
   57–68 (1992).

2. THE FEDERALIST No. 83 (Alexander Hamilton).

3. *See supra* notes 189–90 of chapter 1 and the accompanying text.

SUBJECT INDEX

CASE INDEX